GREAT TIMES & TAN LINES

How I Created **Hawaiian Tropic**,
Turned it into a Billion-Dollar Company
…and Had a Blast Doing it!

RON RICE
with JEFF SNOOK

No part of this publication may be reproduced in whole or
in part, or stored in a retrieval system, or transmitted in any
form or by any means, electronic, mechanical, photocopying,
recording, or otherwise, without written permission of the author,
except for the inclusion of brief quotations in a review.
For information regarding permission, please write to:
info@barringerpublishing.com

Copyright © 2022 JEFF SNOOK
All rights reserved.

Barringer Publishing, Naples, Florida
www.barringerpublishing.com
Cover, graphics, layout design by Linda Duider

ISBN: 978-1-954396-26-5

Library of Congress Cataloging-in-Publication Data
*Great Times and Tan Lines / How I Created Hawaiian Tropic, Turned it into a
Billion-Dollar Company . . . and Had a Blast Doing it!*
By Ron Rice and Jeff Snook

Printed in U.S.A.

ACKNOWLEDGEMENTS

First of all, I want to thank my best friends in life: David Rickman, Kent Lominac, Ronnie Henderson and Wink. We had so many good times over the years and I want each of you to know how much you all mean to me.

I also want to thank some of my key employees and vice-presidents over the years, such as Bill Darby, Larry Adams and Corky Surrette as well as my administrative assistants Lara Butera, Janet Chesser, Cindy Harbuck, Theresa Laios and Alexia Meadows.

Undoubtedly, my father was the most difficult man to please on this earth, but he still had a tremendous influence over me, especially when it came to my work ethic. My mother was a good wife and housekeeper to my dad, and she graciously handled all the behind-the-scenes things that women of her generation did. She was a great mother to me.

Two other family members I always admired: Uncle Lon taught me some lessons in business which later proved valuable to me and Grandma Grace taught me so many things. I really loved that lady.

To my daughter Sterling, I am so proud of you and I want to tell you that you were a joy to raise. You made being a father so rewarding.

And here, finally, I want to thank the following people from all walks of life who I admired or who impressed me enough to be mentioned. This is an amazing list of people who influenced me one way or another. I always believed in the butterfly effect and I hope that explains the length, and sadly, many on this list have passed.

But thank you all for all the great times you provided me or the laughs we shared:

Amanda Henkel, Angel Boris, Angie Smith, Aoife Grant, April Vegas, Asa Bagitta, Barbi Benton, Bit Bit Bridget Gerson, Britt Ekland, Brooke Burke, Candy Brown, Caris Stonge, Carrie Masters, Cecilia Horberg Cheryl Gentry, Darshell Stevens, Debbie Dunning, Denice Kinlaw, Donna Stokes, Gina Lee Nolin, Hanna Day, Holly Hoosline, Janet Garrison, Jasmyn Huntington, Jazz Monroe Huntington, Jeanna Mathis, Jen Cooksey, Jennifer Corliss, Jennifer Rovero, Jennifer Yon, Jessica Hixon, Joan Severance, Jody Thompson, Judy Phillips, Kalin Olsen, Karen Martin, Kasey Head, Kianna Robertson, Kim Choma, Krista Handmaiden, Kristen Achee . . .

La Gena Lookabill, Danny Greene, Lauren Hutton, Lee Ann Strasser, Linda Faulkner, Linda Rice, Lisa Petty, Liz Kirkness, Lora Huckabee Martin, Lynn Blythe Dorsey, Marla Maples, Mary Riley, Melissa Tingley, Michelle Stanford, Milam Gudmanson, Miranda Music, Nakia Martinez, Nicole Bennett, Nicole Collins, Pam Dymmek, Petra Korbay, "Opossum" Rachel Richards, Rebecca Dipietru, Remada Brito, Renata Brito, Robin Zourelias, Sandra Bergman, Savanna Lynx, Shana Hiatt, Shana Prevette Shanon, Sherry Paulk, Sheryl Shade, Sondra Harkey, Sophia Bowen, Steve Hickey, Suzanne Lee and Teresa Blake . . .

Tracy Stinette, Valerie Piazza, Venessa Bednar, Wendy Smith, Shari Lane Edwards, Jessie Conaster Devlynne Neimeister, Malin Gudmundsson, Carey Masters, Carrie Morton, Tanyin Zhang, Chanell Lee, Laura Croft, Michelle Damm, Melissa Germain, Erica Leonard, Shari Edwards, Rochell Lowen, Shelly Forgus, Cindy Van Meenen, Denise Sexton, Linda Wagner, Nickie Black Annie, Lou Andino, Linda Santos, Carrie Stroup, Charity Hodges, Amber Lancaster, Kerri Morton, Tenby Turner, Lidia Santos, Michelle Vaden, Natalie Witt, Donna Sexton, Maiki Maddix, Brooke Paller, Sandra Hubby, Asa Ankerbrink and Ashley Smith . . .

Aaron Carter, Kareem Abdul-Jabbar, Adnan Kashogie, Al Embry, Al Gore, Al Harrington, Al Jardine, Al Joyner, Al Masini, Al Schories, Alberto Tomba, Alec Baldwin, Alice Cooper, Alicia Richter, Alonique Van Voreen, Alonzo Alonzo, Alto Reed, Amy Raley, Andrea Tierney, Andreas Leberle, Andy Bailey, Andy Robinson, Andy Warhol, Andy Williams, Ann Jeffries, Anna-Nicole Smith, Antonio Ferrari, Archie Manning, Arland Deese, Art Mann, Artis Gilmore, Ashley Massaro, Ashley Olsen, Audrey Landers, Augie Busch, Barb Scarborough and Barbie Benton . . .

Barry Gibb, BB King, Bela Karolyi, Benny Hill, Bernie Kosar, Betsy Gasi, Betsy Groner, Bev and Doug Kays, Beverly Shook, Bill Anderson, Bob Anderson, Bill and Jill Stevens, Bill Dandridge, Bill France, Bill Mack, Bill Stanley, Billy Baldwin, Billy Carter, Billy Kidd, Billy Tubbs, Billy Zane, Blake Pickett, Bob and Anne Wolfe, Bob Anderson, Bob Hall, Bob Hewko, Bob Hill, Bob Seger, Bob Snow, Bob Wheeler, Bobby Allison, Bobby Brown, Bobby Freeman, Bobby Kennedy Jr., Bon Jovi, Boy George, Brad Krevoy, Brandy Anderson, Branscombe Richmond and Brian Curry . . .

Brian Dennehy, Brian France, Brian Kelly, Brian Snodgrass,

Brooke Burke, Bruce Johnston, Bruce Pearl, Bruce Popeani, Brandon Bruce, Rossmeyer Bruce, Bruno David, Bud Moss, Buddy Bond, Buddy Davenport, Buddy Lazier, Burt Cabanas, Burt Reynolds, Butch Stewart, Buzz Aldrin, Buzzy Kerbox, Byron Allen, Cary Tagawa, Carl and Susan Persis, Carroll O' Connor, Caroline Berniero, Casey Bennett, Casper Vandeen, Cathy Virzi, Charles Barkley, Charles Bronson, Charles Durning, Charlton Heston, Charlie Daniels, Charlie Fleischer, Charlie Sheen, Cheech Marin, Cher, Cheryl Bachman, Cheryl Cannella, Cheryl Ladd, Chris Butera, Cris Collinsworth, Chris Farley, Chris Penn...

Christian Lassen, Christopher Mitchum, Cindy Harbuck, Cindy Keil Evans, Claudia Schiffer, Clint Eastwood, Coach Shuford, Cody and Jen Preston, Commodore Diaz, Corky Carroll, Cory Everson, Craig Foley, Crash Corless-Frist, Jen Cynthia Bloomquist, Dabney Day, Dad Hoyle, Dale & Diane Dupenthaler, Dale Brown, Dan Cleary, Dan Haggerty, Dan Jenkins, Dan Ackroyd, Danny Angel, Darcy Lapier, David Brenner, David Carradine, David Charvet, David Chokachi, David Chow, David Cohen, David Copperfield, David Crosby, David Faustino, David Garland, David Hasselhoff, David James Elliott, David Keith, David Mecey, David Rickman, David Summerville, Dean Martin, Debbie Schwartz, Deborah Fondren, Deirdre Shaw, Dennis Haysbert...

Dennis Haskins, Dennis Hopper, Dennis Riese, Dennis Rodman, Denny and Susan Crum, Danny DeVito, Derek and Misty Bell, Derek Bell, Dick Clarke, Dick Steadman, Dolph Lundgren, Don Bova, Don Camp, Don Johnson, Don Rickles, Don Shula, Donald Trump, Doug and Alice Wigley, Doug Schwartz, "Downtown" Julie Brown, Dr. Mark Larson, Dr. Richard Schatz,

Dr. Ruth, Drew Carey, Wilma Dushnik, Ed Begley Jr., Eddie Cibrian, Eddie Murphy, Edward James Olmos, Elaine Reeves, Elias Ellen, Ellen Judge, Elliot Adkins, Elton and Noah Brunty, Eric Dickerson, Erik Eagle, Ernest Borgnine, Evander Holyfield, Fabio . . .

Farrah Fawcett, Franz Klammer, Fran Drescher, Franco Harris, Frank Gifford, Franz Weber, Gary Busey, Gary Coleman, Gary Kawesch, Gary Proper, Don Eisenberg, Gene Hackman, Gene Simmons, General Norman Schwarzkopf, George Burns, George Dagazau, George Raveling, George Richardson, George Slattery, President Gerald Ford, Gerald Wood, Giensen Hearst, Gina Leenolch, Gizelle Kovac, Glen Campbell, Glenn Wilkes, Jan Angel, Brenda Doan, Grace Crosby, Grant Cramer, Greg Kinnear, Hank Williams Jr., Hansi Hinterseer, Hedwige Sluss, Mark Hemingway, Holly and DJ Caruso, Hoyt Axton, Hugh Grant, Hugh Hefner, Hulk Hogan, Hussein Khashoggi, Ian Ziering, Jack Black, Jack Elam, Jack Garrity, Jack Sherman, Jack Surrette, Jackie Gleason, Jacque Cousteau, Jake Busey, Jamie Russell, James Brown, James Worthy, Jane France, Nanny Jane Leboeuf, Jane Seymour, Janette Webb, Jason Priestley, Jay Leno, Jean Allen, Jeanette Vostrish Webb, Jeff Bridges, Jeff Daniels, Jeff Evans, Jeff Franks, Jeff Garcia, Jeff Goldblum, Jeff Gordon, Jeff Snook, Jeff Moss, Jenna Webb, Jennifer Capers, Jennifer Gareis, Jennifer Rae, Jerome Bettis, Jerry and Susan Preston, Jerry Arqovitz, Jerry Bruckheimer, Jerry Buss, Jerry Lee Lewis, Jerry Pimm, Jerry Seinfeld, Jerry Tarkanian, Jim and Anna Lagerstadt, Jim Belushi, Jim Carrey . . .

Jim Champion, Jim Edge, Jim Edwards, Jim France, Jim Gibson, Jim Stockton, Jim Valvano, Jim Whitehead, President Jimmy Carter, Jimmy Corley, Jimmy Stewart, Jimmy Valdez,

Jo Owen, Joan Severance, Jody Thompson, Joe Bonk, Joe Lazar, Joe Pesci, Joe Pinner, Joe Piscopo, Joe Pullin, Joe Williams, Joey Fatone, Joey Pants, John Candy, John Casablancas, John Davidson, John Denver, John Elway, John Goodman, John Griffin, John Griffin, John Groner, John Havlicek, John Neyrot, John O' Hurley, John Paul DeJoria, John Travolta, Jon Voight, John Wooden, Johnny Rivers, Johnny Tanner, Johnny Cash, June Carter, Jon and Joel Rendle, Jon Lovitz . . .

Julia Louis-Dreyfus, Julio Iglesias, Julio Iglesias Jr., June Whitman, Junior Seau, Karen Cox, Karen Jessie, Karen Martin, Karen Streichert, Kat Wheatly, Kathy Bitzer, Kathy Lee Gifford, Kathy Lee Crosby, Kato Kaelin, Keith David, Keith Hefner, Kenny G, Kenny Loqqins, Kenny Rogers, Kevin Berlin, Kianna Robertson Kid Rock, Kierston McDaniel, Kiersten Zurstadt, Kim Jones, Kimberly Driscoll, Michael Douglas, Krista Frazier, Kristy Swanson, Larry Adams, Larry Bird, Larry "Bud" Melman, Larry King, Laura Squires, Lauren Hutton, Laurie Gibson, Lawrence Harvey, Lee Majors, Lefty Driesell . . .

Lennox Lewis, Leonardo DeCaprio, Leslie Nielsen, Lexy Capp, Liam Neeson, Lilly Beth Rodriguez, Linda and Dave Conroy, Linda Kramer, Linda Mitchell, Linda Rice, Lionel Richie, Lisa France, Lisa Marie Presley, Lloyd Bridges, Lorenzo Lamas, Lou Rawls, Louis Gossett Jr., Lowell and Nancy Lohman, Lyle Lovett, Magic Johnson, Muhammad Ali, Maria Menounos, Maria Penninger, Marie Beale Fletcher, Mario Lopez, Marjoe Gortner, Mark Hamill, Mark Hughes, Mark Robertson, Mark Rypien, Mark Saginor, Mark Martin, Martin Lawrence, Mary and Peter West, Mary Curry, Mary Jane Thomas, Mary-Kate Olsen . . .

Mary West, Matt Dearborn, Matt Dillon, Matthew McConaughey, Matthew Perry, MC Hammer, Meat Loaf, Meg

O'Malley, Melanie Kerr, Melissa Brewer, Michael Bey, Michael Burke, Michael Jordan, Michael Madsen, Michele Butin, Michelle and Gary Connors, Michelle Stanford, Mickey Rooney, Mike and Mike Ballew, Mike Dye, Mike Love, Mike Myers, Mike Palleu, Mike Snyder, Mimi Sommers, Monica Lange, Monica Soares, Mr. T, Nancy Owen, Ned Beatty, Neil Allison, the Van Patten family, Nick and Kelly Polling, Nicki Sniezek, Nicole Collins-Freeman, Oliver Reed, Olivia Squires, Pam Anderson . . .

Pam Hasselhoff, Pat and Brenda Thomas, Pat Boone, Pat Kennedy, Pat Parnell, Patrick Lewis Patsy Burgess, Paul McCartney, Paul Shaffer, Paul Taylor, Paula Miles, Paula Prentiss, Pauly Shore, Peyton Manning, Peaches & Herb, Pete Fountain, Pete Lofton, Peter and Shena Insul, Peter Danberg,

Peter Fonda, Peter Frampton, Peter Stringfellow, Phil Knight, Pierce Brosnan, Priscilla Presley, Prince Albert, Rachel Spence, Ralph Bellamy, Ralph Wolfe, Randy Peskin, Raquel Welch, George Raveling, Ray Myers, Rebecca DiPietro, Reggie Jackson, Regis Philbin, Renee Russo, Rhonda Sher, Richard Branson . . .

Richard Collins, Richard Kiel, Rick And Ellen Orfringer, Rick Ferritto, Rick Hornsby, Ricky Martin, Riley Wallace, Ringo Starr, Rob Cortis, Robbie Knievel, Robert Davie, Robert Earl, Robert Levy, Robert Loggia, Robert Mitchum, Robert Shapiro, Roberto Canessa, Robin and Alan Thicke, Robin Anger, Robin Leach, Robin Williams, Robin Zourelias, Dwayne "Rock" Johnson, Rod Stewart, Rodney Dangerfield, Roger Clinton, Ron and Anne Henderson, Ron Berkel, Ron Ellwood, Ron Popeil, President Ronald Reagan, Rosanne Woodard, Roseanne Barr, Ross Clarke, Roy Firestone, Roy Hahn, Russ and Tiff Moran, Rutger Hauer, Ryan Reynolds, Ryan Seacrest, Sally Field, Sam Kinison, Sam Tang, Sammy Davis Jr., Scott Sabella . . .

Sean Astin, Serena Fleitz, Seth Lynch, Shari Jenson, Shari Parnell, Sharon Bach-Book, Sharon Gentry, Shawn Thompson, Shell Ferren, Shep Gordon, Sherry Fergus McNeil, Sherry Fuqua, Sherry Jensen, Sidney Dees, Skip Moore, Sondra Harkey, Sonny Bono, Stanley Ho, Stefan Johnson, Stefanie Craig, Steve Kaufman, Steve Lindquist, Steve Mick, Steve Puglisi, Steven Baldwin, Steven Seagal, Sue Ann Hibbs, Sybil Danning, Sylvain Brovillette, Sylvester Stallone, Tara Reid, Ted Turner, Teresa Laios, Terry and Carol Fleming, Terry Moore . . .

Tia Kurek, Tim Culbertson, Timothy Buschfield, Timothy Dalton, Tina Marie Nielsen, Todd Ferren, Tom Arnold, Tom Callahan, Tom Hatcher, Tom McMillen, Tom Robinson, Tom Roush, Tom Selleck, Tom Vesser, Tommy Baker, Tommy Durrance, Tommy Fisher, Tommy Walters, Tony Curtis, Tony Enqadahl, Tony Pike, Tori Spelling, Tracy Bingham, Tracy Embry, Tracy Stinette, Trevor Matich, Troy Aikman, Troy Hilton, Tubby Smith, Valerie Egan, Vanna White, Vicki Foley, Vince Cavataio, Vince Neil, Vincent Price, Vicky Foley, V.J. Armitraj, Walter Snell, Warren Moon, Wayne Gretzky, Wayne Newton, Webb Pierce, Wendy Smith, Wendy Walsh, Wesley Snipes, Whitney Houston, Will Smith, William H. Macy, William Shatner, Wimp Sanderson, Wynona Squires, Wolfgang Puck, Wolfman Jack, Woody and Carol Woodruff, Woody Harrelson, Woody Hayes, Whoopi Goldberg and Zeev Dushnik.

■ RON RICE

CONTENTS

Chapter One 1
    IF I DIDN'T LIVE THROUGH IT, I WOULDN'T
    HAVE BELIEVED IT MYSELF

Chapter Two 12
    FROM THE MOUNTAINS OF
    NORTH CAROLINA

Chapter Three 40
    LEAVING HOME

Chapter Four 54
    FROM INSURANCE TO ENGINEERING TO
    TEACHING AND LIFEGUARDING

Chapter Five 68
    MY IDEA SHOWS PROMISE

Chapter Six 89
    HELLO "HAWAIIAN TROPIC"

Chapter Seven 109
    "GUERRILLA MARKETING"

Chapter Eight 134
    GIRLS, GIRLS, GIRLS

Chapter Nine 184
THE SALESMEN

Chapter Ten 200
THE WORLD OF CELEBRITY

Chapter Eleven 232
HAVING FUN WHILE FIGHTING OFF
THE VULTURES

Chapter Twelve 240
BACHELOR LIFE

Chapter Thirteen 263
"MARRIAGE" AND FATHERHOOD

Chapter Fourteen 278
THE PERKS OF BECOMING WEALTHY

Chapter Fifteen 299
IT'S TIME TO SELL MY BABY

Chapter Sixteen 312
YESTERDAY, TODAY AND TOMORROW

AFTERWORD 330

Chapter One

IF I DIDN'T LIVE THROUGH IT, I WOULDN'T HAVE BELIEVED IT MYSELF

Damn, I really think I may be dying, but I am way too young to die, especially like this. This turned out to be an incredibly stupid thing to do, leaving my life in somebody else's hands. I can see tomorrow's headline in my hometown newspaper: "North Carolina Man Dies in Accident on Florida Beach."

It is a nice, sunny afternoon in the late 1970s, one of those Florida postcard days, and my body now is lying crumpled on the hard sand of Ormond Beach.

Through no fault of my own, I have just crashed this contraption called a "Delta Wing," spiraling from about ninety feet in the air onto the beach in a matter of seconds. My body feels exactly as if I have landed on concrete, which violently forced the crossbar of this apparatus into my diaphragm, collapsing it.

For some reason, my friend Duffy had suddenly stopped his station wagon that was pulling me along, causing me to stop flying. I had nowhere to go but straight down to earth.

Duffy, why did you stop driving? Not that I can even utter those words. I cannot even get one breath. I am in agony, trying to breathe, but I can't. I can hear fine though. Someone behind me is screaming, "ARE YOU OKAY? CAN YOU HEAR ME? TALK TO ME . . ."

Then I remembered my paramedic training from my days as a lifeguard. What was I taught to do in situations like this?

Okay, just relax. Do not think about dying. Relax. Do not think about Duffy's stupidity or tomorrow's newspaper headlines. Relax. Just try to take that one small breath. Relax. Now take another.

That was more than four decades ago, as I write this.

I still believe all these years later that my lifeguard training saved my hide that day. I eventually took a small breath before I started turning blue. Then I look a larger one and knew I would survive.

It wasn't my day to die.

These days, there are times when I sit in my favorite reclining chair in my living room and I cannot stop staring at that beach where it all happened.

My living room overlooks the Atlantic Ocean and when I had this house built, which took five years, I wanted the windows facing it to stretch from the floor to the ceiling to enable the perfect view, just for sunny days like this one.

Day after day, the surf rolls in as the pelicans and seagulls fly by my line of vision. Surfers come with the sunrise and go with the sunset. Tourists and locals walk by constantly, some headed north, some headed south, dogs or kids in tow.

But it is the beach that usually holds my attention, no matter how much the phone rings, or what questions my assistants have for me, or what is happening in the world on my ten televisions that are always turned on.

So much of my life happened out there on that beach.

I saw it for the first time from the back of my daddy's Hudson when I was only nine or ten years old.

We would take frequent trips from our home in Asheville, North Carolina, to my grandma's house in Key West, and one time along our way south, Dad drove over to that beach.

From the early days, cars had been allowed on the beaches of Daytona Beach and Ormond Beach and this particular day left a lasting impression on me in more ways than one. As Dad drove that Hudson slowly and the rest of the family talked about the beauty of the ocean, I opened the back door and leaned out to scoop up some sand into my little green fruit jar.

As soon as I shut the door, I felt the back of my dad's large hand deliver a thud across my head. I may have figured I could just reach out and get some sand and get away with it, but I was sorely mistaken. Dad had collected one rock from every state we had visited and made a bird bath out of them, so I thought he of all people could relate to me wanting some Florida sand. I guess he was angry because I had opened the door while the car still was moving.

I stared at that tiny green bottle of sand in my bedroom for years. The more I stared at it, the more I wanted to be by the ocean, the beach and live in the sunshine of Florida. I really dreamed that I would live somewhere by the beach, if not on it, when I grew up and I hoped the contents of that little bottle symbolized my future.

You know what?

I still have that little, green fruit jar filled with sand. It sits on the mantle by my fireplace.

Every time I look at it, I know it was well worth that slap to the head.

That little green bottle held my dreams.

And they came true.

When I first moved here, I lifeguarded on that beach for years, and along the way, I saved a few tourists in distress.

From my lifeguard chair, on the slow days, I daydreamed. I brainstormed there, too. I made business decisions on that beach. Of course, I met so many pretty girls on that beach during sunny days over the years and later walked hand-in-hand with several of them on moonlit nights there.

And on that one day when I made a poor decision, I almost died on that beach.

These days, when I look around my living room, I am surrounded by hundreds of memories.

To my left by the window of where I sit is a large stuffed alligator on which the actor, Joe Pesci, would lie to get his picture taken. There are stuffed tigers, bears and two lions around me. I did not shoot any of them—they were all gifts from someone.

And behind my chair is a walkway to an indoor pool with a swimming canal leading to two outdoor pools overlooking the beach, a circular bar and a large dance floor that used to be the hub of Ormond Beach nightlife, or as Robin Leach once said on an episode of "Lifestyles of the Rich and Famous," my house was "Daytona's party-hearty headquarters."

It was.

I threw parties which movie stars, most the world's top comedians at one time or another as well as famous musicians attended.

Jerry Lee Lewis sat at that bar. So did Benny Hill and Sam Kinison. Jerry Seinfeld was here, too, long before "Seinfeld" became a TV sensation. And before it went off the air years later, Jerry put me in a scene with his buddy George Costanza during the next-to-last episode of the final season.

Rodney Dangerfield sat on the couch over there in the middle of the room many times, usually alone, and I always wondered what he was thinking or why he did not mingle more. He was certainly funny enough and people loved being around him.

Comedians.

I loved being around comedians. I loved to laugh, and they made me laugh. I loved to play practical jokes on my friends and family members, and they understood that side of me.

Leslie Neilsen started his career as a serious actor and then turned funny in those "Naked Gun" movies. Let me tell you, he was as funny off-screen as on it and he was here often.

So was his co-star O.J. Simpson, who danced in there under that giant silver disco ball at one time or another, back when the world still thought he was a great guy as I once did. So did Julio Iglesias, who became one of my closest friends.

Burt Reynolds was here a lot in the old days, too. He always loved the times when I took some beautiful girls with me to the sets of all those "Smokey and the Bandit" movies and he would put them in the background of scenes as extras.

I sometimes glance around the tables or walls at all the framed pictures to remember the best of times of my life.

There are pictures of me with Paul McCartney, Dean Martin, Jimmy Stewart, Robert Mitchum, Chris Farley, Jim Carrey, Drew Carey, Lloyd Bridges, Sammy Davis Jr., Paul Newman and John Denver, just to name a few.

Those last two I mentioned?

One was an arrogant jerk and the other was a miserable asshole. But I will get to that later.

Behind me by the fireplace sits a garbage can of all things, the centerpiece of my living area. No, I am not eccentric, at least I don't think so and I am definitely not crazy.

That can is not for collecting trash.

But back to the beach.

It is the same beach where my life happened to change forever.

I really don't believe even the Beach Boys can claim their lives were changed more by the beach, or at least the concept of it in their case, than I can.

And I happened to become business partners with them for a while and knew them well in their heyday. And by the way, none of them actually surfed. Or even swam in the ocean for that matter, maybe other than the drummer Dennis Wilson, and unfortunately, he drowned in it.

Speaking of jerks, I once almost engaged in a fistfight with a drunken Dennis in the middle of an airplane some 30,000 feet in the air, but that is another story I will get to later.

I have quite a few stories like that.

God knows, I have a million of them. I sometimes forget many of them, to be honest with you. But once in a while, one will pop into my memory and I will smile. Great memories. Wonderful memories.

Being eighty years old does that to you. So much time has passed that it makes it nearly impossible to remember it all. I do believe they were years well-lived. I admit I have had quite the life. I really never dreamed it would be so good, so fun, so rewarding.

But most of all, it was never, ever boring . . .

Sure, there were the usual pitfalls. I was not successful at marriage, even though I was married twice and divorced only once. That, too, is a complicated story.

In between those momentary setbacks, I dated some of the most beautiful women in the world. In fact, I created my own beauty pageants which became well-known throughout the world.

If you are over the age of sixty when you read this, you probably have been asked at one time or another, "Where were you when JFK was assassinated?" or "Where were you when man first walked on the moon?"

Take July 16, 1969, for example.

It was 9:32 in the morning as I drove my van south on A1A in Daytona Beach, Florida.

The sun was shining brightly that day and through the windshield, I noticed a shiny silver object shooting upward. I squinted to make sure I was not hallucinating. It looked similar to a big silver bullet leaving a vertical white trail.

What the hell? I muttered to myself.

I had been so immersed in my work, I had absolutely no idea what the rest of the world already knew: Three astronauts were shooting into space on a mission named Apollo Eleven, launched seventy-five miles away at Cape Canaveral to place the first man on the moon.

At the time, I did not know their names—Neil Armstrong, Buzz Aldrin and Michael Collins—until I watched the news later that night. But those brave men had to be nervous as hell at that very moment, not knowing if they would ever return to earth in one piece.

I know I was nervous, too.

In fact, it was the biggest day of my life.

As I said, I had been just your average high school assistant football coach, chemistry teacher and part-time lifeguard until that July day in 1969 when everything changed for me.

It was the day I introduced my new product, something that changed my life forever.

That trash can I had mentioned.

It was a key piece of equipment during my transformation from a poor lifeguard and part-time chemistry teacher to a successful business owner, which I will explain. It also symbolizes the very beginning of four billion dollars' worth of business. That is *billion* with a B.

Don't get the idea that I had just fallen into overnight success without some stroke of luck. I had worked like a mule for a few years. Later, I built my company brick by so-called brick and I helped it thrive with my marketing and advertising ideas. It really was amazing how it all happened. It was a matter of good timing, really, as well as that good luck and hard work. And there was a uniqueness to it, too.

Success opened a lot of doors for me. Having money didn't hurt, either. Or having dozens of the prettiest girls in the world, either as my company's models, employees or girlfriends, always helped, too.

I really can't remember all my interactions with the rich

and famous of the world because there were thousands.

And beside the ones who came to my parties or just dropped in over the years, I skied with Sonny Bono on the same mountain in Lake Tahoe on which he died just weeks later. I double-dated with Simpson on one New Year's Eve, the same night before he apparently beat his wife Nicole when she made that infamous 911 call, pleading for help as he was attacking her.

I had a hand in introducing President Trump to his second wife. I hired Paul Newman for one very successful marketing venture. I counted Burt, Michael Douglas and Sylvester Stallone, among several other actors, as friends. I was good friends with the explorer Jacques Cousteau and once gave him one of my large sailboats.

I related to *Playboy* founder Hugh Hefner very well and admired him to no end. Then he became a good friend, but I also cringed when the media compared me and my life to his.

They sometimes called me "The Hef of the East Coast."

I never liked that, simply because I respected him immensely and did not think it was fair.

Sporting events? I think I have been to most of them, at least the ones that interested me—from Super Bowls to the Olympics to NCAA Basketball Tournaments to the biggest college football games. And when I decided to sponsor race car teams from the Indianapolis 500 to the Daytona 500 to the 24 Hours of Le Mans, I became part of that sport.

I hung out with royalty and got to know Prince Albert and Princess Stephanie well.

I have traveled to the most remote parts of this world, normally in the never-ending search for business opportunities.

I also survived my share of and near-death experiences, like the one I mentioned. Do you know how someone has a close call in a car accident or perhaps survives a heart attack, and subsequently says: "I saw my life flash before me."

That happened to me about fifteen times.

When people ask about my life, I say, "You will have a hard time believing what happened to me. In fact, I would never have believed it myself unless I lived through it."

It all was one unbelievable, amazing, wild ride.

How else can I explain that decades after Apollo 11 launched that very day when my life changed, one of those astronauts, Buzz Aldrin himself, would become a close friend.

And you know the large alligator by the window that Pesci loved to lie on? For a photo op one night during one of my parties, Buzz stuck his head inside that alligator's mouth. Like plenty of brave men, Buzz owned a big personality and a great sense of humor and I loved the guy.

Still do.

He would see me at charitable functions over the years and immediately launch into the same old joke . . .

"Yep, as we left the launch pad and headed into space, I glanced toward Daytona and I saw my friend Ron driving down the street in his white van," he would say. "Before we took off that morning, I had taken some of that sunscreen gel he had come up with, rubbed a little of it on the nose cone of Apollo 11 so we could slip through the atmosphere a little easier . . ."

Of course, he really had no idea who I was back in 1969, because I was just your common everyday high school chemistry teacher, assistant football coach and part-time lifeguard back then.

As a skinny kid growing up poor in the mountains of North Carolina, I never would have imagined what a wonderful life I had in front of me.

As I grew older and rubbed elbows with celebrities, CEOs, politicians and people who were very successful in just about every walk of life, one thing always bothered me: Those rich and famous or very successful people who conveniently forgot where they came from.

No matter where they lived, or what car they drove or how large their mansion was where they lived, or how rich and famous they became, how could they forget their roots?

I know I never forgot mine . . .

Chapter Two

FROM THE MOUNTAINS OF NORTH CAROLINA

I sometimes tell people I grew up just like John-Boy Walton.

I did not have near as many siblings as the TV character of the 1970s, but I can guarantee you he did not work as hard as I did as a kid, either.

Anyway, I grew up just a poor country boy from the mountains of North Carolina and just like "The Waltons," we had our own mountain, too. By the time I was born, we lived in a small log cabin. Dad had saved some money after the Great Depression and used it to purchase an entire mountain east of Asheville, since land was pretty cheap in the 1930s.

There was no official name to our mountain, so we just referred to it as "Rice Mountain." As I grew up, I learned every part of that mountain. I knew it so well that I could run up and down it in the dark of midnight and never run into one tree.

How the Rice family came together and settled there is quite a story. My mother's side of the family, the Crosbys, were Mormons originally from Utah. My father's side, the Rices, had settled in the mountains of North Carolina in the 1800s.

My grandfather on my mother's side, a man by the name of Joseph Crosby, had partnered with Bill Cody, famously known as "Buffalo Bill," and they owned sheep herds and gold mines together. Joseph and his wife Grace Crosby, my grandmother, settled in Lovell, Wyoming, shortly after the time my mother, Pauline Edith Crosby, came along in 1907.

Mom used to tell me stories of playing with Buffalo Bill's grandchildren and swimming in the Great Salt Lake. She said it was impossible to drown in that lake because of the high salt content, how buoyant it made her and how safe it made her feel.

Her stories of her youth were fascinating to me and I couldn't get enough of them...

When they had traveled by wagon train from Salt Lake City to their home in Wyoming, they had to cross a plateau that dropped off about one-hundred feet, so they used ropes to lower the wagon train and horses to the bottom, hooked them up, and off they would go again. She would describe watching it all from inside the wagon, her small hands gripping the side of the door as it was lowered to the bottom of the cliff.

And I would picture what she described in my mind, as if I were living it myself.

As a kid, I got to know an uncle who had been a real true cowboy in his prime. Uncle Lon, who had married one of Grandma Grace's sisters, was my second-favorite distant relative. He would tell me stories of the Old West and what a mean guy Joseph Crosby was. From what I heard, my grandpa was considered a man who had money from his business ventures with Buffalo Bill and he was feared in the region. Apparently, those two men took no guff off anyone.

However, Grandpa Crosby also had taken part in something I always thought was fascinating: The construction of the original Mormon Tabernacle in Salt Lake City in the mid-1860s. The builders did not use the type of nails we are familiar with today to put the pews together. His job was to hand carve the wooden nails used to attach the pews. I toured the building once in the 1990s and like anybody who has been inside, thought it was one of the most amazing places I ever saw. I was always proud that my grandpa had a hand in building it.

Anyway, Joseph Crosby had a stroke and lapsed into a coma at the age of forty-one. It didn't take long for Grandma Grace to be swindled out of all the money he had left her by unscrupulous attorneys.

He died three years later.

She was a former teacher and later became a tutor, so she and Mom, who became a hairdresser after she graduated from high school, would drive from Miami to New York with nothing but the clothes on their backs to make money during the Great Depression. When they drove back and forth between New York and Miami, they usually stopped at a place called Brimmer's Boarding House in Asheville, North Carolina.

During one of their stays at Brimmer's, a man named Clyde Wade Rice just happened to be renting a room after having recently graduated from Georgia Tech. Apparently, their room wasn't ready one night when they checked in, and this Rice fellow had been out hunting, so the owners let them stay in his room until theirs was ready. While in his room, my mother snooped through his scrapbook and learned all about him, things such as that he had perfect attendance in Sunday school.

The more she read and the more she looked at his pictures, the more she liked this young man she had never met.

My mother was a very pretty blonde at the time, but apparently this Clyde fellow wasn't as smitten with her as she was with him. One day, he had caught a string of fish and brought them back to the boarding house and as the story goes, she didn't think much of his fish. So that initially turned him off, she claimed.

But I guess he would always stand up from his seat in the common dining room whenever Mrs. Brimmer entered the room. One day, he heard the high heels on the floor and figured it was the owner, so he stood up. Instead, Mom came walking around the corner.

"Oh, it's *you*," he said.

Anyway, they continued meeting in the dining room until she eventually won him over and they began dating. When Mom returned home to Miami, I guess he wrote her a letter almost every day until one day he proposed, and she accepted.

They married in 1928 and settled down in Asheville. And that's how my parents got together.

And at that point, my grandma Grace settled as a widow in Key West, Florida.

I came along on September 1, 1940, just little more than a year before the Japanese would bomb Pearl Harbor, sending the country into the thick of World War II. As the middle child, I was six years younger than my brother Crosby Clyde Rice.

They named me Ronald Joseph Rice, my middle name after

Grandpa Crosby.

I shared a bedroom with my brother in that small log cabin. He was named in honor of both Mom's maiden name and Dad's first name.

I was such a little troublemaker, at least that's what they told me, that my parents sent me to live with my aunt Edna and uncle Glen at their farm in Hendersonville, North Carolina, for a while when I was four years old so Mom could peacefully give birth to my sister.

They named her Barbara Pauline after Mom. Obviously, my parents never ventured from outside the family tree when it came time to choosing our three names.

My brother and I were always at odds with each other for one reason or another, perhaps some of it was because of our age difference. For starters, we shared a bunk bed and he slept on the upper bunk. Every time he jumped up there or turned over, a big plume of dust would fall on either my face or on my pillow. He was also bigger and heavier than me because I grew up to be a tall, skinny kid.

I would sometimes do something just to aggravate him so he would chase me, but he rarely caught me. I may have been younger, but I was still faster than he was. But when he did catch me, I knew I was in trouble, until I could scream for Mom or Dad to force him to let me go.

By the time I was twelve, Crosby had moved out of the house while attending North Carolina State. We never really were close after our childhood. It just seemed we always competed in one thing or another, and then later, we had some major financial disagreements over Dad's estate.

My dad was a man's man—by that I mean a *real* man.

Born in Highlands, North Carolina in 1905, he graduated from Georgia Tech with a degree in engineering and was considered very educated for someone of his era because few went to college in those days. He went to work for the American ENKA Company, the largest rayon and nylon manufacturer in the world, in Asheville and remained there his entire life, most of his career as the head of the building department.

Dad never entered the military like a lot of other kids' fathers I knew, but his job and that company were especially important toward the U.S. war effort in the 1940s.

He was not only highly intelligent, but very personable and outgoing. While he was in college, he would hitch a ride to cover the 130 miles from Atlanta to his hometown just so he could call the weekly Friday night square dances. A square dance caller is somewhat like an auctioneer, needing the talent to call a dance as fast as it happens and to know all of the cadences. I don't think you could do that job, especially when you were of college-age and be very shy.

Above all else, he was probably the most honest man I ever knew, to the point of getting taken advantage of way too often as he grew older.

Anyway, as we grew up, Dad was the disciplinarian of the house and I received a few welts over my childhood years to prove it. He was a big guy, too, probably six-foot-three and 240 pounds. He had big hands. Huge hands. And he used them whenever we got out of line, or at least he thought we had gotten out of line.

He was a hard guy to please. It seemed that nothing was ever right as far as he was concerned, and I guess a lot of that attitude rubbed off on me and made me the way I was later in my business life. I had tried to do anything and everything to please him, but I never could. If I did one hundred good things and one bad thing, he would always bring up that one bad thing. I believe I realized much later in life what he was doing, probably trying to make me a better person and that was just his way of motivating me.

When I wasn't catching a smack from one of his huge hands whenever I did something wrong, I got the switch treatment. All three of us received it at one time or another. We would have to fetch a switch off the Privet bush on our property before pulling our pants up past our ankles. Dad would take that Privet switch across the lower part of our legs.

Ours wasn't exactly a handholding, hugging, lovey-dovey-type of household.

I don't think we ever said something as simple and meaningful as "I love you," but I do believe we all knew it and we all felt it about each other. We ate dinner together every evening. I can still see my dad eating: If he had four things on his plate—perhaps a meat and three vegetables—he would eat one item entirely, rotate his plate, eat another, rotate it again, and eat another, and so on. Just one item at a time until his plate was clean. Then he would get up and leave the table.

Our log cabin was built with wormy chestnut, which was a very expensive wood. The two bedrooms were upstairs, and the garage housed a coal heater. One of my many jobs was to shovel coal into that heater to keep our cabin warm in the winter. I never considered us poor when I was a kid, but looking back, we just didn't have a lot of material possessions as other families did.

I remember one day when I was about six, Dad told me,

"When you go to the bathroom, you can only use three sheets of toilet paper!"

I think about that all these years later and just laugh. Only *three* sheets? I don't know how he would have counted or caught me if I used more, but I did follow his rules.

That was no problem for me, because I always found a way to get by and get things the old-fashioned way, just by working for them. I improvised whenever possible, too. As I walked to school every day through cow pastures, I would make it a point to stop by the apple orchard and grab an apple off a tree to give to my teacher.

I guess I needed all the buttering up of my teachers I could muster, because I spent a lot of my time in school daydreaming and staring out the window.

That is, when I wasn't staring at a girl named Paula Elkins, who competed with my daydreaming during the fourth and fifth grades. I knew even at that age that I was an incurable romantic, although I was scared to death of girls.

Paula was a tiny but really, pretty girl. Finally, after staring at her for so many weeks, I decided to make my move one day. I wrote "RR + PE" on a piece of paper, drew a heart on it, stuck a piece of Juicy Fruit chewing gum inside, and quickly handed it to her when school ended. Then I ran out the door.

She hardly looked my way the following day.

I thought, *"That move didn't work at all. Paula wants nothing to do with me."*

At the end of the day, each row of kids headed to the back of the room to get their coats and her row had gone before mine. Well, she had waited in there, because as soon as I walked into that coat room, she jumped out and kissed me.

You never forget your first one.

From that point on, we were just like Mutt and Jeff together. I was tall. She was short.

And we were inseparable.

One time, we were snowed in for three days and school had been canceled. I wanted to write her a letter but I couldn't mail it, so I woke up at two in the morning, peeled off my pajamas, put on some heavy clothes and walked two miles in the snow in the middle of the night to place it in her mailbox. Trucks honked at me along the way and as I think back on it all these years later, I realized what a dangerous thing it was. Then I walked the two miles back home.

Dad had noticed my pajamas on the floor and was mad at me for doing such a stupid thing.

Like I said, I was an incurable romantic and that was true love to me.

Paula's family kept a tent in their backyard and one day we crawled in there together, long before we knew anything about sex. We were just innocent kids, laying there and talking, but when Mom and Dad found out about it, they repeated, "Oh no, oh no, oh no."

I wondered what in the heck we did wrong.

On May 17, 1955, I went to the Mountain Youth Jamboree, which was an annual festival at the Civic Auditorium. People came out of the woods from all around Asheville for that one night to audition whatever talents they had, to either play their banjos, or sing gospel music, or dance. And that night, Paula and I square-danced together.

The reason it is so memorable: The guest entertainer was none other than Elvis Presley. He was pretty much unknown then, but I remember he sang gospel that night and we all got to meet him after this show.

The following year, Paula's family moved to Davidson, North Carolina, and I didn't see her again until I happened to be driving through there when I was about twenty. I pulled the car up to her driveway as her mother came out to greet me. Then her sister also came out to say hello.

When Paula finally came out, I was absolutely shocked: She had not grown an inch! I think she was the exact same size she was back in the fourth grade. I even think she had on the same clothes from the fourth grade.

As far as work goes, I guess you could say I was a born workaholic from the very start.

Dad gave me daily chores, so I worked. If I had any spare time, I worked. In fact, I loved to work, and I guess that made me somewhat different from most kids my age.

I started a roadside stand at the bottom of this hill on Route 74, right in front of Johnny Matthews' Gulf service station. I had built three tiers of shelves, stacked on bricks and wood for support. The road curved to the right and then back sharply to the left—this was exactly where my stand was located. If any driver went out of control and didn't make that curve . . . I really had to pay attention.

I think that Mister Matthews figured that if customers stopped to buy things from me, they often would come into his place to buy gas, too, so he liked having me and my stand there.

I sold all kinds of stuff: apples, cider, honey, grapes, peaches, cracked nuts and just about anything we could harvest off the mountain. We had an old cider press with a big crank on the side. The apples would slide down into the hopper and the juice ran out of the bottom of it. I would bottle the juice into gallon jugs during the September-to-December months and then just wait for the cider. Some of my friends would show up with empty jugs, and if they helped me make cider, I would pay them with a free gallon.

I would rotate the gallon jugs, according to their age. I quickly noticed several of my regular customers made special orders to buy the cider which was five days old. They wanted the cider exactly five days old. Being young and naive, I had no idea why they wanted it on the fifth day. Then I realized they were drinking it to get drunk as skunks. Five-day old cider was at the beginning of something called "Applejack." They would buy it on the fifth day and drink it over the next few weeks.

If you wait too long, it starts to turn to vinegar—and vinegar wasn't in high demand.

Each December, I made Christmas wreaths by using coat hangers and pine needles, stringing together berries or pine combs to decorate them. My brother, sister and I would walk to the housing areas around Asheville, peddling our wreaths. Crosby was what I called "the mule"—he would carry the samples we made on a home-made rack. I was the salesman. I would knock on the doors, as he stood behind me, holding up the sample wreaths.

And my sister's job was to close the deal without saying a word.

I would tell her, "Now just stand there and look poor . . ."

She really did play her role very well. It was not that I was deceiving my customers. The fact is, we did look like poor kids from the mountains and we certainly needed the money.

We took orders for wreaths the people wanted to buy and

then I would deliver them the next day.

We raised chickens in our coup and I also raised rabbits and sold them for forty cents each, skinned or alive. That was good money back then. I would design traps and place them around the mountain, then stick a carrot inside and when the rabbit went in there, the trap door closed behind it. I would wake up at four a.m., walk around the mountain to check my traps, or gums as I called them, sometimes heading home with three or four rabbits bouncing around a gunny sack slung over my shoulder. At times in the winter, I trudged around that mountain in deep snow before sunrise, realizing all of my friends were warm in their beds.

In the summertime, we would gig bullfrogs at a nearby lake and Mom would fix the legs in a frying pan.

That reminds me of a story which illustrates just how sharp Dad was. A man who had claimed to own the lake had told him one day, "I'll let you gig frogs out of my lake, but only if you give me 'half' of the frogs you get."

Now Dad and I both knew he didn't own that lake and the guy was well known around town for being a Class-A jerk. He just happened to live close to that lake, but nobody really owned it. Once, after a productive day in which we caught several frogs, Dad cut each of them in half. He left the front halves—the worthless part—from all those frogs on this guy's back porch.

We kept the meaty back legs, the only part of a frog worth anything. When I noticed what Dad was doing, he didn't say a word. He just gave me a sly smile. I realized then that not only did he have a great sense of humor, but he could outsmart most people.

The important thing was, he had fulfilled his promise, giving the man "half" of our frogs.

I also had a large pen that housed about forty dogs, mostly Beagles and bird dogs. I bred them, raised them and took them hunting. When I had them trained, I sold them to hunters around the area. I can't remember how much I got for them, but I remember people paid good money for a trained bird dog.

Even though I worked long hours, I was not a loner—I had some good friends growing up.

The one kid near me whose family had some money was a boy named Roger Faulkner, who lived at the bottom of our mountain. His father, a pilot who had searched for German submarines during World War II, owned a dry-cleaning business.

Roger was the middle kid in his family, just like I was. He received an allowance while I never got a penny for all the work I did for the family. He had two bicycles. I didn't have one. They had a television. We listened to the radio. Often, Roger would go downtown, and I would tag along just to watch him spend his allowance.

However, Roger was overweight even as a kid, with a big round face, and all the other kids were mean to him, calling him "Fat Roger."

One day, Mom treated Roger and me to a movie at the only theater in town, the Paramount Movie Theater, when we were ten or eleven years old. Roger bought this big box of chocolate-covered cherries before we sat down. He opened that box and I could smell them at once. I tried not to look at them, but I noticed there were two layers of cherries in that box. I always had a good nose and I spent the entire movie smelling those chocolate-covered cherries, just hoping he would offer me one.

But Roger sat there and ate the entire box all by himself.

Mom didn't get one, either, even though she had paid for our tickets. When the movie ended, Roger had an awful look on his face.

He whispered, "I have to go throw up."

Mom looked at me and smiled.

"Serves him right," she said.

Soon after that, Roger was diagnosed with diabetes.

We would pay nine cents at the theater and stay all day long on a Saturday, watching as many movies as we wanted. They showed a lot of series, too. I would be on the edge of my seat as some villain stood on a cliff, just ready to fall off and then the film would end. We had to come back the following week to see if that guy fell off or lived to fight another day. I guess that was smart business by the movie people.

As we grew older, Roger taught me how to play chess and I started beating him rather regularly. He didn't take that too well. He later became a tuba player in the school band. I was a defensive end on the football team. We argued constantly about why fans attended the games. He swore that fans came to the games just to watch the band. He claimed we players played the first half just to get the fans ready for the halftime show.

I may have been as much a prankster as I was a hard worker. And I never changed after I grew up.

I pulled silly pranks around the house all the time and my family members were my victims. My sister Barbara, whom I affectionately labeled "Space Monkey," was my most frequent target. One time, she had tried to make a turkey sandwich following Thanksgiving. She raided the fridge and set out the mayo, turkey, bread and lettuce. After she toasted her bread and made the perfect turkey sandwich, she turned around to put all the ingredients back in the fridge.

Just when she turned her back, I came by and scooped up the sandwich and the glass of milk she had poured and hid them both. I then placed an empty plate and empty glass on the counter and stuck two pieces of bread in the toaster. She turned around and saw that bread in the toaster and the empty plate and empty glass. She just shrugged her shoulders and unloaded the fridge again, wondering if she really had made a sandwich and had poured a glass of milk in the first place. I waited until she made the second sandwich, poured a second glass of milk and headed for the dining room. I grabbed the originals and sat down right beside her and ate my lunch.

For some reason, even today, Barbara claims that I was somewhat tough on her as we were growing up. She once told me that I got so tired of her wanting to tag along with me and my friends that I tied her to a tree one day and left her behind. She also claimed I shot her in the shoulder with my BB gun. I had one of those pump-action BB guns and I was a pretty good shot with it, but I don't remember doing either. To balance it out, however, she also told me I had protected her from any other kid who was ever mean to her.

She wasn't my only target. Mom would boil a dozen eggs, pour cold water on them, and leave them in the sink to cool. I would grab a raw egg and sit it right on top of the others, so when she went to peel the eggs, she would grab the raw one first. I stood around the corner of the kitchen just to watch as the yolk ran everywhere, and she stood there wondering how in the world that egg was still raw after she had just boiled it.

Finally, she caught on to me and chased me around the kitchen.

Like I said, we didn't have a whole lot, and since toilet paper was regarded as a commodity in our family, I certainly didn't want to waste too many eggs with that trick.

My days at the YMCA influenced me a great deal in various ways. Besides learning how to swim, which would later lead to many great things in my life, I became pretty good at archery. When I was ten to twelve years old, Mom and Dad sent me to a summer camp, Camp Daniel Boone, where I practiced almost daily and won medal after medal after medal. In fact, in one competition, I defeated three kids my age from the Cherokee Indian reservation.

I guess swimming and pools were always a big part of my life, as I will explain later, but you would never think that would be the manner in which I would discover my sex drive, so to speak. One time at the YMCA when I was only thirteen, I was swimming like hell to catch up to the kid I was teamed with, when all of a sudden, I started to feel a sensation that every boy must feel at a certain point on their way to adolescence.

Let me put it this way, there was a strange feeling going on in my swim trunks.

I slowed down in the water and wondered, *Oh man, what is this going on here?*

The swimming instructor blew the whistle for us to finish the laps and get out of the pool. Everybody else did, but I couldn't very well do that at the time, so I just stayed in the pool and got yelled at. I just had to wait it out.

As far as the opposite sex goes, other than my grade school courtship with little Paula Elkins, I was scared to death of girls.

The Navy operated a recruiting center down the street from

the YMCA and the counselors would walk us down the street to watch these war documentaries. One particular documentary about World War II somewhat traumatized me for a long time. The film documented real footage of battles in the islands off of Japan, such as on Okinawa, and it was very, very graphic and gruesome. I would watch those intently as if I were there, and suddenly, the camera view would jump and then would be pointing motionless at the blue sky. I realized the cameraman had just lost his life in that very instant. Seeing those battle scenes, the faces and bodies of the wounded and the dead was something that always stuck with me.

I had three older cousins who had fought in World War II, and after seeing those films, I had gained another level of respect for them and what they had endured.

My uncle Dick, Dad's older brother who had a tough side to begin with, had brought back the most gruesome pictures you could imagine from the war, showing decapitation of enemy collaborators by some of our allies in the Pacific. He had photographed them getting beheaded and he showed them to me when I was just a little kid. They were a series of photos in time, similar to what ISIS has done in recent years, showing a man with a huge sword as his would-be victim was slumped over in front of him. The next photo showed the man wielding the sword and the final photo showed the man's head on the ground.

Those images will be burned into my memory until the day I die, helping shape my opinion on war in general, and especially the one that was to come later that divided my generation.

I had mentioned Uncle Lon, the old retired cowboy, as my second-favorite relative. There was no competition for the first.

She was Joseph Crosby's widow, my Grandma Grace. Whenever Mom and Dad told us we were headed to Key West to visit her, usually for Thanksgiving or Christmas, those became the road trips I looked forward to the most. We three kids would pile into the back of Dad's old Hudson, riding south to the Florida Keys. There wasn't much between North Carolina and Key West in those days, so I laid in the backseat staring at the blue sky as the telephone poles passed by. I loved those trips.

Dad was a very good fisherman and a great hunter. He grew up in the mountains and he could have lived off the land back then if he didn't have a college education, a good job or a family to support. We fished off bridges in the Keys, mainly because we couldn't afford to rent a boat.

One day Dad battled and battled something on the line for several hours. When he got it to the surface, it was a giant stingray. He had no choice but to cut the line to get rid of it once he saw that it wasn't the giant red snapper or grouper we had been hoping for.

When he wanted to splurge, he would go in with some other fishermen to split the costs of a boat and we would go deep-sea fishing. We weren't doing it for sport. Whatever we could catch would be our dinner that night.

I cherish those memories now.

Grandma Grace owned a four apartment house in which she lived, and she rented the other three apartments to Navy people who were stationed at Stock Island. She was a real skinny lady, wiry and quick, too. I mean quick in both senses: physically and mentally.

She once gave me a silver dollar from the year 1880 and told me, "I wanted to give you one from the year I was born, but I couldn't find one from 1879 . . . this is as close as I could get."

That coin is still one of my prized possessions.

Grandma belonged to one of those little ol' lady groups in Key West which protested pornography. Her job was to read books first and report back to the group on whether they were acceptable for public consumption, or on the other hand, if they needed to be banned by the local bookstores.

One day, being the curious kid that I was, I got a hold of one of her books. It was titled, *Pelican River*.

Well, she must have realized it, because suddenly, I couldn't find that book to finish it. I figured she hid it from me, but I never mentioned it. We were ready to head back to North Carolina, so I thought I would try a little reverse psychology on her and use her frugality to my advantage.

"Don't worry Grandma," I told her. "When we get up to Miami, I will see if I can buy it somewhere."

I had no intention of buying that book. Miraculously, before we pulled out of the driveway, the book just reappeared on the backseat of the car. By today's standards, that book was very tame. I thought it had to be at least one book she had approved to her book review committee, but it didn't stop her from hiding it from me.

Besides having the puritan interests of her fellow citizens at heart, Grandma also worked at the Key West Museum and did plenty of volunteer work. Those were a few of the reasons she was voted Key West Citizen of the Year more than once. I like to think she probably was a Key West legend among the Conchs, as they call the locals.

Lon would travel all the way from Wyoming to stay with

her for six months every year, pulling his little trailer behind a '49 Chevrolet. He would park that little trailer, which came with a little cooking unit and a sleeping compartment, in her yard and basically live off the land. Being around him, I learned you could live on very little money. He would go out and catch fish and other things and he could cook just about anything and make it taste great. I learned a lot from that ol' cowboy.

On those road trips back from Key West, Dad would sometimes drive through Daytona, because he had a friend who owned a grapefruit orchard there. We stocked up on free grapefruit, giving them to all our friends once we got home to Asheville.

One thing about Dad: He was always teaching us something. As we traveled in that old Hudson, he would point at a spot in the distance.

"How far off do you think that is?" he would ask.

We would each take our guesses and be way off from the correct answer. Then Dad would explain how to gauge distance. He was a very intelligent man and knew something about almost every subject there was. I do not think he ever let an opportunity pass without a teaching moment.

When Grandma fell and broke her hip in 1960, my parents flew down to bring her back to North Carolina, so I hitchhiked down to Key West to bring her car back. While she recovered, the doctors taught me how to massage her hip and leg as a form of rehabilitation. The method worked, because after a while I got her up walking again. I always thought we had a special bond and I would have done anything for that lady. When she died three years later, they buried her above ground in the old cemetery right near Duval Street in downtown Key West.

To this day, I always take the time to visit her grave whenever I am down there.

Anyway, she was the only grandparent I ever knew, and I loved her dearly.

As far as religion in my family, Mom took us to Central Methodist church every Sunday and Dad went with us only on the religious holidays, like Easter and Christmas. Church was a fun, social gathering in my eyes where I had the chance to meet a lot of girls.

Mom had been a Mormon, but I think Dad was more of a realist when it came to religion.

When I was not learning about God at church, I was learning to drive when I was only fourteen or fifteen.

While everybody else was inside, I would sneak out of the back of the church and drive our car around the parking lot. Mom never knew where I was. I think she probably thought I went to sit with a friend somewhere else in the church. The funny thing was, after church, the car usually was in a different parking space, but she never caught on.

One thing Dad did not have: The patience to teach me how to drive. One Sunday, Mom took me out to a softball field as I drove, listening intently to all her instructions. With every Sunday, either in the church parking lot or on the softball field, I improved greatly behind the wheel.

Although I liked going to church, it was a brush with Billy Graham's organization that really turned me off of organized religion. I was fourteen when the Reverend, who happened to grow up about twenty miles from Asheville, came through town to give a sermon. We could get out of school that day if we attended his sermon and everybody wanted to get out of school.

Especially me.

I sat in the balcony that day hanging on Billy Graham's every word. By the end, he had me convinced of his message and I was more than ready to pledge everything I had to his cause. So, I did. I ran down three flights of the stairs from the balcony to become the first one in line afterward to pledge, just as he had asked the audience.

For whatever reason, I gave into the moment and pledged $300, even though I didn't have thirty cents to my name.

"Where are you going to get three hundred dollars?" Dad bellowed at me when I got home and told everyone what I had done.

Then 'wham' . . . I felt the back of his hand as I fell right into the wall.

It instantly occurred to me that maybe giving hard-earned money to traveling preachers wasn't a great idea after all.

Anyway, as time passed and I never sent any money, I received plenty of letters from Billy Graham's group. They wanted me to follow through on that pledge, but I didn't have the money. The notices continued arriving, as if I was overdue on the electric bill. They were just relentless.

And so was Dad.

With every letter that arrived, I received another smack. Then the letters turned to telegrams. When you got a telegram in those days, it was serious. Finally, I received a telegram which basically read, "We'll let you off the hook if you pay half of what you pledged. Pay $150 and we will consider the matter closed."

Another smack.

Wish I had received just half a smack.

Other than getting married or attending a few weddings or funerals over the years, I am not sure I have been inside a church since I became an adult. I looked at it this way: You don't have to go to church to worship God.

Neither one of my parents even drank alcohol or swore. In fact, I can remember Mom drinking only once.

It was right before Crosby was to leave for his freshman year at North Carolina State. Dad had handed Mom five hundred dollars a few days earlier to give to him before he left. She had hidden it somewhere in the house. I guess she was cooking that day, using cooking sherry and she apparently got into it. The cooking sherry took hold of her and she had forgotten where she hid the money.

We spent days turning the house upside down searching for that five hundred dollars. I remember lifting the carpet, furniture, desks . . . searching inside pillowcases, desk drawers, cabinets, under plates and dishes. Everybody searched, except Dad who was busy raising hell and ready to hit somebody with the back of his hand.

We could not find the money, so Crosby scraped together a few bucks elsewhere and headed to Raleigh for his freshman year.

Years later, Mom opened one of the encyclopedias on the bookshelf and out dropped the cash. It's a good thing she wasn't a regular drinker, or we would have spent our time constantly conducting search parties.

When it came time to leave junior high for high school, I should have gone to the county high school where most of my friends were because of where we lived. However, I wanted to play football and I thought that playing at a bigger school would give me a chance at a college scholarship, so I attended Lee Edwards High (now Asheville High). Our "Maroon Devils" football team was just so-so. We didn't have great coaching and I was a tall, skinny defensive end who stood six-foot-two and weighed only about 150 pounds. I was not that good of a player, either, but most of my buddies were.

The important thing to me is I really loved the game of football.

David Rickman and I had become best friends, largely because we sat next to each other all the way through school because of the spelling of our last names. Kent Lominac was another friend and he absolutely loved cars. He could listen to an engine and know immediately what was wrong with it. I really think he forgot more about cars than most mechanics would ever know. As we grew into teenagers, we cruised around town in his 1955 Chevy.

Ronnie Henderson, another high school friend, was the toughest guy I ever knew in my life. Pound-for-pound, he's probably still the toughest guy I know. He could beat up guys twice his size and after a while, nobody ever messed with him.

As a teen-ager, I listened to the radio a lot since we didn't own a TV. I was into any Rock 'n' Roll that was being played at the time, like Bill Haley and the Comets. I wasn't that big on Elvis back then, but all the girls were. If I had a girl in the car, she always wanted to turn on the radio just to listen to him and I didn't much like competing with Elvis for a girl's affection.

It seemed as if a new hit song would hit the airwaves every three days and we just thought that was normal. We had no idea that music was changing before our ears and we were right in the midst of it. I know our parents all hated Rock 'n'

Roll. When Mom listened to that crap like Frank Sinatra's songs, I couldn't stand that, either. (Many years later, I met ol' Blue Eyes a few times and grew to hate his music even more because he always acted like such a jerk.)

Besides Billy Graham's sermon, the only other time I ever missed school was when I was seventeen and *Thunder Road*, starring Robert Mitchum and Keely Smith, was being filmed in my hometown. Rita Grice, whom I was dating then, and I skipped school to go watch them film it. The movie, centered on a former Korean War veteran running a moonshine operation through the North Carolina Mountains, became a classic. And Asheville and its surroundings were the perfect setting for that movie.

What I always found interesting is that police cars in those days where I grew up were adorned with a huge clasp on the front bumper. They called them "bumper snatchers." If the police could get close enough to a moonshiner's car, they would employ that clasp to grab onto their rear bumper. In one scene of the movie, it did not work, and the rival moonshining car went off the cliff near Tallulah Falls on the Georgia state line. 'Shining' was serious business back then and fortunately, the law never got wind of my side business of pedaling my five-day-old cider.

I never did skip school other than that or get into any real trouble, other than some minor mischief now and then, but the truth is that I wasn't a very good student mainly because I didn't apply myself. In fact, I barely squeaked by, but I knew how to cover it up, too. I usually had two report cards—the actual one from the school that had C's and D's and the fake one I made up of B's which I gave my parents to sign. I knew a girl who had my parents' signatures down pretty good.

The bottom line is that I figured out how to do enough to graduate when the time came.

Anyway, I am proud to be from Asheville, North Carolina, also hometown to 1962 Miss America Maria Fletcher, as well as Charlie "Choo Choo" Justice who became a College Football Hall of Famer after a great career at North Carolina.

When people talk about "dating the girl next door," I did that, but the fact is there was no next door to our house. Maria lived down the ridge in one direction and another, Jean Patton, lived down the ridge the other direction.

Jean was a year younger than me and a little tomboy, and when I was fourteen, we ran around those hills together like two best friends. But she blossomed into a real beauty when she grew up. We dated some after high school.

Maria was my age, but she attended a different high school, the county school, and I dated her before we graduated, and we remained very close as the years went by. Her family owned the Fletcher School of Dance and after she won Miss America, she became a Radio City Rockette.

When I think of those formative years, I think of my father often. Years earlier, even before I was born, Dad had plans to build his dream house, which would someday become our much larger home on the very top of the mountain.

As I became a teen-ager, I had no free time at all. If I wasn't playing football, or selling goods, I helped Dad build his dream house on the top of the mountain. He had completed the foundation before World War II, and I had played up there quite a bit as a kid before he began construction.

One of my jobs was to go up there and kill the rattlesnakes

which had made their home in the foundation, by taking a hoe and chopping their heads off. We took our time and worked on that house for many years, building it piece by piece with hundreds of pieces of beautiful granite. My typical day was to go to school, play football, come home and mix mortar and carry rocks or stone up that mountain. I was strong and lean with big muscles. Carrying rocks and mortar up a mountain is as good as any weightlifting regimen in a gym.

Our family project turned into a big beautiful home, which included four bedrooms, two baths, a two-car garage and a great view down the valley. We were all proud of what we had built. It really could have been considered a mansion by the standards of the times and I got to live in it for a few years before leaving for college.

All in all, it was a good life.

But one day, things changed for us—and especially for Dad.

A representative from the state of North Carolina came to the house out of the blue to break the news: The state wanted the land in which we had built that home to expand an access road to Interstate 40.

"Eminent Domain," the government called it.

Those were the two words that took the life out of my father.

They bluntly told him, "We are going to tear down your house and put a road right through here."

They had given him a few years notice, and over that time, I watched what happened to him as he waited for his dream home to be torn down. The news was just like a slow death to him. It had crushed him. He was never the same again, realizing what was about to happen to the home we had built with our bare hands.

I really believe he slipped into depression in the ensuing years.

The state gave him some money, but it was not near enough for what that house was worth. They did what they said they would do. They tore it down and then took their bulldozers and pushed all that granite, which we had carefully chosen, over the side of our mountain.

Then they built their access road.

Dad had friends in high places with his job at ENKA and he surely could have had the state move that road one degree this way or the other, but he refused to do it. He knew that if he had pulled some strings to save our home, the state would adjust their plans and take somebody else's home. He was the type of man who would never do that to somebody else.

That's just how honest he was.

He took what money the state paid him and bought a stone house in Hendersonville, North Carolina, for him and Mom. A few years after that, in 1975, he died.

The official cause of death was congestive heart failure, but I knew better. I watched what happened to him from the minute that man from the state arrived to tell him of their plans.

Some people may not believe you can die of a broken heart when somebody takes your dream away, but I do.

I saw it happen to my father.

Chapter Three

LEAVING HOME

By the summer of 1958, I was now a proud graduate of Lee Edwards High School in Asheville and I had my entire life in front of me.

But what would I do with it?

My dad had gone to college. My brother had gone to college. So, naturally, I figured my future would be better off if I went too.

I just had no idea where I wanted to go. Dad went to Georgia Tech and my brother went to North Carolina State, which I initially favored.

But remember, my actual grades—not the grade card I forged for my parents—weren't that great to begin with, so I had to take three courses during the summer after my high school senior year just to be admitted anywhere.

Therefore, I headed to Raleigh, some 240 miles from home,

for summer school.

I sat in those classrooms at N.C. State with no air conditioning that summer and was just plain miserable. When kids say that they "sweated through" math, or whatever course, usually they are just using an expression. I really *sweated* through math, English and I believe the third course was history.

The conditions were almost inhumane.

Vines ran down the windows of the classrooms and they happened to be full of gnats. I tried to concentrate on what the professor was teaching while I had gnats swarming my eyes and nose. I couldn't take it much longer, sweating and fighting off gnats, so one day I wrote a letter to Mom. As I was writing it, a gnat just happened to land on the paper.

I went 'bam' with my fist and squashed it. Then I took a little piece of tape and taped it down, securing the gnat and its specks of blood on the paper. I drew a little arrow to it and wrote, "If I flunk out of school, this is the reason why."

Sure enough, I flunked out, failing all three courses.

Obviously, I did not get into North Carolina State, but you know what? I did not care much. I thought, *"I will just take a year off and party."*

And that's exactly what I did.

When I got that out of my system, I called the admissions department at Western Carolina and then took a trip to Cullowhee, North Carolina, to see the school, which was only sixty miles from home. It was a desolate area, let me tell you. There was not much to do in Cullowhee and I still was looking for a good party or girls to chase.

It really was one of the most boring places on earth to me, so I flunked out of there, too.

I had little choice at that point, other than to return home to attend Asheville-Biltmore College (which was later renamed UNC-Asheville). I took night classes only to bring my grade point average up to where it needed to be, so I could get admitted to a larger school someday.

During the day, I worked at the Biltmore Hotel, teaching archery, horseback riding and swimming to little kids. That camp was called "Little Beaver" and it was managed by a man and his wife. One day I had noticed he had a number tattooed on his wrist.

"What's that?" I asked.

He told me his story—he had been a prisoner in a concentration camp in Germany during World War II.

I was always amazed by the interesting people you meet as you proceeded through life.

I spent the next two years taking classes at Asheville-Biltmore and even played basketball there one season, even though I wasn't very good. To this day, I joke, "I played basketball at the University of North Carolina." Then I wait a few seconds and add . . . "Asheville."

But I was always a great swimmer, so it was only natural that I started lifeguarding. Of course, I had no clue then how that skill, and that part-time summer job, would eventually change the direction of my life.

I started out at the beach in Myrtle Beach in the summer of '62, making sixty dollars each week. I got used to dragging people out of the surf, because the waves there were higher than the surf in Florida. The riptides made saves common, but fortunately, I always had help. At least two guards usually worked together in saving people in distress.

While I was sitting in a lifeguard chair that summer, and pondering my future most days, my former girlfriend Maria Fletcher was becoming Miss North Carolina. And then she became Miss America.

At least I could always tell my buddies, "I dated Miss America!"

I had very fair skin and never used any sunscreen back then. I am not sure I really knew what it was, or that it was even sold anywhere. We all just tried to slowly build our tans and get darker from May through August as each summer progressed. Following each winter, in which my body turned back to lily-white, I would start the process all over and do it again.

The most important thing I learned that summer was that all the lifeguards on the hotel pool decks got all the girls first, before the beach lifeguards ever had a chance. They were able to discover who was checking in at the front desk and if they saw four or five pretty girls, they called their buddies right away.

Still not enrolled anywhere when that fall came, I did not do much at all.

So, that next January, my buddy, Steve Santoro, and I hopped into my '55 convertible and took off for New Orleans. I babied that car. I loved that car. It was turquoise-green and had a white canvass top. Along the way we stopped in Tuscaloosa to check out the University of Alabama. We also visited Baton Rouge to see LSU. Finally, we made it to New Orleans, where I visited Tulane University.

But mostly, we were visiting Bourbon Street every night.

We liked it so much that we decided to rent a tiny little apartment right there on Bourbon. It was during Mardi Gras, so you can imagine what we did every night. We drank. We partied. We had a blast. The apartment wasn't so nice—we had to crawl over pipes to get to our beds—and there was a huge rat which lived in there with us. We got to know him so well, we tagged him "Mortimer."

We didn't have jobs which meant we had little money, but we found ways to improvise. One night we walked into a bar on Bourbon Street, using a bottle of bourbon from my back pocket to supplement our drinks. The first drink was free at this place, but we had to pay for the rest. The bartender would come back over and over again that night and wonder why we hadn't finished our first drinks yet. We just kept filling our glasses up when he wasn't looking, and that system was working fine, until I dropped our bottle on the floor. As soon as that bottle hit the floor and caused a loud crash, our scheme was up, and we dashed for the door.

Finally, after partying for so long, I came down with a bad case of croup.

I told Steve, "We got to get back to warm weather and the ocean so I can get well."

I wanted the warmth of Florida, too, and I remembered Daytona Beach, from scooping up that sand as Dad whacked me on the back of the head. Fond memories.

I told Steve, "Let's get to Daytona Beach and the sun."

We drove to Florida and I was sick as a dog along the way, but we did stop to visit Tallahassee to see Florida State and Gainesville to see the University of Florida. Remember, I was on a mission to find a college.

I had completed my tour of college campuses, had a blast and got sick in New Orleans, and now it was time to just get healthy and rest up.

Route 92 ran right through the heart of Daytona and ended at the beach, sort of a main East-West road in the city. After we arrived, we found a little split-level cottage on the south side of 92 at the Ferran Villas, right on the beach. We rented a room for the night and I parked that '55 out front near AIA.

By the time we woke up late the next morning, fire trucks were everywhere, and hoses ran over and under my convertible. It turned out that there had been a huge fire in the cottage right next to us and it had burned to the ground overnight. We were so tired, and I was so sick that we slept right through the commotion and the firemen couldn't find us to move my car.

The next day, I negotiated with the hotel owner for us to stay the entire month since it was something like only four dollars per night.

I discovered that I could buy a gallon of orange juice across the street for only ninety-nine cents. I just loaded up on it, drinking glass after glass after glass until I slowly got better. I lay in the sun, played shuffleboard and drank orange juice all day long. And that's how I recovered. That's what we did every day—sun, shuffleboard, pool and beach.

At night, of course, we tried to pick up girls.

That was the life, I thought.

And Daytona Beach was where I wanted to live.

Now I just had to find a job. I scanned the want ads for jobs and noticed this item called "The Teaching Machine." It was a mechanical device that supposedly helped students learn. So, they hired me to sell it. I went door-to-door and announced, "You can be the only one in the neighborhood to own this 'Teaching Machine,' for the ridiculously low price of . . ."

At that point, I usually broke out laughing.

Every single time I got to that point in my reciting sales pitch, I couldn't finish it without laughing out loud.

As you can imagine that job didn't last long.

One day I walked into Baker Shoe Store in the Bellaire Plaza.

They hired me and it didn't take too long to become a pretty good shoe salesman.

I worked under an assistant manager by the name of Mister Murbot. He was like an old mother hen who all the employees somewhat made fun of. Whenever a customer walked in the store, he would automatically tell them, "Please have a seat."

"Please have a seat . . . please have a seat . . . please have a seat."

I got so tired of hearing his voice utter those same four words, over and over each day, I wanted to scream.

I also could tell that customers wanted to walk around and look at all the shoes—they didn't want to have a seat. An older guy who also was a salesman and I would walk by each other all day, muttering, "Please have a seat," mocking Murbot.

I didn't make much money—I think I earned fifty cents for every pair I sold—but I did sell a lot of shoes, mostly because I never told anyone to have a seat.

One good thing came of my shoe-selling days: I met a girl named Nancy Owen who also worked there, and we started dating. She had come from a very poor family in town. Her father was a carpenter and they were good, hard-working, honest people. During lunch at her house one day I asked for a glass of milk. They didn't have any, so I settled for a glass of water. Nancy later told me later her mother never had extra money to buy milk and I could tell she was embarrassed by it.

It didn't take long for Nancy to want to get married, and

I wasn't ready for that, so we broke up. She soon married a lifeguard.

It seemed I was on a never ending search for a job, or a career, or a future.

Whenever I got a college degree, that is.

After a while, I realized that I couldn't lay around the beach forever and our money was running out fast, so I eventually had to get back to a college and get that degree my dad and brother had.

I had visited Florida, Florida State, LSU, Tulane and Alabama but still hadn't decided on any of them. I had heard good things about the University of Tennessee. One problem for me was that *Playboy* had just come out with the top party schools in the country and Tennessee wasn't on the list. And I wanted a party school.

When I visited in Knoxville, I asked a student about the omission from *Playboy.*

"Well," he said. "They can't mix the amateurs with the professionals!"

That was good enough for me.

I think I could have been accepted at any of those schools I had visited earlier, but when I found out that Tennessee would award me more credits, or transfer points as I called them then, than I thought I actually had accumulated in my two years at UNC-Biltmore, that clinched the deal for me.

I was accepted and enrolled, already a junior.

From the start, I loved Knoxville and the university. I even went out for football as a walk-on during my first few weeks on campus. Basically, I was a piece of meat or a live tackling dummy for the starters.

One of the assistant coaches came to me one day and said, "Sorry, we are looking for someone twice your size and twice your ability."

It wasn't my first experience with Volunteers' football. When I was fifteen or sixteen, someone had given Dad tickets to a game and I remember sitting in Neyland Stadium in awe that day. Johnny Majors played then, and it was an incredible experience for a kid my age.

One of my first roommates, Jim Turner, was from a little town near Asheville. He was a very smart kid and very neat. His side of the room was immaculate while mine was an absolute mess. He knew where everything was, even my stuff.

One day, somebody knocked on the door and said, "Ron, you got any band-aids."

"I don't think so," I answered.

"Oh yes, you do," Jim piped up, ". . . right behind the Listerine bottle in your medicine cabinet."

He was so organized that he knew where my stuff was more than I did.

One of my roommates later, a guy by the name of Benny Silvers, I had nicknamed "Goat Man." The Goat Man would sleep naked and would get up and come over to my bed often and then fart in my face. Now, I had as good a sense of humor as anyone, but that was just childish.

And finally, one night I had had enough.

"Goat Man," I said, "if you do that one more time, I am throwing your pillow out of the window."

And yet, he did it again.

I opened the window and tossed his pillow out into the snow.

He then ran naked downstairs outside to grab his pillow. By the time he headed back into the dorm, the main dorm leader was walking down the hall. There he was—stark naked, shivering and holding that pillow over his most-strategic area.

Let's just say that Goat Man never farted in my face again.

I admit I too pulled shenanigans that could have gotten me kicked out of college. One day, I picked up three girls who were hitchhiking from Cincinnati to Florida. All three were under eighteen and had run away from home. They were all beautiful and they needed a place to stay, so I brought them back to my apartment, trying to figure out what to do with them.

I told them I didn't want them out there hitchhiking on the interstate where it was dangerous. But when some of the guys found out about who I was hiding, I knew I had to get them out of there. I finally found a guy at school who could take them as far as Atlanta.

I didn't have any trouble finding girlfriends at Tennessee, either. I started dating a cheerleader named Carol Edwards and we became very close. She was a real beauty and I liked her very much. We would hang out at her house in Knoxville and her mother liked me, and I knew that was important because she was everything to her mother. There is no way Carol could be friends or date anyone seriously without her mother's approval.

After graduation we later drifted apart and didn't see each other much.

But there were always girls.

And during the summer, I returned to Daytona to lifeguard.

I worked at the old Desert Inn, a tiny little motel right on the beach, in 1963. It was owned by two brothers with the last name Weiser. Hotel guests would order food while relaxing on the pool deck and the owners had jacked up the price from a local restaurant and have somebody go pick it up for them. By the time they returned, their food was always cold.

It wasn't something that made me fond of the Weisers.

I was walking from the pool deck to the kitchen one day, with my tips resting next to a set of dishes. The owner's wife saw the tray and started to scrape off the tip money, while saying, "This goes to the house."

"No, no, that's my tip money," I said.

She absolutely refused to give it back, and one of the brothers just happened to walk into the kitchen at that moment.

"I need my paycheck," I told him. "I am out of here."

It was two weeks into my employment there.

He said, "Well, first you have to pay for the T-shirts we gave you, so you owe us money!"

I became enraged, pulling a Hulk Hogan on the shirt I was wearing, ripping it off, tearing it into a few pieces and gently laying it on the counter. I headed to my car, which was parked on the beach. Then the owner told me, "Well, you can't go out this way, since you are no longer an employee."

He started to follow me toward the beach.

I turned and told him, "If you follow me as far as the pool, you are going in it!"

I got to my car, drove down the beach and found an exit to the beach road. I also started thinking about a girl I had been seeing who just happened to be staying at their hotel.

I saw her that night and told her, "I have to get back at these guys. They treated me like shit. Got any ideas?"

She said, "Let's roll them."

Toilet-papering a property owner's trees was a big thing

back then.

So that night, we rolled every tree on the property with rolls and rolls of toilet paper. I wanted to go one step further. I took a huge blanket to the beach and filled it with sand. I dragged that blanket back to the pool and dumped all that sand to the bottom of the pool.

As she and I drove down the street the next day, we looked over to see several workers surrounding the pool area, trying to figure out how to remove all that sand. I hate to admit I have a vindictive bone in my body, but something inside of me clicked whenever I felt wronged.

I hated to see people treat other people like shit, and that included me.

Another time when I rented a place in Miami briefly after following a girl there (I will get to that later), the apartment came with very cheap furniture. "Dutch modern" the landlords called it. You would sit down on it and it would wear clear through. When it came time to move out, the owners inspected it and then refused to give back my $200 security deposit, claiming I had ruined the furniture.

That thing inside me clicked again, so I backed up my van to their pool and loaded $200 worth of deck furniture and drove back to Daytona.

But that wasn't even my best "get-even" tactic in Miami. I once sold a motorcycle to this guy on nothing but trust that he would pay me. Sure enough, he stopped making payments to me after a few months. I went to his house, hired two laborers to lift the motorcycle into my buddy's 1958 Chevy. I stored it in his garage in Hallandale. Naturally, the guy started calling my apartment in Daytona screaming, "WHERE'S MY

MOTORCYCLE?"

"Come up with the five hundred you owe me and you will get it back," I told him.

He paid me the money the following week.

I figured he had it all along but just decided to stop paying, figuring I wasn't a repossession company and could nothing about it.

But back to my days in college when I got along with most people.

One time I got so sick that I couldn't function. I just lay in bed with the flu. A girlfriend had brought me chicken soup for a few days, but I kept getting worse. I had no choice but to call home. So, Dad drove over, got me, took me home and loaded me up with penicillin. I was better in three days. My dad was great that way. He never said it, but he was a very caring man with a big heart, and I knew he loved us kids.

When it came to academics and my classroom work (I majored in natural sciences), fortunately I had matured somewhat from my days at North Carolina State, Western Carolina and UNC-Biltmore. I knew Tennessee was the time and place I had to get my degree and to stop letting a great party get in the way of my future. That doesn't mean I didn't have fun, but I was focused on what mattered, too.

I did have buddies who did whatever it took, including one who would dumpster dive for carbon-copies of tests and exams that professors had tossed out. He knew just where to look. Remember that scene in *Animal House* when John Belushi and his buddies are searching for the answers to a test? It was just like that.

By the time he graduated, he had an entire file of courses

of which he had the exact tests certain professors were giving their students. I don't know what he ever did with that file.

The hardest course I took in college was something that seemed so easy—Music 101. The professor made it difficult, requiring us to learn all these various operas. I couldn't stand opera, so I barely squeezed by that course.

When it came to my final quarter, I took a whopping thirty-one hours, which was exactly what I needed to graduate, while most students took no more than twenty-one in any given quarter.

But I needed a degree and I had to do whatever it took at that point in my life.

It seemed that I went to class and studied around the clock that quarter.

But I survived it.

At least now I had a college degree.

As I look back on that experience, I owe the University of Tennessee a lot. Here we are more than five decades later, and I remain an ardent supporter—both financially as well as emotionally at football games—of the University of Tennessee. I am a Volunteer at heart.

After all, it took many stops, detours and tribulations to get that degree.

Therefore, I was very proud of it.

What I would do with it was anybody's guess, including mine.

Chapter Four

FROM INSURANCE TO ENGINEERING TO TEACHING AND LIFEGUARDING

Now that I was a college graduate, it doesn't mean everything in my life was gravy, or groovy as kids my age said during the 1960s. I was about to enter the "real world" and the real word was sometimes a mess in the turbulent times of the Vietnam War.

The U.S. was deeply involved in the war and I also knew that at twenty-four years old, I had to find a job in order to receive a deferment from the military or I soon would be fighting in a jungle thousands of miles from home.

In my opinion, it was a senseless, meaningless, stupid war back then—and it always will be.

And those gruesome World War II pictures I had seen as a kid had left a lasting impression just how awful war was.

I was young, but I was smart enough to know I didn't want

to go to Vietnam and get shot at and I sure didn't like authority. In other words, I wouldn't qualify as your typical good soldier. I figured the Air National Guard was the best way to go, but I took the test thirteen times and couldn't pass it.

It got to be a running joke. Every time I failed, they put me at the bottom of the list, and I had to wait some time to take it again.

Dad had once told me that the last four years of your business career is when you make the most money, so if you can extend those years to the latest age possible, the better off you will be.

Tennessee had hosted a job fair when I graduated and it seemed every oil company in the country wanted to hire me right on the spot, but every offer dictated that I would wear a three-piece suit and travel the country telling service-station owners what kind of oil to sell to their customers.

I didn't get a college degree for that, so I turned them all down.

I soon decided to enroll in a six-week training course in the insurance business in Atlanta, even though I figured insurance wouldn't be my future. I had met some new friends in the course, and we partied just about every night. I don't think I ever got six or seven hours of sleep each night during those six weeks, but I somehow passed the course.

I learned a lot about the insurance business and a lot of it I didn't like. I didn't know what I would do with my life, but I knew it wouldn't be in insurance. But once I passed the course and graduated, they sent me to Miami. I quickly learned, as I had suspected earlier, that the insurance business was a bunch of crap. I believed it was a business designed to screw people over left and right. I would have to visit a car accident scene and I was supposed to slide a paper under an overturned car for the injured driver to sign. I am not kidding, either.

So, that didn't last long.

In fact, I quit that job hours into my first day of work in Miami.

In reality, I just wanted the company to pay for my move to Florida.

So, I hung around Miami for a while, just goofing off. But I got bored and left to spend the summer of 1964 in Valdosta, Georgia—working at the planning commission of Lowndes County of all places.

After that, I then decided to go back to Knoxville to enroll in a graduate course in geology. I still was sending out resumes and that is when the boss of an engineering company in Orlando responded to one and called me.

I scheduled an interview and drove my old Mustang to Orlando, getting lost in the downtown area searching for this engineering firm. I pulled over to the side of the street to ask for directions when this guy walked up to my car to help. He had an all-over tan and looked like he had just spent two weeks on the beach.

"Yep, this is where I want to live," I thought.

I finally found the place and the boss told me that day, "We got a big government contract and we need employees. We will hire you."

I immediately accepted the offer, but I knew once again that I was simply trying to buy time, since I never pictured engineering as my career. I drove back to Knoxville, loaded up my car with all my possessions, then drove back to Orlando to begin my engineering career, however long it would last.

I walked in the door for my first day and was promptly informed things had changed—the company had lost their government contract and there was suddenly no job available for me.

"No, no, no, you promised me a job and you are going to give me a job," I demanded.

"But we lost our government contract," the guy said.

"Well, that's your problem," I told him. "I am beginning work today. Where do I sit?"

They must have felt sorry for me because they didn't resist after that.

They first assigned me to draft plots for the Beeline Expressway, east of Orlando. I was making sixty dollars per week. My boss was a strange man who always wanted to pitch horseshoes during lunch. I would spend my lunch hour sitting in the sun, trying to get a Florida tan like the guy who had given me directions a few weeks earlier, while all my co-workers pitched horseshoes with the boss.

I soon grew to hate the guy, because it was obvious to me that he wanted everybody under him to kiss his ass. And I was never good at ass-kissing the boss.

One day, they had me represent the company as the governor cut a ribbon opening the downtown Interstate-4 extension. I held those big ceremonial scissors for Florida Governor Claude Kirk, who then cut the ribbon. The following day, a picture of me and the governor appeared on the front page of the *Orlando Sentinel*.

I was still hanging around the beach in Daytona every weekend and one day there I met a lifeguard by the name of

Jim Edge. We started hanging out together. He was a tall, good-looking guy who attracted a lot of pretty girls and had a great personality. He had a way of coming on to girls and they never seemed offended no matter what he said.

One day, he told me about one of his buddies, a guy by the name of Richard Winkelman, whom everyone called "Wink," who also lived in Orlando.

"You got to meet Wink," he said. "I know you guys would get along great."

He gave Wink my number and not too long later, this guy pulled up to my apartment in a Ford Mustang, dressed as neat as he could be, while wearing a button-down collared shirt and penny loafers.

From that moment on, Wink, who was a recent Rollins College graduate, became a huge part of my life as one of my best, lifelong friends.

But the engineering gig wouldn't last. After just two months, I quit that job and headed back to the beach in Daytona. I still needed something to do to stay out of Vietnam and sitting on the beach watching people swim or the girls walk by was much, much better than drafting plots for sixty dollars per week.

Even with my fair skin, I loved being at the beach and getting sun all day. And I was a great swimmer from the time I was a kid, so it was only natural that I work as a lifeguard. Maybe this is my future, I thought, and not just a stopgap thing or a summer job.

My living conditions back then were right out of a frat-house playbook. Me and some lifeguard buddies moved from apartment to apartment. One time we even rented a large house with six bedrooms and there were always girls coming and going day and night.

I remember that one day we all had picked up some girls on a pool deck and had plans to go out on the town. But first, they all came back to the house. I fell asleep when I heard a loud banging at the door. I jumped out of bed and went running to the front door. There was the landlord standing there with his hand stretched out.

"I need the rent!" he demanded.

The other guys had forgot to pay me their share, so I headed outside to the trunk of my car, wearing nothing but my underwear. I opened the trunk, pulled out the money from where I had hidden it and paid him.

"You keep money in your trunk?" he asked me.

I was still half asleep, but then I heard him say, "While I am here, I want to inspect the house!"

He came back into the house, started to walk around and every time he opened a bedroom door, there stood a girl in her underwear, either doing her makeup in the mirror or something else that offended him.

He looked and me and just blurted, "I can't believe you people live like this!" and then he stormed out.

I guess it was only normal to us, being red-blooded American boys who happened to be lifeguards.

Most all my friends and subsequent roommates were lifeguards, too.

And along the way, I roomed with some real characters.

A guy named Paul Jacobs, who was one year ahead of me in school, moved in with me. Paul and I went as far back to my days of running that roadside stand when he would help me make cider and we swam in all those lakes around Asheville.

He was a chemistry major from the University of South Carolina and like me, had moved to Daytona. He was a funny guy and very mild-mannered with a great sense of humor. One day, he just showed up at the Plaza Hotel on the beach, grabbed a paint brush and started painting.

Somebody asked him what he was doing.

"I am your new painter," he said.

I don't think they ever officially hired him or even paid him, but eventually they started to pay him with meals from the coffee shop.

One day he was outside painting and he noticed the beach patrol conducting lifeguard tests. To become a guard, you had to swim certain distances under a certain time. He watched the tests that day and thought, *"Hell, I can swim faster than those guys."*

He could, too, so he took the test, passed it with flying colors and became a lifeguard.

When the owner of Plaza bumped into him the next time, she asked, "I thought you were our *painter*."

He responded, "I was, but now I am your new lifeguard."

He and I were roommates in four or five different places, and he set most all the timed swimming records on the beach for the lifeguards. He was barrel-chested and strong as a bull and if you were drowning, you wanted Paul nearby.

Your income, as a lifeguard, was always dependent on "beach weather." That in turn meant it was seasonal. You always had to find other means to support yourself, other sources of income. It was common then for lifeguards to peddle products to tourists or locals on the hotel pool decks to supplement their income.

On the pool decks in Daytona back then, I always met all kinds of characters and interesting people. There was a lady named Dottie Schagalis who made and sold jewelry. There was a guy named "Scotty the Hatmaker," who weaved and sold those straw hats you see the tourists wearing to protect them from the sun.

But one day I got talking to Dottie and her husband Bill, who sold other products on the pool decks.

He had one interesting background, to say the least. In his earlier days, Bill had been a pilot and when Fidel Castro took over Cuba in 1959, Bill would make good money on the side by flying people in and out of Cuba.

Apparently, someone had tipped off Castro's regime to Bill's flights and one day his troops were waiting on him. They started firing at Bill's airplane, causing his co-pilot to panic, as he steered the plane off the runway into some bushes. They were unhurt but Bill was apprehended and stuck into a Cuban prison, where he soon contracted a virus and lost his hearing in one ear.

Rather than let her husband rot in jail forever, Dottie took it upon herself to plead to Castro himself.

She flew to Cuba and met with Castro in person and somehow convinced him to release her husband. They then returned to Daytona and started up their pool deck sales business. I became good friends with Bill and Dottie, and like everybody else, had a common dislike for a man named Paul Burke.

Burke sold suncare products, such as something called Deep Tan, up and down the beaches of Daytona and had an easy time of rubbing people the wrong way.

After dealing with Burke a while, I thought, "If this jerk can sell all of these products and make all of this money with his personality, then I could really out-sell him."

So, I decided to go into competition against him. In the summer of 1965, I reached out to whatever contacts I had and discovered that I could get oils, but no lotions, from the suppliers in Fort Lauderdale. At the time, I also decided to attend graduate school at Stetson, about twenty miles east of Daytona, taking some courses to get my teaching degree to go with my liberal arts degree from Tennessee.

That's also when Jim Edge and I decided to form "Rice and Edge Enterprises," a two-man company that sold beach products to lifeguards, who in turn sold them to tourists.

And that's how we came across a guy named Harry Sampson, who sold suncare products in Miami. Sampson owned a gift shop there and could get just about any products for us that we needed to sell.

He soon referred me to two brothers, Ken and Jim Collier. Their father had sold red veterinarian petroleum to the government, which placed it in survival kits for our pilots in the Pacific during World War II. If they ever were shot down, and survived, they had to put something on their skin to protect them, so they used this red stuff that came in a little tube. It was more like axle grease. There were no real protective chemicals in it, but it covered the skin enough to prevent severe sunburn.

That substance known as "red vet pet" served the most rudimentary stage of sunscreens.

After the war, Benjamin Greene used it to help Coppertone develop its first lotions in the late 1940s, but that was it as far as the American market and suncare products, until Sea & Ski came around in the 1950s.

Anyway, the Colliers were in the music business, organizing rock concerts but they also owned a business that sold suncare products and other items. I started buying a product called "SunScreen" from them and I became one of their biggest accounts, then turning around and selling most of their products to other lifeguards who I had relationships with.

Jim and I started making money right away during the day, but he had a habit of going out every night and spending too much. I was telling everyone we weren't making much, because I wanted them to feel sorry for us and buy more products. At the same time, Jim was telling them we were killing it and that we had plenty of cash while he was buying everyone drinks.

One day, I happened to be on a pool deck in Daytona when there was a large group of girls wearing Tennessee shirts. I found out they were cheerleaders and majorettes from the university. My former girlfriend Carol had been one of them.

"Carol Edwards wouldn't happen to be with you, would she?" I asked one of them.

The girl took a step backwards and lowered her head.

"Carol is dead," she said. "She was riding in a car in Knoxville when it ran off the road and rolled over on her..."

I was stunned.

I went home with tears in my eyes and wrote her mother a letter, but never heard back from her. Carol was everything to her mother, so I am sure it was devastating to her. I know it was to me.

That wasn't the end of the heartbreak, either.

Tommy Fisher, who was three years younger than me, had

been a great linebacker for the Volunteers, and the two of us would ride together from Knoxville to Florida when we came home for the holidays from school. He was from Brooksville, Florida.

He had just been drafted in the third round by the NFL's New York Giants and came to visit me during spring break in March of 1966. He brought two other former Tennessee teammates with him and we had a great time together that week. But on their way back to Knoxville, their car collided with a tractor-trailer head-on while heading around a curve in the road. Tommy and the other guy in the front seat died instantly.

The headline in the *Tennessean* newspaper the following day read: "Fisher was destined for greatness."

I thought so, too. I think he would have had a long NFL career. Both Carol and Tommy were in their twenties, were great people and had their entire lives in front of them.

And their deaths hit me hard, especially Tommy's since he had just been with me days earlier.

My lifeguarding/sales business ended when each summer did, so now that I had my teaching certificate, I thought I would try teaching and I soon landed a job at Mainland High School. They needed an assistant football coach and a chemistry teacher, and I qualified for both.

I was making about $4,300 a year—$4,000 from teaching and another $300 from coaching football.

I coached the JV football team at Mainland, and we went undefeated in that first season, but the varsity coach—a guy named Paul Andrews—couldn't stand me or the way I coached. We had seven or eight assistants, and each of us had to take a teacher's exam at the conclusion of my first year. We had to score at least a 500 to pass the test and remain employed.

For some reason, it seemed that Andrews liked every one of them but me.

The day he received our test results, we all were sitting in a big circle as he passed them out one by one.

"Fail, fail, fail," he said, as he looked at each coach. "Fail, fail, fail, fail . . ."

Then he handed my test to me, still with a disappointed look on his face.

I had scored a 501, making me the only assistant who had passed, so he couldn't fire me. At least not for that reason.

I also taught history and math at Mainland and was stuck in one of those portable classrooms that sat separate from the main school building. I had three students in my math class that I will never forget their names.

They were Rusty Sizemore, Barney Smith and Raymond Tiffany. They were in that same class and remarkably, they all died in Vietnam within a year of each other soon after they graduated. Not that I needed any further reasons to hate that war, but their deaths so close together really hit me hard.

After one year at Mainland, Andrews made it clear that he didn't want me back and I was not offered a second contract, so I was left unemployed again.

I mentioned my departure to one of my roommates, Richard Krause.

"There's a job open now—go apply for it," I told him.

Richard, who was a lifeguard, too, drove over to the school and told them he had played football at Auburn. I knew that he had really been a cheerleader. (Richard later became an attorney and would work for me.)

Jobless again, I didn't panic because knew I wouldn't have a problem getting another teaching and coaching job, so I met the principal who was named McMillen of Central Junior High (it is called Holly Hill Junior High) in 1966 and I helped coach football and taught science for two years.

After two years at Central, the school couldn't afford to let me receive tenure as all the teachers did by reaching their third year, so they let me go.

McMillen, who had been stricken with cancer by then, felt so bad about it, but I told him, "Don't worry about it. I will find something."

He had been extremely nice to me and I liked him, so I didn't want him worrying about me or my situation and he died shortly after that.

I then went to Campbell High, an all black school, and when I applied for a job the principal there told me, "Good timing! We can use you—we just happen to need an assistant coach and chemistry teacher."

I started teaching and coaching there in the fall of '68. That team I helped coached at Campbell had an offensive line that averaged about 280 pounds, as much as many college teams today. We had an incredible team that lost only two games that season. It seemed that everywhere I went we had great football teams.

That teaching job at Campbell wouldn't last long either, but for a good reason.

My teaching stints all were very short, and I realized that cliché about life being short also was very true.

Carol Edwards and Tommy Fisher had been killed in auto

accidents. Three of my students from the very same class had died in Vietnam.

It got me to thinking really hard about my life.

And I figured . . . I just knew . . . there had to be more to my life than teaching, lifeguarding and eating condensed soup and peanut butter for dinner.

Chapter Five

MY IDEA SHOWS PROMISE

The Collier Brothers soon started focusing on promoting concerts and the musicians they represented, such as the rock band, Spirit, as well as Tiny Tim among other performers, more than they did their sales business.

They were always hosting events at this bowling alley near their store in Miami which always seemed to draw large crowds. They even handled a singer by the name of Jim Morrison before his popularity with the Doors exploded worldwide.

And they became somewhat famous for what happened on the night of March 1, 1969, when Morrison went nuts at a concert in Miami, exposing himself on stage in a near-riot. Ken Collier jumped on stage and grabbed his microphone in an attempt to prevent Morrison from causing a disaster.

In the meantime, with their nightclubs and concert promotions, they pretty much forgot about their suncare sales business.

Unfortunately, that left me hanging for a good product to sell to the customer base I worked so hard to develop. Jim Edge had been drafted into the military, so it was just me now and I didn't have to worry about a partner blowing the profits at bars buying drinks.

Another druggist and wholesaler in Fort Lauderdale sold me a product called Sky Blue, but nobody liked it—and I didn't realize that inconvenient fact until after I bought a bunch of it. That misstep really set me back financially.

I also had tried Coppertone and Sea & Ski, but I wanted to sell something of "high quality."

I really didn't think there was such a thing on the market.

Coppertone was a big company and sold well in stores, but I never understood why. I always considered it an inferior product. It didn't sell well on the pool decks in Daytona Beach or anywhere that I knew of. For starters, the smell in sunscreens, lotions and oils is a huge, huge factor in whether the customer likes it or doesn't.

And I for one just hated the smell of it. It was mass-produced and included a chemical called Phenyl Salicylate, which produced the smell that turned me off.

At the time, I didn't have much money, and I never could have afforded to fly to Hawaii, but a friend of mine had booked a flight there and couldn't make it for some reason. Back in those days, anyone could take somebody's airline ticket and use it as their own.

So, I headed to Hawaii in the spring of '66, rented a car and went out exploring the islands.

I was sitting on a beach on the backside of Oahu one day,

not thinking about anything really and I noticed some native Hawaiian girls cracking opening coconuts. I figured they were doing it just to eat them. But then I noticed something startling—at least to me—these girls were rubbing the coconut oil all over their bodies.

I always loved the smell of coconut. Who doesn't love the smell of coconut? It was as if a thunderbolt hit me: So why not smell it all over your body as you lie in the sun?

As I said, there weren't many sun tan products on the market that I cared for, and I figured the public had to feel the same way. When I returned from that trip, I started brainstorming almost every day. What if I . . . and I tried this . . . and added this . . . my mind was in overdrive. And those native Hawaiian girls were always in the back of my mind.

That idea was stuck in my head for a while, but I didn't quite know what to do with it.

Meanwhile, my personal rival in sales on the beach, that guy Paul Burke was doing well peddling that Deep Tan product. In fact, because of his success, I had lost all of my previous sales accounts.

Not everything was terrible in my life, however.

I did find a wonderful place to live and it wasn't costing me a penny in rent.

When I first arrived back in Daytona to stay, I had rented apartment after apartment, house after house, usually sharing them with several other lifeguards to split the rent. It was the only way I could afford anything decent. I counted once and I think I had moved thirteen times by 1965.

By that fall when I started teaching school, all my lifeguard-roommates went off to college and I had to find yet another place to live.

That's when I stumbled upon this circular house sitting atop a sand dune on the beach near the Daytona Beach-Ormond Beach border. It included a three-car garage on the bottom and two other levels.

It was owned by a character by the name of Myra Reed.

"You can rent the bottom half of the house for $150," she told me. "It is very Bohemian and when it rains from the South, you may have to move your bed, because it will rain in through the roof and come down into your room."

I later learned the house was designed and built by one of Frank Lloyd Wright's chief architects. What's more, that guy for whatever reason, had committed suicide by jumping off the top of the house and landed head first on the cement.

I affectionately called it the "Round House" and it and my new landlord soon became a big part of my life. And as time went by, everyone who knew me also called it by the same name.

As far as my new landlady, Myra, I will try my best to describe her accurately, but it is very difficult.

To say she was eccentric would be an understatement. She was very rich, owning several properties along the beach, and very, very strange. The story was that Myra had been financially liquid when the Great Depression hit in the 1930s, so she was able to purchase a lot of land and properties with what cash she had for virtually nothing. She bought several properties in Ormond Beach, Gainesville, Florida and Charleston, West Virginia. It was very smart business, I thought.

And did I say she was eccentric?

She wore two diamond rings on every finger, and they were

always dirty as hell and I am not sure she ever bathed herself.

Myra had married some guy named Larry, who was about twenty-five years younger. She would collect everything she could get her hands on, such as sticks and strings and bottle caps and wrappers of any kind. I would catch her going through my trash and I was as poor as a church mouse while she was a multi-millionaire.

She kept all her money in one local bank in Daytona, which as I learned while doing business and banking later was a very stupid thing to do. Banks were insured for only $100,000, but she had millions of dollars in one account. If that bank had gone under, she would have lost everything but her one hundred grand.

She had all this money, but no friends whatsoever, so she did whatever she could to fill the void. Get this: She coerced the bank to throw a party for her once a month. The bank employees would host it in an upstairs room that had one table and one bar where they would serve finger sandwiches, Myra always carried a large purse and that came in handy when it came time to gather up the leftovers.

Larry invited me and my friends to her monthly bank party, I suspect only so the bankers would believe she actually had a few friends. All the tellers would attend this party, have a drink in their hand, and socialize just to be in on the act. When Myra walked by the food table near the end of the party, it was understood to everyone working to turn their backs, so they wouldn't see her as she raked all the leftover food into her large purse.

She did this every month. I really believed she and Larry would dine on those finger sandwiches for the entire month, until the next party. That was just how cheap she was.

To take advantage of the Florida tax laws, she would live in Ormond Beach for six months and one day, so she could declare it as her residency. Then she and Larry would drive their motor home to Charleston to spend the other five months and twenty-nine days.

One time as they were about to leave, she handed me six grapefruits.

I thanked her, but then she said, "No, they are not for you to eat—keep those for me until I come back."

I thought, *"For six months? Are you kidding me? This lady really is crazy."*

I ate them within a week, and sure enough, when she returned six months later, the first thing she asked me was, "Where are my grapefruits?"

By that time, I had completely forgotten about them, so I ran down to the store to buy her six more and brought them back to her. That made her happy.

Anyway, as I said, the Round House became a huge part of my universe.

It was there when I really started to believe that ghosts exist. Maybe it had something to do with that architect killing himself there, I don't know, but soon after my Grandma Grace died, her image came to me in the middle of the night. I could see her face clear as day in my room even though it was late and completely dark. Then she came again, and again, and again. And I wasn't dreaming, either. I was wide awake.

I liked to think that she was coming to check on me, to watch over me, because we had been so close. She was probably my favorite person in the whole world and her posthumous visits made me feel good. It also got me to thinking about the afterlife, believing it existed after all.

Anyway, I rented the bottom half of the Round House from Myra for $150 per month. I turned around and sub-leased half of that to another lifeguard named Dave Hampton for $150 while my buddy Wink took the living room sometimes. I charged him only one dollar per night for every night he slept on the couch. From the living room and from my bedroom, we both had awesome views of the Atlantic.

In other words, I lived on the beach for free—for seven years. Wink wasn't there for the entire seven years.

Meanwhile, Burke and Deep Tan were still going strong.

I didn't like the fact that he was doing well, and nobody really liked the guy anyway. I had to do something about it. The Round House had a three-car garage—that very garage where I like to think I made history in the suncare market.

I had all these ideas that had been floating in my head and it was time to put them together and do something about it, so I went out and bought a silver galvanized garbage can. It cost only four dollars.

I took it to a shop teacher I knew at Holly Hill Junior High where I had taught school.

"Can you cut a hole in the bottom of this and add a plug?" I asked.

"Easy," he said.

I knew just enough chemistry to be dangerous, or in this case, successful.

After tinkering with the various ingredients—coconut oil that originated from seeing those Hawaiian girls, avocado and Aloe Vera among other things for example—I got the consistency and smell just right. The most important thing, I thought, was that it was all natural. There was nothing artificial in it. There were no chemicals like Coppertone used.

By the time I had it just right, the formula was all in my head, too, and I poured all the ingredients all by hand to get the perfect amounts of each.

I didn't even write it all down, but I had a good memory. I always remembered it all to a tee.

My new tanning concoction smelled wonderful.

I cut the end of a long broom-handle and used it as my stirring stick.

Maybe I never expected it to go anywhere. Maybe I just wanted to earn a few extra bucks in the summertime to supplement my measly income, but I would never know if I didn't try.

So, I called Dad to ask for $500 to get it all started and he came through for me.

I soon discovered a company called FE Mason in New York, which produced labels for bottles. I started tinkering around trying to come up with a design for the label of the bottle. At first, I wanted a label shaped like a coconut, but I couldn't make it look exactly right. I started playing around with a Tiki hut design, and I knew I was on to something. I figured the Tiki design would be perfect.

I had to decide on a name, and I knew I had to have "tropic" in it somehow. Tropic means something exotic to me, like the tropics. And the desired effect was a golden tan, so I called my invention "Tropic Tan."

I then hired several kids who were about eleven or twelve years old to fill bottles with my mixtures. There were always surfer kids hanging around the beach every day who would work if you paid them well. And I did pay them very well, at least way beyond what minimum wage was at the time.

They would come in early and then I would open the garage door of the Round House at lunch time and shove a bunch of Burger King burgers under there for them and I also made sure they had plenty to drink.

They really couldn't get out of that garage. I had them locked in there. I think back on that now and if there had been a fire . . . it was dangerous, but I never thought of the worst-case scenarios back then. I cringe about it now.

I like to think now that I helped those kids, who are in their sixties today. They were making money and I tried to teach them what I knew about business. Their names were Ken Loubriel, Kevin Masters, Charlie Messer, Robert Mitchell, Larry Saufl and Carl Livingston.

Kenny was a real hard worker. He started for me when he just eleven years old. (I trusted him, and his entire family later worked for me at some point.) He never complained one bit. When he grew up, he moved to the Florida Panhandle, became a preacher, got married and had kids—and I still stay in touch with him today. I know that Robert died a few years ago, but last I heard the rest of them are doing well.

These were the kids that helped me make history.

It didn't take long for the city of Ormond Beach to figure I was manufacturing something in the Round House, but they didn't know what, so they sent this inspector out to spy on me. I would see him sitting in his car, across the street, watching the house most days, but I also knew he had to cut off every day at five o'clock.

I am sure Burke had tipped him off in the first place. That guy was more obsessed in stopping me than making his product better and trying to outsell me.

Anyway, as soon as the clock hit five every afternoon, we would raise the garage doors and let air in there for the kids. My buddy, Paul Jacobs, who now worked as a chemist for a big carpet company in Dalton, Georgia, stopped by to see me one day.

He was well-versed in all the county's health and safety regulations.

"You can't do that," he would tell me.

Then he would notice something else.

"You can't do that, either," he said.

Paul noticed all those things, so I eventually hired him. He would become my lead chemist, but much later, he had a terrible traffic accident and had collided with a Coca-Cola delivery truck head-on, which resulted in a head injury and a long hospital stay. (When he returned to work for us, I made him a safety engineer at our factory. Today, he is retired and still lives in Daytona.)

I had to hire an assistant to help me. Her name was Karen Streichert, a tall, beautiful girl who all the guys had been chasing. Well, one day as a big truck was pulling out of our driveway at the Round House, this city inspector pulled up. The truck had just delivered a shipment of glass bottles.

As the guy walked up to the house, Karen was shutting the garage door. All of a sudden, a box fell, and all of those glass bottles were breaking and making a lot of noise, but she never let him in to inspect the place.

Now that I had production rolling, there was only one

question: Will sunbathers like what I had created enough to spend their money on it?

I loaded my old Ford Mustang convertible, a car which had been eaten alive by the salt air and took the product out to the beach and the pools up and down Daytona Beach and Ormond Beach and approached all the lifeguards.

"This is a great product and I know it will sell if you give it a chance," I told them. "It's much better than anything on the market now."

Here's how the hotel pool deck sales business worked back then in Florida: The hotel owner would give the lifeguard the right to sell products at their pool. The lifeguard would sell the product, take care of the pool and watch over its sunbathers and swimmers, especially the kids, and generally try to make everybody happy. As lifeguards, we knew if the tourists were happy with their pool experience, they would return to that particular hotel in the future.

If you didn't make everybody happy, and the hotel owners heard complaints, lifeguards would lose your right to sell products at that pool.

Fortunately, my new oil took off right away.

It was a sales hit.

Soon, I had many lifeguards selling it for me and they would get a cut of whatever was sold each day. I would collect it all and then distribute it daily, strictly on a cash basis.

I eventually had the rights to four hotels at once.

We also sold bathing caps, tiki necklaces and floats. But the main product, of course, was this new suncare oil.

It was a good deal for the hotel owners because nothing came out of their pockets. They didn't have to pay us. We essentially were getting paid by the hotel guests and that was a win-win for everybody.

Our risk when it came to saving lives was dramatically reduced on the pool decks as it was on the beach and in the Atlantic Ocean. We always tried our best to enforce the parents to watch their own kids, but we still made sure we had at least two guards at each pool. If one lifeguard was distracted by a pretty girl at the time, we had another one there to pay attention to what mattered most.

(Compare that to today's beachfront hotels, or hotels anywhere for that matter. There are no lifeguards working at all unless it is a top resort. They just place "Swim at your own risk" signs everywhere—and people buy their suncare and beach products at a CVS or Walgreens across the street).

Now that I had a popular product, I would constantly work deals with fellow lifeguards, who would peddle it to tourists on the pool decks up and down Daytona and Ormond Beaches.

It was nothing for a lifeguard to sell anywhere from $150 to $500 worth of products on a nice, sunny day at the various pools up and down the beach. I learned that a tanned, good-looking lifeguard makes a heck of a salesman.

And the importance of lifeguards would become paramount to my success as the years progressed.

At the old Summit Hotel, right on the beach on the south side where Route 92 (now International Speedway Boulevard) ends at the beach, I landed the rights to the pool concession. The Riviera Hotel was on the opposite corner, or the north side.

Ironically, it was the exact same spot where that cottage burned down when I first arrived in Daytona from being sick in New Orleans a few years earlier. And that was where I installed my first billboard.

It read: "Tropic Tan" and you couldn't miss it as you drove out to the beach from the mainland. But I soon had a running battle with the city and their permit people were always trying to force me to take it down, but I had befriended an older attorney who was staying at the Summit Hotel.

I also had gotten into the float concession business as well. I bought thirteen surfboards, but I had no idea how to surf. I would rent them out for the day to tourists who were learning to surf. Problem was, there was a guy who already had a float concession business near there and he was trying to shut me down, too.

So, this attorney dreamed up the idea to sell them—but just for a day.

I would "sell" the boards in the morning and then buy them back when the surfers were finished with them that same day.

I still hadn't made any inroads in getting the product in stores, even after I created a sales brochure from the copying machine where I had taught at Mainland High. I mailed it to fifty retail stores up and down the Daytona Beach coast and I received one reply—from a tiny drugstore in Ormond Beach.

When it came to determine a price for my new product, I also used some philosophy. I always wanted my oils and sunscreens to be priced one quarter to fifty cents higher than any other product on the market. It was simple: I believed if customers saw it was a little more expensive, then they naturally would figure it had to be better. And I believed it was better, so It wasn't as though I wanted to fool the customer.

It turned out that it was a smart thing to do because that strategy worked.

When I started, Coppertone had a set price of $2.75 to $3.75 for most of their products. I went a bit higher and even had a set price from the factory for our deluxe Royal Blend at five dollars.

I knew that since Tropic Tan was popular around my home beaches, it surely would sell elsewhere, too. I just needed the contacts and salespeople to help me. And from lifeguarding days in Myrtle Beach, I knew it was the perfect place to spread my wings.

"Sun Fun" was an annual festival there that marked the official beginning to each summer, was perfect for our product. It centered on having fun at the beach, getting sun, sort of the official kickoff to each summer. It would be the perfect market.

I decided to write a letter to the head football coach of Myrtle Beach High School, thinking maybe I could expand my product through fellow football coaches. I basically explained what I was producing and how it was selling in Daytona and I asked, "If you want to do the same thing and sell this product in Myrtle Beach, write me back."

I soon received a letter from a man named Elton Brunty.

"I am not the head coach, but I am his assistant coach," he wrote. "Do I qualify?"

I then drove up to South Carolina to visit with Elton, arriving at his school at about ten in the morning. I walked into his classroom and introduced myself.

"What are you doing? You will get me fired!" he said. "Come back after school at three!"

Naturally, I headed to the beach. Within a few hours, I had sold more than $2,000 worth of my Tropic Tan. When I returned later that day, I showed Elton my ten-cent book full of sales receipts.

His eyes grew large and he told me, "Okay, I am in! What do I have to do?"

I hired another guy named Gene Perkins, who came to me one day and said, "I think I can sell some of this stuff in the New England states."

I had enough money coming in that I had hired Gene Perkins and I also decided to head to France, Portugal, the south coast of Spain, Monaco and Italy, looking for markets in which I could sell Tropic Tan. I saw a lot of Europe in a very short time. I would fly into a city, rent a car and just start exploring. And my product proved to be popular overseas, too.

As my success grew with Tropic Tan, my competitors—mainly Burke—grew more worried.

And much more ruthless.

He would sneak into stores, or hire someone to do it, and open a bottle of my Tropic Tan and insert a cockroach.

He figured one roach found in the product would lead to negative publicity and put a big hurt on my sales, so he had inserted one in a bottle of my product at Liggett's Drug Store. When the manager caught him doing it, he lost that account—and it was a major account.

I called this practice, "roaching the aloe," but it never successfully worked the way he had intended.

Another strange thing happened, born out of pure jealousy and greed.

When Steve Santoro and I first moved to Daytona after partying in New Orleans, I had met a guy by the name of John Guyton. John was a beach bum who had recently moved down from Atlanta, just to look for people to pal around with.

So, we became friends and I also got to know a few of his buddies.

But one day he asked to use my bedroom at the Round House with the pretense that he was taking a girl in there.

But it really turned out to be was a spying mission.

He had broken into my files, writing down addresses and looking for my Tropic Tan formula, which as I said, was in my head. He took what he discovered and headed back to Atlanta, thinking he had the smoking gun to a sure fortune. He came up with something called "Island Tan," but it pretty much flopped.

And that pretty much ended our so-called friendship.

One day, I had walked into Liggett's Drug Store in the Bellaire Plaza, right where I used to sell shoes, to deliver a box of products. There was a pretty girl working behind the soda fountain and I noticed her immediately.

I approached her and she told me that she was still in high school. Her name was Linda Kocsis. The more I looked at her, the more beautiful she appeared to me. She had brown hair and I could tell she was very down to earth. I asked her out, but she turned me down.

Every time I went in there, I tried again, until finally, she agreed to go out with me.

Then she told me she had no intentions of dating me, but her friend wanted some free sun tan products from me, so that's why she finally agreed to go out with me. When she graduated from high school the following year, she moved to Miami to become a stewardess for National Airlines.

But it didn't take long to miss her, so I followed her to Miami.

I remember that while she was working for National, I really pissed off her boss one time at a party which one of the flight attendants hosted. His name was Lewis Maytag, the heir to the Maytag Appliance family fortune, and he owned the controlling interest in the airline. But the flight attendants were striking again. He hadn't been invited to the party, but he showed up anyway.

Linda had told me that he always wanted to play around with the pretty flight attendants, who wanted no part of him.

As a publicity stunt during the strike, he had lined up all his airplanes with the rear of each facing LeJeune Road, the main artery in and out of Miami International Airport.

So here we were at a party of flight attendants and the owner who they were striking against showed up against their wishes. Naturally, I think it was in my nature to try to piss him off.

And I succeeded.

"You know what you should do?" I asked him rhetorically. "Cut off the noses and tails of all of your airplanes, load the planes with your washers and dryers and let all the poor Cubans in town come over and wash their clothes."

Of course, he didn't laugh and left in a huff.

One Sunday, Linda flew into Daytona and I had to pick her up at the airport, but first I had to load a U-Haul truck full of product so Perkins could deliver it to stores in other states north of Florida up the eastern seaboard.

After we finished loading, I hopped in my Mustang and took off out of the parking lot from our building, headed to the airport to get Linda. Little did I know that I had FBI agents tailing me as I headed through Holly Hill. I must have been late to pick up Linda because I had driven so fast that I had lost the agents, although I didn't know this until later.

Once I picked her up, we headed to Perkins' grandmother's house to pick up some bicycles. As I pulled into her driveway, Perkins was there with the rental truck and it was surrounded by sheriff's cars, local police cars and FBI agents. I could see agents pulling bottles of my product out of boxes and dumping the contents on the ground.

Suddenly, I heard someone call my name.

The voice came from Ronnie Morgan, who just happened to be one of my former football players at Mainland who now was an Ormond Beach police officer. The FBI agents in charge were parked across the street and Ronnie talked to them convincing them that I was no drug dealer. This went on for a while as Ronnie would come back to me with questions from the FBI and I would answer them and then he would walk back across the street and deliver the answers.

One of my messages to them was this: "I have already written one sales order for you for all the product you dumped out on the ground. If you want to dump any more, I will start writing the second one."

As this went on for a while, I learned that the agents had been hiding behind the railroad tracks, watching us through binoculars earlier as we loaded the product into the rental truck.

Finally, after a lot of explaining, they were convinced they had been had and had received a bad tip.

It was a tip of vengeance.

What I learned was that Burke had called the police earlier and claimed we were drug dealers about to haul a huge shipment. Our building just happened to be next door to another building where drug dealers had been nailed earlier, so the police gave his tip some credence.

Even though Tropic Tan was succeeding, I still wasn't being taken seriously in the business community.

When I walked into a bank to make a deposit from Topic Tan sales, I usually had nothing on but a straw hat, bathing suit and a pair of flip flops. There was no dress shirt, let alone a suit and tie. There were no fancy shoes.

Bankers must have looked at me and thought, "You are nothing but a local yokel, a real fly-by-nighter, aren't you?"

That was my image and I knew it.

The local banks collectively considered me nothing but a local beach bum.

I would constantly apply for loans to get the business rolling even more only to be turned down each time. I always thought: *There is going to come a time you will want my business and I will be turning YOU down!*

But I never told them that.

I had a friend named Jack Tasker and he loved my lifestyle and what I was doing, so he put me in touch with a banker named Ed Brown at NCNB in North Carolina and Ed saw the future and potential in the company. He soon came through, loaning me $20,000 as a line of credit and I took that money and bought even more bottles, bottle caps and labels.

I also found a chemist in Miami by the name of Ben Friedman and he helped me develop a lotion for Tropic Tan to go with my oil. So now I had two products to sell.

I had never taken any business courses in high school or at Tennessee. I was into sports, and chemistry, and science. What the hell did I know about running a business? I just did whatever came to my mind on a certain day. So, what if I made a mistake? I would learn from it. If I screwed up, I screwed up.

I still didn't have much spending money in my pocket since I was pouring almost every cent of profit back into the business. Me and my buddies still cut corners when it came to eating out, entertainment, parties and attending sporting events on the cheap.

And I was still teaching.

I had been using the weekends to drive to Miami on Fridays, filling fourteen of those large, fifty-five-gallon drums with lotions, and returning each Sunday night. I often drove into the Campbell parking lot early Monday morning, slept in my car for a few hours and then woke up on time to get to class. Or other times, I didn't wake up on time.

The humiliating thing was, I had to sign a pink piece of paper if I was one minute late.

The principal, Jack Surrette, never cut me any slack, either. He would be standing there by the timeclock just waiting for me to be one minute, if not seconds, late for my class.

So, he soon fired me, just like the others had before him.

Getting fired never got to me much, because I knew every time it happened it was only temporary.

Anyway, on Friday, January 11, 1969, my roommate Wink and I threw my little dachshund I had named "Skinny von Weiner III" into my delivery van and we drove to Miami in my old beat-up beige Ford '65 van I used for deliveries, figuring we would somehow find a way into this relatively new event they called the Super Bowl.

Nobody expected much of a game as Don Shula's powerhouse NFL team, the Baltimore Colts, were supposed to steamroll the

AFL champion New York Jets, but we wanted to see it anyway. We loved to take road trips and just goof off having a good time, trying to meet girls. We didn't want to spend money for a hotel that weekend, so Wink and I threw down some large pads in the back of the van and parked in it the parking lot of the Newport Hotel.

That day at the beach we ran into two pretty girls.

"Where are you staying?" they asked.

"Oh, we are over at the Newport . . . just thought we would try a different hotel this time," I said, acting as if we visited Miami Beach often.

We were at the Newport alright—the Newport parking lot, sleeping in the back of a beat-up van. We woke up the next day, took a nice swim in the Atlantic, then grabbed a bar of soap and showered at the hotel pool's outdoor shower before driving that beat-up van over to the Orange Bowl Stadium.

Somehow, we scored some cheap tickets and sat in the bleachers in the open end of the field. We had a great view as we watched sports history being made in front of us, as Joe Namath directed the Jets to the biggest upset in football history in Super Bowl III.

That shocking outcome turned Namath into a major celebrity and changed his life forever.

Little did I know it at time, but 1969 was about to become the year that changed mine forever, too.

Chapter Six

HELLO "HAWAIIAN TROPIC"

A few months later when the weather warmed up, I was minding my business, sitting in my lifeguard stand, thinking about Tropic Tan and what move I had to do next to sell even more, while looking at the girls and the ocean, as well as just daydreaming the time away . . .

That's when this nerdy-looking guy approached me.

I had noticed him hanging around my stand earlier, but he never said a word—until now.

"How are you?" he asked. "Nice day, huh?"

To my knowledge, I don't think I ever had a gay friend growing up, or in high school or college for that matter, so I had no experience with recognizing who may have been gay.

But I was positive this guy was gay because he seemed to be hitting on me in a subtle way. More importantly, it turned out that he was a lawyer on vacation from Washington, D.C.

I always prided myself in being very nice to people whom I don't know, because the majority of people you come across throughout your life are nice, decent people. Why be a jerk to someone you don't even know? I already had plenty of candidates, like Burke, and those city code people, to be a jerk to if I had wanted.

Anyway, we started to talk, and I started telling this guy the details about Tropic Tan and how I developed it and how well it was selling.

Then he asked, "What about your patents and trademarks?"

"What do you mean?" I asked.

"Well, you have to register your patents and trademarks," he told me.

I had no clue what he was talking about—patents and trademarks—but I also could tell that he knew exactly what he was talking about.

"I tell you what. I'll do you a favor and check on it for you," he told me.

I gave him my phone number, he returned to D.C., and sure enough, he called me a few days later to deliver the news. It wasn't good.

"Ron, not only do you not own this name 'Tropic Tan,' but it was registered in 1951 to some family in New Jersey," he told me.

My mind started racing: *Oh my God, here we go . . . I have been selling a product for a few years and I don't even own it?*

I was crushed, panicked and dumbfounded all at once.

My panic lasted a few days, before I brainstormed a little while about how to try and fix this suddenly gigantic problem. I had to confront it head-on, so I decided to take a trip to New

Jersey. The lawyer had given me the owner's address and I thought maybe I could buy the name from him.

One of my students had given me this beautiful little German Shepherd puppy, so I loaded my Mustang with boxes of Tropic Tan to sell along the way, put my puppy in the backseat and took off driving North. My car didn't have air-conditioning and it couldn't have been hotter that summer day that I left Daytona. I dropped off boxes of products in Myrtle Beach for Elton Brunty the following day and it seemed even hotter if that was possible.

As I drove, my window was rolled all the way down, but I had the passenger's side windows about halfway down.

All of a sudden, my puppy just jumped out the window. All I could think of later was that he must have been hot and needed water. I looked into my mirror to see him tumbling down a hill off the side of the road. I pulled over into the dirt and went to find him. He apparently had come back up the hill and then was hit by an oncoming car on the freeway. As I ran back toward him, a motorist had waved to me not to bother. He was gone.

I went back, picked him up and wanted to give him a proper burial under some rocks in the river. When I finished, just as I was about to walk back to my car, I heard a yipping noise and followed it, discovering a burlap sack of dead puppies in some shrubs by the riverbank. However, one female, black-and-white Terrier was somehow still alive. Some jerk must have thrown the bag off the nearby bridge intending to kill all the puppies.

I cradled this lone survivor, put her on the floor on the passenger side and drove off to find a vet. Once I found one in the nearest town, the vet made it more than obvious he cared about being paid more than saving the dog's life, so I drove off to a convenience store and bought some milk.

It was obvious she had been starved, but I also could tell that she was going to make it.

It also didn't take long for her to have diarrhea all over the car's floor.

After I reached New Jersey, I found the house of the man who owned the rights to Tropic Tan and knocked on the front door. The maid answered.

"Sorry, he's in California," she told me.

But the trip wasn't fruitless—she did give me his phone number. Soon after I returned to Daytona, I finally reached the guy on the phone.

"I won't sell you the name, but I'll lease it to you," he told me.

"No, I want to own it," I told him.

"That name is a family heirloom!" he said. "There's no way I can sell it!"

Heirloom? I thought. It's a name, not a diamond ring or a painting. I could tell there was no bargaining with him, but there also was no way I was going to pay rent for a name for years to come, so now I faced a new dilemma.

I had to come up with a new name for the product I already had been selling for a few years.

I knew I wanted to keep "Tropic" somehow. I considered it a tropical product, and it also had a romantic aura to it. I also always loved Hawaii and I suddenly remembered those native girls on Oahu, cracking open the coconuts in that scene that had inspired me in the first place. My idea originated right there that day, so it was "Hawaiian," right?

The new name just came to me and it was that easy.

"Hawaiian Tropic."

I don't even remember the other possibilities I had bounced around in my head, but these two words had a ring to them together and it just seemed . . . well, natural.

I worked day and night with FE Mason about a new logo, new labels for my bottles and had all of them quickly shipped and ready to go. Then I had the kids working overtime to fill them.

On July 16, 1969, I drove south down A1A with the first boxes of Hawaiian Tropic in the back of my delivery van. It was 9:32 in the morning and I was about to make history; little did I know, I was also *witnessing* history.

I suddenly noticed this big silver-like streak heading straight up into the air in front of me.

What the hell? I thought.

I had been so busy with my product and its new name, I hadn't paid any attention to the news, what was happening in the world or what I was seeing.

What I was witnessing was real history in the making: Apollo 11 had blasted off from Cape Canaveral, about seventy-five miles south of Daytona. Five days later, Neil Armstrong would walk on the moon, moments before Buzz Aldrin did.

Wow, that's pretty neat, I thought.

Then I went right back to business of delivering the first-ever bottles of Hawaiian Tropic to the beaches and pool decks. I had an oil, a gel, a lotion and an aloe, but I was skittish and apprehensive. What am I going to do if this new name doesn't sell? What if customers want Tropic Tan instead? What do I tell them?

Within an hour, I realized I had no worries.

Sales took off like crazy. I sold out of what we had bottled very quickly.

The best thing was that I had beaten Paul Burke to the punch. My product was being gobbled up all over Daytona Beach while he was taking his time getting his new oil—something he was calling "Native Tan"—on the market, and thinking no competition was imminent.

I remember seeing him on a pool deck, storming around with his face as red as a tomato. It was my first major victory in the suncare wars; I can't describe how rewarding it was. It was pure fun working so hard so fast to beat a guy like him to the punch and it suddenly had paid off handsomely.

Looking back, I guess that's what drove me. I didn't want anybody to out-think me or out-work me, least of all a guy like Burke.

It is funny because I admit that when I worked for someone else, I watched the clock every day and lived for the weekends. Then once I started working for myself, and now that I had my own business, I thought nothing of working eighteen-hour days. In fact, I suddenly loved to work. I worked, ate, worked, slept and worked some more. And there was very little eating and sleeping in between.

I can only guess it's that way for most business owners. Employees watch the clock and business owners work like a dog, at least in the initial stage of their business.

Now that I had a great product and an exciting new name people seemed to like, I had to figure a way to get it into local stores.

And I tried just about anything.

There was a gift shop chain called Craig's Beach Hut in

Daytona, so one day I just paid the store a visit.

"Sorry, we only buy from the big boys," the manager told me. "We just don't mess with small-time guys like you."

I was persistent, but the guy wouldn't give in, so I just about gave up on convincing him.

A few days later, I noticed five girls all wearing Ohio State shirts on the pool deck at the Summit Hotel. They had "tourists" written all over them, and suddenly, I had an idea. I approached them and bluntly told them, "Okay girls, I have a great proposition for you! I am going to give you and your friends an entire summer's supply of this new product that you never heard of. It's called 'Hawaiian Tropic' . . ."

They had to think I was just using a new line and coming on to them, especially when I added, "But I am going to need you for about thirty minutes tonight."

Then I explained the entire scheme: I would return to pick them up at seven o'clock. They were right where I told them to be and I gave them a script to read and memorize. We drove back to that gift shop and I dropped the girls and then parked out of sight. I waited outside behind a palm tree, peering through the window to the gift shop as the girls wandered around inside. One of them picked up a panama hat with an alligator on it. Another looked at T-shirts.

Then they all went to the aisle with the tanning oils and sunscreens.

They were reciting the script . . . "Doesn't Janie want two bottles? She wants the expensive one, right?"

I saw the manager pick up a bottle of Coppertone and showed it to them.

"No, we don't use that crap," the girl said. "We only use

Hawaiian Tropic. You don't have Hawaiian Tropic?"

Of course, against all my sales overtures, I already knew he didn't, so they walked out in a huff just as I had scripted. I drove them back to their hotel, thanked them and handed them a big box full of Hawaiian Tropic products.

As soon as I walked back into the Round House that night, my telephone was ringing.

"You are the worst salesman in the world!" the voice said. "You haven't been in to see me lately."

It was the manager of the gift shop.

"Okay, I will be there first thing in the morning," I told him.

"No, no, you come down tonight," he demanded. "And bring some Hawaiian Tropic with you."

I quickly loaded the car and headed there. Within two weeks, that store sold so much Hawaiian Tropic that he agreed to put up two big displays—one in that store on North Atlantic Avenue and one in his other store on South Atlantic. I suddenly had both ends of the beach road covered.

This was the perfect example of how good the product was. It was just a matter of getting the buying public's attention. Once I got it placed on the store shelves, it sold like crazy and there was no turning back.

I could have stopped teaching school, because I was making so much money with the company, but I continued because I loved coaching football and loved being around the kids. And there still was this little thing called Vietnam going on—and teaching school guaranteed my deferment.

So, I continued it.

I coached football but didn't teach at Father Lopez High in 1970-72, although the school provided the necessary paperwork to continued deferment. Then I moved to Seabreeze High as a part-time chemistry teacher, for the 1972-73 school years. I would teach two classes and a lab, which took no more than three hours of my day.

That was enough to satisfy a woman I had never met or never even talked to for that matter, but I knew her name very well. She was feared by most men my age who grew up in or around Asheville. If you got a letter from her, you dreaded opening it.

Her name was Geneva Early Fox, who happened to be the head of the draft board in Buncombe County, North Carolina.

I still believed I needed verification from schools where I worked to send to Geneva, in order to justify my deferment each year. But after those two years at Seabreeze, Hawaiian Tropic was doing very well, and I figured I was pretty much in the clear as far as Vietnam went because of my age, so I decided to quit teaching altogether.

The war department had to want eighteen- and nineteen-year-old boys fresh out of high school as soldiers, rather than a thirty-three-year-old part-time chemistry teacher, lifeguard and suncare salesman.

When my teaching/coaching career finally was over, I had taught at seven schools for nine years, been fired a few times and quit on my own a few times. It was a great experience all in all and I hoped I helped hundreds of kids along the way and I stayed in touch with many, and I later hired many of them, too.

And that career probably prevented me from getting shot at, or worse yet, buried in some unmarked grave somewhere in the jungles of Southeast Asia.

Those three kids in my class—Rusty, Barney and Raymond—

who died there shortly after they had graduated and had their entire lives ahead of them were always on my mind and in my memory.

Without teaching on my plate, I became even more of a workaholic. All that time and energy I had put into coaching football or teaching chemistry for hardly any pay, I now could put into building my new and ever-expanding company. I knew my hard work over the next year or so would be the key to its success.

I hired people at all levels and continued working. I started to develop ads and continued working. I developed a marketing strategy and continued working.

By my final year of teaching school, 1973, four years into Hawaiian Tropic, sales were still growing fast, and I created a parent company to our products and called it Tanning Research Laboratories, Inc.

Also, I relied on something called the Thomas Register, which was basically an encyclopedia for American industry and business owners. I could look up where to buy just about any ingredient or product I needed for our production.

All we needed was a factory to keep up with the production demand.

So, I scouted around for possible land in which to build a small factory. I found a perfect piece of land in Ormond Beach and paid $25,000 for it. I then had to build the factory. I shopped around and started talking to this construction company about the specifics and then decided I should call Dad to see if he would come down and help negotiate a deal for me.

After all, he was head of one of the largest building departments in the world and he knew much more about building and construction than I ever would. By the time he was finished talking to them, I think he had scared the hell of them into giving me a great deal. When they were finished, we had a nice little factory of about 9,000-square feet.

What was important is how much land it came with because I knew we could expand over time if we needed to.

Now that I had a facility, I also attended trade shows to learn about production, equipment and the latest technology of manufacturing. At the first one in Chicago, I was overwhelmed by the various kinds of equipment you could buy to update your factory.

We happened to need an automatic tube filler at the time. There was a vice president there demonstrating this tube filler, wearing a suit and tie and trying to act like he knew what he was doing. He put the tube in the machine upside down, just as the lotion came spitting out all over his face, down his shirt and tie. The crimper then caught fire because it was upside down, too.

I calmly said, "Sir, I really don't think we want to fill our tubes like this."

I had a couple of my workers with me and we slowly walked away smiling. By the time we got thirty feet away, we were into a full, gut-busting laughter.

The key employees I hired became such a big part of my life and many of them were real characters.

A guy named Bill Darby—whom all his friends simply called "Darby"—had come to see me one day, trying to sell me an incentive plan for a reward-type program similar to green stamps. Way back when, shoppers would receive stamps when they bought groceries, then paste them in a book and turn them in for more groceries. Anyway, after talking to Darby for a while, I saw his potential for an incredible salesman.

"Look, I am not buying your program," I told him, "but let me sell something to *you*."

I told him everything about my new business and then I offered him a job. He took it on the spot and eventually became my vice president of marketing.

Darby had grown up with a guy named Larry Adams and it just happened they had attended Tennessee a few years after me. As Darby worked for me, he continued telling me about this guy Larry, who was a great attorney in Lewisburg, Tennessee.

Then on one trip back to Knoxville to go to a Volunteers football game, we invited Larry to join us and we soon grew to be good friends.

Earlier, I had made the mistake of hiring a former lifeguard-roommate to do some legal work. Well, he had screwed up just about every lawsuit in the beginning that he ever touched for us, so I was looking for a new one.

I hired Larry.

As I would learn through the years, Darby had the personality and mischievousness to create all the problems before Larry would come along and clean up his mess. And that is how their friendship worked. Whatever Darby could get away with, or at least thought he could get away with, he tried.

However, Larry would become one of my most trusted executives for decades to come. Another guy came along and handled the accounting and I made him a vice-president, too.

Even though Linda had moved to Miami, I continued seeing her. I made sales calls to Miami all the time anyway.

Then I did something really stupid.

I asked her to marry me. I guess I just thought, "All my friends are doing it, so I might as well, too."

I really can't remember a big romantic proposal or anything like that, but I had placed her engagement ring inside a small box and placed it inside a larger box and that box inside even a larger box and so on. There must have been ten boxes for her to go through before she realized it was a ring and that I was asking her to marry me.

Maybe that's what I thought I should do at my age and stage in life.

We had a very small wedding at a church in Ormond Beach.

She had come from sort of a kooky family. In fact, her father was a total kook. He once locked his son in a walk-in freezer when he got mad at him. The family had four kids, and Linda was really the only sane one in the group.

I remember sitting next to her father at a Thanksgiving dinner one time when they served Brie Cheese as an appetizer. I ate the inside, leaving the chalky outside part on my plate. He became incensed because I wouldn't eat it all. He went on and on about it, until I finally picked up the chalky part and put it on his plate.

"Here, I want you to have the best part of the Brie cheese," I told him.

He stood up and stormed out of the room.

By the time we got married, Linda had grown tired of the Round House and all the commotion that went on there, and the frat-like atmosphere, so I told her to go find another house for us. She found this little house on Hollywood Street she liked, about four blocks off A1A, near the beach, so I bought it.

When we moved in there, I didn't realize one of my ex-girlfriends lived next to it, ironically.

After all, Linda chose the house in the first place.

After we married, we also rented an apartment in Coral Gables because of her stewardess job, which allowed both of us to fly anywhere in the world for only five dollars. Staying there was quite an adjustment for me because I had grown to love the Daytona area. But I had been commuting back and forth between the two cities all the time anyway, while teaching, dating her and running the business.

Later, I also bought a beach house in Daytona, with a pool table in one room, and it became somewhat of a party house for my friends and top employees. I learned later that Linda had spied on the place a few times, looking through windows hoping to catch me at something illicit.

It was a strange situation and within two years, she wanted to end the marriage.

"Okay, whatever you want," I said.

I then made another mistake. I let her hire a much better attorney than I did. For some reason, I signed an agreement that would have me making alimony payments for the rest of my life. Today, she is a social worker living in Denver and we still talk once in a while. She never remarried, but then again, she didn't need to financially, because I still pay her alimony, even all these years later.

Like I said, she had a much better lawyer than I did.

When Hawaiian Tropic sales exploded in the coming years, Linda tried one time for us to get back together.

"No, I don't think so," I told her.

Then again, I hadn't learned from my mistake enough not to do it all over again many years later.

I did score one major head-to-head victory in my new venture.

One day in the early 1970s, I had noticed Burke had placed his "Royal Oil" signs all over the pool decks up and down the beach, but he had not yet released his new product. He was taking his time, thinking there was no competition for it in sight. I wanted to beat him to the punch with a similar product I had already worked on so I made the kids work extra-long hours to get my new product which I would call by the same name.

So, I immediately called FE Mason and ordered them to work up some labels with the new name.

"You have to make this label as quickly as you can and ship them to me so I can compete with this guy," I told them. "I want the words 'Royal Tanning Blend' on the label directly under the words "Hawaiian Tropic."

We went to work and produced hundreds of bottles filled and ready to go, just waiting on the new labels. They arrived within a few days and me and the kids worked all day and night, attaching them to all the bottles. That next day, I delivered them to the pool decks and at once saw Burke scurrying around in misery, completely befuddled that I had beaten him to the punch.

By 1975, Hawaiian Tropic was entrenched as a thriving company, sales were huge, money was flowing in and I was working around the clock. And people were noticing.

One day when the popular *All in the Family* was running on CBS, I opened a letter at the office, and it was from Rob Reiner. His letter complimented us on the product.

I took it and superimposed a picture of him on TV and put it in our sales kit. Buyers were very impressed that the "Meathead" would use Hawaiian Tropic and it helped with sales.

I sent him a big box of products and about two weeks later, I received a letter from the actor Peter Boyle, who became famous later for his role on *Everybody Loves Raymond*.

"Can you send me a box like the one you sent the 'Meathead?'" he asked.

So, I did.

I knew we were making waves when I went to a trade show once at People's Drugs in D.C., and two high-level Coppertone reps approached me. Their names were Lanny Chase and Will Smith, just like the actor.

One of them asked, "Do you really want to hop on this merry-go-round?"

"What do you mean?" I asked.

"Well, once you get on, you can't get off of it," he said. "It's a tough business . . . a really tough business."

I knew they were trying to discourage me because Hawaiian Tropic's increasing sales were making them extremely nervous.

I even had the money coming in to enable us to lease two large aloe fields, one in New Mexico and one in Texas, through a third party, a company in Melbourne, Florida. I knew that we had to be a big promoter of aloe and we used a lot of it. We probably controlled the aloe market in those early days, so much so that we often sold it to other companies that needed it.

What most people don't realize is that it takes six years from the time an aloe plant is planted until it can be harvested. We had the aloe processed at the fields and had it shipped back to Florida in large drums on tractor-trailer flatbeds.

One day, I received a nasty letter from a guy named Rodney

Stockton, the owner and CEO of a Fort Lauderdale company called Aloe Creme Laboratories, Inc. It was addressed to "Ron Rice, Assistant Plant Manager, Hawaiian Tropic."

It was basically a "cease and desist" letter regarding the use of so much aloe, since I guess he deemed us a threat to his company's bottom line. Knowing it was bogus threat, I wrote him back stating that we would do no such thing, but the funny thing was that I addressed the letter: "Rod Stockton, Assistant Stock Boy, Aloe Crème Laboratories."

Legend has it that Cleopatra used aloe to keep her skin looking so young, and if that is true, I agreed with her, so I knew full well that aloe, just like coconut oil, was a key component of what we were producing.

What I did learn though was that I couldn't just stick the name 'Hawaiian Tropic' on any product and it would automatically be successful. One such failure was a line of cosmetics. We tried to create it, and I thought it was very well done and very well packaged, but it just did not sell.

I learned you had to roll with the punches and adapt. If you tried something and it failed, that doesn't mean you stop trying.

Meanwhile back home in North Carolina, Dad was getting sicker and sicker with congestive heart failure.

I flew up and walked into his hospital room.

"These people are killing me, Ron," he told me. "Get me out of here."

The doctors walked me out into the hallway. They explained the painkillers were taking effect.

"When people are dying, that is normal," they said. "They say things . . . they say anything."

I knew that he was *dying*. I flew back to Daytona. After I got back home, Mom called with the terrible news: Dad was gone.

This was years after the state had taken his house from him and I knew then the news had started killing him prematurely, as I said earlier. Now it was official. He was gone forever. As far as I was concerned, the state of North Carolina officially had finished the job. I drove back to Asheville and went straight to the mortuary.

"Open it up," I told the worker at the mortuary. "I want to make sure it's him."

They opened the casket. I lifted one of his hands and held it. It was twice the size of mine. That was one of those large paws that had caught me across the head a few times when I was a kid, like when I scooped up that sand the first time I saw Daytona Beach.

I loved that man.

You may wonder why I wanted to open his casket. I guess I just wanted to make sure it was him, and that we would be burying the man who was my father. I learned over the years that you can't trust some people and I really wanted to make sure it was him. I had heard that funeral workers or mortuaries sometimes substitute bodies or bury the wrong person in the wrong grave.

Soon after, Mom told me, "Ronny, he was so happy that you went into business for yourself. That is something he always wanted to do."

I never realized that.

He had stayed at American ENKA all those decades for his entire career. I had no idea he wanted to own a business. Was he proud of me? Well, if he was, he never said so. I just like to think it was implied. As I said, we weren't a family which told each other, "I am proud of you" or "I love you" . . . I like to think it was just understood.

For some reason, my brother, Crosby, handled his estate. I never did find out if Mom had given him that duty, or if Dad did.

But I soon discovered that my brother was greedy, greedy, greedy.

During Dad's funeral, he and his wife left early, and I could not figure out why they would do that. It turned out they had gone to Mom and Dad's house, taking all his hunting and fishing gear . . . everything . . . they just cleaned it out.

I had wanted one of Dad's guns, a .22 rifle, which he once told me I could have. I had used it when I hunted growing up and I really liked that gun. Dad had a lot of guns, but that is the only one I really cared about. It was gone, too.

Crosby also took some of the estate money and built an extra room on his old farmhouse where he lived in South Carolina. After Mom moved in with him and his family, he then took some of her money and built a swimming pool. He used up a lot of her money for other things and when I found out about it, I was not happy at all.

Finally, he kicked her out of the house, claiming she was a bad influence on his kids. I knew he just made it up, so he had an excuse to get rid of her. I drove up there to settle things. It was the final straw for me.

"Mom, just come down and live on the beach with me," I told her.

She liked that idea, so we drove back to Daytona.

I felt so bad about how my brother had treated her. She was

our mother and I had to take care of her, even though I was building a company and my time was limited to tend to her needs.

For the next five years, I took her everywhere and she had a blast. I took her to Hawaii with me three times. I took her on supersonic jets and helicopter rides. She would sit right up front as the pilot dipped down mountains or into a volcano. She loved every minute of it.

In her final year or so, as her health deteriorated, I hired a nurse to look after her. She would wheel her out to the living area every day so she could sit and look at the ocean. She spent her final years mad at my brother, too, enough that she had made me executor of her estate.

When she finally died and it was time to divide her money, which was about $200,000, I just gave it all to my sister Barbara. Crosby didn't deserve a penny of it. I figured he had probably drained about a third of her money earlier anyway.

My brother and I were estranged at that point and we remained that way, until the day he died. I never spoke to him again. He died mad at me and I was certainly mad at him. I did go to his funeral, however, because I loved his two kids and I owed it to them.

Does it all bother me to this day?

It bothers me to a point because I am a family guy. I would have loved to have had a close brother like other people do, a brother for whom I would have lived and died, as he would have for me. But I didn't.

It just wasn't meant to be for us.

And I accepted that.

Chapter Seven

"GUERRILLA MARKETING"

Once I realized that this product line, Hawaiian Tropic, was going to make it, and make it big, I never really set any sales goals or had a stated desire to be the No. 1 suntan company in the world.

That was never in my thought process.

I had only one thought: *"Let's just see how far I can take this thing."*

I also realized that to increase sales and keep it sustainable, I had to come up with some savvy marketing and advertising to further its growth.

With ads and marketing, I just operated by the seat of my pants.

I did not know a thing about advertising or marketing. I had never taken any advertising courses in college, so like everything else, I learned on the fly through trial and error.

I had the product in local stores everywhere in the early 1970s, but I had to come up with a strategy to get the products into the major outlets. One of the first things I did was buy advertising space on every billboard I could find in Bentonville, Arkansas.

You may wonder, why would a Florida-based company do such a thing? Bentonville, Arkansas?

It was simple. That's where Walmart's headquarters are located.

I had learned that Sam Walton would not let his employees travel much, so when they were driving to and from home and work, they would be seeing all our billboards. So, those key people at Walmart had to figure that they also were plastered all over the nation as well.

That was the furthest thing from the truth. I had a few in Daytona and several in Bentonville and that was it even though you couldn't buy it there.

Sure enough, my strategy worked, and I soon landed a major account with Walmart.

But other than that idea specifically targeted for Walton's company, I focused locally, sponsoring just about everything to do with spring break in Daytona Beach in the 1970s and '80s. I figured that I had to build the name recognition and brand right there in its birthplace and hometown and then build outward.

I started spending as much as $200,000 every March, which covered events, signs and banners featuring our name and logo practically everywhere spring breakers were.

I tried everything and anything to make Hawaiian Tropic a household name in those early days. Some of the smaller things on a local scale were very cost-effective toward first getting our name out there. We even paid to pull Hawaiian Tropic banners behind airplanes flying over the beach, to placing our ads on sailboat masts and then having the sailboats just crisscross each other all day in front of the crowded beaches. Those things never cost much, and it was great exposure.

Daytona Beach became the mecca for spring break in the 1970s and '80s once Fort Lauderdale's city leaders shut theirs down to nothing but a small party. Some Florida location had to pick up the slack and fortunately, it was Daytona Beach, because it is right where I lived, and where the company was headquartered.

It was only natural to me to use every spring to market Hawaiian Tropic to college kids. I always believed that you could develop life-long customers if your product appealed to buyers at an early age.

There was a guy named Allan Cohen, whose parents owned a string of hotels up and down the beach. The city leaders came to hate Allan for various reason, but he and I worked together on many projects, so I would work with the city to pull permits for him while telling the city it was for a Hawaiian Tropic promotion.

I owned a large portable stage, which cost me $30,000. And whenever the cities of Ormond Beach or Daytona Beach needed a stage, I loaned it to them for free. All I asked was that they hung a sign that read: "Compliments of Hawaiian Tropic."

We even sponsored a comedy showcase event on the beach in 1984 at the New Moon Grill which featured Jerry Seinfeld—way before his TV show debuted—and Billy Crystal. Leslie Neilsen, who later became a good friend, was there. So was his

Naked Gun co-star by the name of O.J. Simpson

We hosted concerts by the Moody Blues, Three Dog Night and The Fixx one year.

And with that came being exposed to rock stars and some rock-star attitudes.

We had sponsored a river cruise to entertain some of the entertainers before the event that week. I spent a lot of money on food and drinks and we invited all of our secretaries and several of our top Hawaiian Tropic models. We used a large van to transport everyone to the boat that day and first stopped at Daytona Beach's nicest hotel to pick up Graeme Edge, the Moody Blues' drummer. We waited and waited and waited. Finally, after forty-five minutes, he appeared in the valet area holding a Bloody Mary.

He stumbled over to the van and held his hand out, as if he were a princess and needed help getting into the van. So, I reached out and helped him into the van just as if he were Queen Elizabeth.

Then we stopped by a cheap motel to pick up all the members of The Fixx. We all boarded the boat that day and within minutes, Edge was demanding a certain kind of vodka that had not been supplied at the bar. I promptly sent one of the girls across the street from the dock to buy it at a liquor store. She found it and came racing back with it.

We started down the river and everybody was having a great time. Then I glanced over at Edge and he was sitting by himself, looking miserable. Suddenly, he ripped off his clothes and started to place pieces of fruit all over his body. Apparently, he was waiting for all our models on board to come over to service him, figuring they were all prostitutes.

I looked at the top deck of the boat and all the models and secretaries were standing there, watching him, just laughing hysterically at his antics. He was completely drunk. Then it got even better—he started screaming, "I AM A BLOODY ROCK STAR! I WANT OFF THIS BOAT RIGHT NOW!"

He continued that for a while as everyone laughed, until I calmly walked over to him and whispered, "If you want off this boat, you had better know how to swim!"

But the concert later was one for the ages in Daytona Beach and everybody had a great time.

And of course, we sponsored bikini contests and just about any organized event that goes hand-in-hand with spring break.

Suddenly, I was the fair-haired child of Daytona and could get permits pulled for just about anything. When MTV discovered Daytona, spring break exploded as about 400,000 college kids poured into town every March. And as it became one large beach party, especially for those four weeks every March, right in my own backyard, it was only natural that we would be a large part of it.

When it came to advertising, I could envision what I wanted in an ad. I wanted that curve on the beach, and a certain way a palm tree looked. I wanted the sand of the beach a certain color. I wanted models who looked a certain way. I wanted the sky a certain color of blue.

So, I took that vision to Hawaii and got started on producing our first national ad.

Two kids named Bob and Patsy were our very first full-time Hawaiian Tropic models.

Patsy was an absolute beauty whose parents lived on the backside of Oahu while Bob lived way out on the southwest side of the island. We had hired this small ad agency in Honolulu to mostly produce some small ads for local drug stores and other gift shops. But I wanted to have some pictures for one big national ad.

The beginning of it all got off slow.

The day we were supposed to shoot it on Waikiki Beach, the photographer was a no-show. We had paid for our two models to spend the day at the beach, which happened to be a perfectly sunny day, but we had nobody to take the pictures.

Mickey Devine, whom my Hawaiian sales rep had hired, was there with an old Pentax camera but he didn't have any film for it, so I told him to run across the street and buy some.

I thought, *"Who needs a professional photographer? We will shoot this thing ourselves."*

"Mickey, do you know how to use this thing?" I asked.

He did not.

How hard could it be?

So, I took things upon myself. I loaded the film and then I formed a big trough in the sand and told Bob and Patsy to run toward that trough. Diamond Head, the extinct volcano you see in all the pictures of Waikiki Beach, was in the background, just as I had envisioned, and bottles of Hawaiian Tropic were stuck in the sand in the foreground.

I shot picture after picture that day and just wore those poor kids out, as they ran back and forth all day long. By the end of the day, as the sun was setting, they must have run toward that trough one hundred times.

Early in the shoot, I had noticed some lady in the background who constantly brushed her hair and stared at the camera. Finally, I had no choice but to go talk to her.

"Please, lady . . ." I asked. "Just act natural and don't look at the camera!"

"This is a public beach!" she snapped. "I can do anything I want!"

I walked away politely but muttered "bitch" under my breath.

When I got the film developed, there she was in the background, staring at the camera in every shot. I simply edited her out completely and transformed her image into sand, so to speak (I would have just loved to see her face when she saw the ad later in her favorite magazine, wondering where the hell she was).

As we left the beach that day, the sun was setting over the Pacific Ocean—and who shows up but the photographer we had hired?

"Where the hell have you been?" I asked.

He started screaming at me.

"This is the exact time the ad agency told me to be here!" he protested.

We went back and forth, and this huge argument ensued. I never did find out who screwed up, but I doubt many photographers get hired for night time assignments on Waikiki Beach to shoot pictures for a suncare product.

I had taken hundreds of pictures, most of them bad or indifferent, but all I needed was that one and I had that one great one.

It was exactly what I was looking for and it soon appeared in several national magazines throughout the world—and undoubtedly helped our initial sales and growth as a company.

And I still have that picture in a very large, frame in my

house today.

Since I did not consider TV commercials to be the perfect medium for us, I focused more on magazine ads. They were perfect at reaching our target audience, I believed. I would send some of my top salespeople to New York to meet with editors and advertising reps, so if we had to pay about $100,000 for a full-page ad in a national magazine, we also were mentioned in a news feature or two. And those mentions helped the company grow even more.

When I designed our first ads, I had targeted *Cosmo*, *Mademoiselle* and *Vogue*—the leading women's magazines—and did most of the photography myself.

After that, I hired some veteran photographers, but I soon found out after working with them that they were so set in their ways that they did what they wanted to do—and never listened to what I wanted.

So, with my Waikiki success fresh in my mind, I flew to Hong Kong and spent $18,000 for three sets of just about everything Nikon made at the time—all the expensive lens and cameras and photography tools. Then I studied photography. I soon became a very good photographer if I say so myself.

Then I hired kids fresh out of college who knew photography and taught them exactly what I wanted.

And we also photoshopped backgrounds and locations if we didn't shoot on location, simply because it obviously was much less expensive.

As the product became more and more successful, and the revenue flowed, it was time to find some exotic locations as backdrops for our ads. Mostly, we focused on Hawaii, naturally. I would head to Hawaii with a group of models and just drive around to find a good remote place to shoot them—all around the Big Island or on Oahu.

I learned one thing immediately: Models were just mesmerized by a camera lens. I called it the "magic of a camera." If you held one and pointed it at them, you held immense power in your hands. They would do anything to satisfy that lens.

After a while, as our success continued, it was the right time for a commercial or two. I obviously had to hire professional videographers to produce national TV commercials. But I always wanted to be a part of the decision-making process, believing I had a feel for what appealed to the buying public.

One time we took a crew to Key Biscayne, Florida, and stayed at a place that once was the "Winter White House" where President Nixon vacationed often during his presidency. We used five models and we were shooting on the beach, and in this one shoot we were using a few guys as props. We arranged three girls lying on a blanket next to the product with another girl walking off to the side. We had dug large boxes under the sand where the guys would stand with only their heads visible as they admired the girls.

Problem was, these guys would always be using stupid lines like "What's your sign?" or "Come here often?" Finally, this one model who was a beautiful brunette just got tired of hearing it and pushed this guy's head down into the sand. I went and looked at the shot under the camera's hood and thought, *What a great idea for an ad.*

I walked over and told the producer to go look at it. He did and emerged from the hood.

"Let's do it!" he said.

It turned out awesome and the entire commercial became very successful. I always knew I owed the model, Katrina Ray, big time for improvising. Either she knew what she was doing, or she just grew tired of hearing those silly pick up lines, which she probably had heard thousands of times before.

When it came to marketing events, if we could put the name "Hawaiian Tropic" on it and I believed that the event, whatever it was, would receive enough exposure, we would do it.

In August of 1978, we even sponsored the marathon swimmer, Stella Taylor, in her attempt to swim from Orange Cay in The Bahamas to Florida. She already had successfully swam the English Channel twice and her goal on this swim was to reach any beach in the Sunshine State, which would amount to about eighty nautical miles, if you drew a straight line to Key Largo. The interesting thing about Stella, despite being forty-eight at the time, was that she was a nun.

Sally Field had played *The Flying Nun* on TV, so the media labeled Stella "The Swimming Nun."

There was plenty of media present at her sendoff in The Bahamas and we had our crew all dressed in Hawaiian Tropic gear in one boat while Stella had her own crew in another. She even wore a Hawaiian Tropic bathing suit.

But as the day progressed, I could tell she wasn't going to make it. The gulf-stream flows so fast in the Atlantic Ocean east of Florida and she happened to be swimming against it on this particular day. We couldn't convince her or her crew to stop, as the hours wore on, and she swam slower and slower. But finally, she had to stop.

It did not end with the successful beach party at the Florida landing spot that we had planned on, with awaiting media giving us tons of exposure, but it still was one of the most unique things we ever did.

One summer day in 1976, I was sitting in my office when a tough-looking guy walked in and introduced himself.

"I am Neil Bonnett and I have a great deal for you," he started.

Neil needed a sponsor for his race car for the upcoming race at Daytona and I guess he figured I had the money to become his. He placed several pictures of his race car on my desk. Now, I didn't know shit about auto racing, outside of how to park cars at the track, which I did a little when I was younger, but I did see some potential in it and I agreed to become Neil's sponsor.

And it did not hurt that I liked him from our first meeting. He was a down-home type of guy and a member of what was known in racing circles as "The Alabama Gang."

It would not cost me much to have Hawaiian Tropic's name and logo painted on the hood and side of his race car.

So that is how I entered the NASCAR racing business.

Neil did really well for those final seven races of that season and once other sponsors realized he could drive a race car well; we could not afford to back him, and he moved on to another car for more money. But he always remained very appreciative of us helping him.

When Neil moved on, another driver, Donnie Allison, came to us and we sponsored him. He provided the greatest moments in NASCAR for us, as he won two races in 1977—at Talladega, Alabama, and at Rockingham, North Carolina. Then in 1978, he won a race at Atlanta.

While we sponsored Donnie, we had another car as a replica that was painted with huge Hawaiian Tropic logos and our name. I paid Bob and Patsy, our two models that I had hired for that first photo shoot on Waikiki Beach, to tour the country in that car one summer as a promotion. They would walk into potential buyers' offices and hand out Hawaiian leis and give them various Hawaiian Tropic samples. That promotion generated a lot of publicity but as those two drove that car around the country, they soon grew to hate each other.

After Donnie left us, we sponsored David Pearson in 1980 and he won a race that year at Darlington, South Carolina. Then we co-sponsored Harry Gant's car for a few races after that. My favorite driver, however, was always Donnie. He was just a good ol' boy who was genuine and we stayed in touch over the years.

And for what we paid back then to sponsor a team in NASCAR, and I don't remember exactly how much it was, it would not even buy a season's worth of tires nowadays. After our fifth or sixth year of involvement in NASCAR, I got burned out on it—and moved on to sports car racing.

That introduced me to the one and only Paul Newman, who raced one of the three cars we sponsored in the 24 Hours of Le Mans. We started sponsoring a car there in 1978 and Newman drove three races for me the following year. I know he was very popular with fans and he was a famous actor, but he was an egotistical jerk to me.

I remember one afternoon we had to send somebody out to get him a new pair of driving shoes. After he put them on, one of my assistants, Bill Darby, remarked how nice and new they looked on him. Newman then took them off in a huff and started scuffing them up on purpose just to make them look worn. But he was part of our winning team at Le Mans and I will always be grateful for that moment.

But the worst part of my racing sponsorship ventures came with a half a sponsorship in 1980, along with UNO, for an Indianapolis 500 car driven by driver Tim Richmond. UNO was owned by a guy named Bob Tezak, who later went to prison for arson. Tim was just a bad egg, as we would learn over time. He later gained stardom in NASCAR but ended up spreading the AIDs virus around to several women before he died of it in 1989.

And one of them would hit remarkably close to home for me, which I will explain later.

Another bad memory from our auto racing ventures began when we sponsored a car named the Spirit of Miami for the Miami Grand Prix in 1983. There was a part-time driver—but not a good one—from Sydney, Australia, a bearded guy who had made his money in construction, but he also was an amateur photographer. He would walk around the racetrack and take pictures of all the pretty girls and many of them were getting a bad vibe off the guy.

It turned out that they had good reason.

His name was Christopher Wilder.

My secretary at the time was Janet Chesser, who had been Miss Florida and competed in the Miss USA contest before she came to work for us.

The following year, Wilder turned into a serial killer known as "the beauty queen killer" and he became fixated on Janet, we learned from FBI agents who called our offices one day.

His killing spree began February 26, 1984, in South Florida where he had lived. He started abducting pretty girls as he drove his way north and then he would dump their bodies with the FBI hot on his trail. Agents had raided his house in

Boynton Beach, Florida, and his walls were covered with photos of pretty women. Apparently, one entire wall was dedicated to Janet and featured her pictures from the Miss Florida pageant.

The FBI called our office and warned us, "We think he is headed to Daytona to find her and kill her."

We were just about to take off for Hawaii at the time for a promotional event and we suddenly had to consider Janet's safety.

I told her to take some time off for work and leave the country, rather than go to Hawaii with the rest of us, so she and her boyfriend flew to the Bahamas. The FBI figured Wilder thought she would be headed to Hawaii, so they had staked out many of the airports looking for him.

He obviously had headed out of state, because they found one victim in Oklahoma and then another in Los Angeles. He had traveled a long way, leaving a trail of dead women along the way. He then kidnapped a seventeen-year-old named Tina Marie Risico at a mall in Torrance, California, and then flew with her to Boston.

Once they reached Boston, strangely enough, he put her on a flight back to Los Angeles. His trail of terror ended April 13, 1984, when agents cornered him in New Hampshire near the Canadian border. He pulled out a gun, shot himself just as FBI agents unloaded on him at the same time. Within days, the FBI claimed he had abducted and killed at least twelve women.

Anyway, Janet and all of us who knew her were relieved when the ordeal finally ended, and she returned to Daytona feeling lucky to be alive.

As far as sponsorships, however, I did not agree to take on every opportunity.

One example was Billie Jean King.

She and her husband Larry had courted me for sponsorship on the women's tennis circuit. Remember, pro tennis' tournament prize money was not very much back in the 1970s, especially for women.

So, they invited me to their Marina del Rey condo for a day of conversation and tennis. As soon as I arrived, I noticed Billie Jean bossed Larry around like an employee, telling him what to do and what not to do. She was always giving him hell.

Then we headed out to the tennis courts.

I was just an adequate player then and she blew me away with her serve, which she called "The American Express." It looked like it was coming at me one way and then it went the other way. By the time I left their condo that day, I had decided I did not like Billie Jean very much. I did like Larry, but maybe I just felt sorry for him.

I never sponsored his wife, but Larry and I actually became good friends and we met often and played racquetball often. As a matter of fact, we were playing racquetball together the day he received a phone call from one of those tabloid reporters. They were about to "out" his wife for being gay. It would not be a big scandal in today's world, but back then, it was a big deal.

And then there was the sad ending to much of our local marketing and sponsorships, where it all had started.

By the end of the 1980s, our golden goose of spring break was about to come to a sudden halt when a local guy named Frank Heckman got involved in bringing it crashing down to earth.

He was a neighborhood watchman/sometime politician who aligned himself with a bunch of little ol' ladies in 1989 and made it clear they would lead the charge to kick local politicians out of office if they didn't do something about the crowds flowing in for spring break, the local economy be damned.

Sure enough, local police started arresting kids for minor infractions, such as public drinking, and that is all it took.

The network *Showtime* televised a documentary called "Spring Broke" that my buddy Allan Cohen produced, detailing the rise and fall of spring break in Daytona. In the documentary, I said, "We had the golden goose here. But then the stupid city fathers had to kill Spring Break . . . and when they did, they killed it."

I really did not care who those comments ticked off, because I meant every word. The local economy boomed and a lot of businesses made a lot of money during that one month or so each year and then it all stopped because local politicians listened to a few people who were offended by college kids drinking beer or coeds flashing their boobs on the beach.

It made no sense to me.

Sure enough, the idiots who ran city hall then chased MTV and its sponsored parties out of Daytona and essentially shot themselves in the foot financially. The crowds of spring-breakers moved on to Panama City, but the weather rarely cooperated up there in the Florida Panhandle. In recent years, the crowds have relocated to Cancun and Cabo San Lucas, Mexico, and South Padre Island, Texas.

I found other marketing outlets, including one on a much bigger scale.

In the early 1980s I had met two guys who really opened doors for me toward sponsoring something that turned out to be one of the highlights of my marketing life.

One was Tom Hulett who had co-owned a company called "Concerts West" which had promoted every one of Elvis' concerts after 1968, as well as the Beach Boys and several other top entertainers in the country.

The other guy was Jerry Weintraub, who was a legend in Hollywood and the entertainment business.

Weintraub was a film producer and concert promoter that worked with Hulett for several years. He also did some acting and later appeared in *The Firm* as the gangster Sonny Capps. Whenever I was around him, he always bragged about how much money he made.

I remember over dinner one night at his house in Malibu, he just flatly said out of nowhere, "I never had a year when I didn't make at least ten million!"

We weren't even talking about money at the time, but he had to throw that out there. And he did it often.

But through Hulett, I was introduced to the Beach Boys, who happened to be looking for a title sponsor for their annual July Fourth concerts on the mall in Washington, D.C. I could not have jumped at the opportunity any faster. I knew that nothing could have fit the Hawaiian Tropic brand better than the Beach Boys.

On July 4, 1980, the NASCAR car we sponsored driven by David Pearson was leading the field near the end of the Firecracker 400 at Daytona. Problem was, we had to leave the track to get on the airplane to fly to D.C., so we had a choice to make: Wait and see if our car wins a major race and be late for the first Beach Boys' concert we agreed to sponsor, or leave before the end of the race.

We left.

We were the main sponsor for the Beach Boys' first-ever concert on the mall in D.C. Before we arrived that day, air traffic controllers in Washington had us in a holding pattern to land and the Beach Boys were ready to play. But Mike Love wouldn't go on stage until we got there, so essentially, we were holding up about 500,000 fans from seeing the concert.

We finally landed and they rushed us to a few limos which dropped us off near the backstage. I wore a black cowboy hat for some reason and when Mike saw me, he tipped his Hawaiian Tropic cap to me, I tipped my cowboy hat to him, and they rushed on stage.

I had never seen half a million people in one place before until I looked straight down toward the Washington Monument. All I saw were people.

And I learned that night that David had finished second, behind Bobby Allison, so we didn't miss a trip to Victory Lane in Daytona after all by leaving early.

It was never boring with the Beach Boys. The other band members would tell me so many stories about Brian Wilson and how they would have to be ready to cut off his microphone whenever he started to rant on about something. Bruce Johnston would turn to the audio technician and do a throat slash gesture.

The following year, July 4, 1981, the Beach Boys played at the mall and we all had a blast once again. Then as soon as it ended, we had to fly straight to Long Beach for their concert the following night near the Queen Mary, which was permanently docked there. I took Kim Jones, a girl I was dating at the time, on the flight with me and that is when their drummer, Dennis

Wilson, had too much to drink. As I was standing in the aisle talking to a few people, he suddenly appeared in front of me.

And for some reason, he wanted to fight me.

I had no idea why, other than I think he was jealous I had this very pretty girl with me, and he was sitting in the back of the airplane by himself.

He just continued, wanting to provoke me to take a swing at him. Dennis was not a big guy and he was very drunk, so I know I could have squeezed his head off like a bad pimple, but I tried to ignore him and continue my conversation. And that seemed to piss him off even more.

Finally, after a bunch of screaming and threatening, Mike, Bruce and Al Jardine grabbed him and dragged him back to the rear of the airplane. They were used to dealing with his excessive drinking and his mood swings.

The following year, President Reagan's Secretary of the Interior, James Watt, complained about the Beach Boys' "lack of wholesomeness," and that forced them to play the next two July Fourths, in St. Louis, in 1982 and then in Atlantic City, New Jersey, in 1983.

Five months after that Atlantic City concert, Dennis had gotten drunk again, dove into the water for some reason one night in Marina del Rey—and drowned.

After Dennis died, the band frequently used guest drummers, such as the actor John Stamos and even Ringo Starr.

But the Reagans, especially Nancy, wanted the Beach Boys back in Washington for July 4, publicly condemning Watt's silly comments. So, when we planned the July 4, 1984, concert in D.C., it was our second attempt at sponsoring two venues back-to-back. Three Dog Night opened for the Beach Boys that afternoon in D.C., and it was an unbelievable concert. The minute that the Beach Boys followed and had played their final note, they jumped off the stage and we all rushed to the airport to fly to Miami so they could play on Miami Beach later that night.

The promoters had arranged two huge tractor-trailer flatbeds to build a stage at Haulover Beach in North Miami.

For these two concerts that day, Ringo sat in as the guest drummer.

As we flew from D.C. to Miami, I moved around the airplane and mingled with everyone as I usually did. I talked to all the members of Three Dog Night and they all seemed like great guys. They asked me about the business and how it operated and how it all got started, and I would ask them all about their backgrounds and their music.

Then I noticed Ringo sitting by himself.

I sat down next to him and introduced myself. I am sure he knew who I was since I was sponsoring both concerts, but I never wanted to take anything for granted.

He did not acknowledge anything I said, and I could tell he was very annoyed just by my sitting in his presence. Finally, I said, "Listen, I won't bother you anymore, but I would love to send you a box of our products for you to use. Just give me your mailing address."

Without even looking at me, he flatly dead-panned, "London . . . care of Ringo."

That was enough one-sided conversation for me. I didn't even respond. I just stood up and walked away and we never spoke again. *What a jerk*, I thought. He couldn't even be cordial to the guy sponsoring two concerts in which he was performing.

Just what was it about famous drummers and me? Graeme Edge of The Moody Blues was the "bloody rock star" I had threatened to throw off a boat once, Dennis Wilson wanted to fight me on an airplane in mid-flight and now Ringo was rude as hell when I was just trying to be friendly.

Those two July Fourths in which we flew to another concert destination made for long days, but they were so much fun and successful that Mike Love wanted to take the concept even further.

"Let's do six concerts in one day!" he explained to me.

"We will follow the sun and head West as we go. We will start in D.C., fly west, then do one in L.A., keep going west, do one in Hawaii, then on to Japan . . ."

I could tell he was not joking—he was dead serious.

"Mike, are you crazy?" I asked him.

His aspiration, almost impossible unless you had an airplane that would fly at the speed of light, never came true, obviously, and the most we ever did was two. But it illustrates that he never thought of the Beach Boy's concerts as true work, even though he probably was a workaholic. They were fun and he enjoyed entertaining the fans.

When the Beach Boys played for the National Association of Chain Drug Stores (NACDS) convention at the Breakers in Palm Beach a few years later, I couldn't wait to see all the guys again to catch up on things. The NACDS was run by a guy named Jim Whitman whom I had a running business battle with for years for one reason or another. For some reason, he hated Hawaiian Tropic and anyone who worked for Hawaiian Tropic. And he especially hated its owner and creator.

After they performed, I was trying like heck to get backstage and security guys were stopping me.

Whitman was standing there.

"You can't go back there! That area is only for the Beach Boys!" he screamed at me.

Then suddenly, somebody grabbed my arm. It was Bruce Johnston.

"Come on Ron!" he said, leading me beyond security.

"That area is for the Beach Boys ONLY!" Whitman screamed at him.

"I AM THE FUCKING BEACH BOYS!" Bruce shouted back at him.

It was one of those brief moments when a jerk gets put in his place that always made me smile, just like when I beat Paul Burke to the market with a royal tanning oil years earlier.

And I never said a word to either when they happened, just letting a broad smile do my work for me.

Another marketing opportunity later came my way.

A businessman named Dennis Riese, whose family owned dozens of restaurants in New York, wanted to open two "Hawaiian Tropic Zone" restaurants, one in New York and then one in Las Vegas. They were in name only as far as my involvement went. We didn't have any money or any input in managing them, so I said, "Sure, why not?"

As the marketing and advertising worked bit by bit, sales increased. And as sales increased, we had to increase production. To keep up with the demand and make shipping easier and less costly, we had to build or buy factories strategically located around the world.

We ended up with thirteen of them, in countries such as

Venezuela, Australia, Brazil, Canada, the Canary Islands, and, of course Hawaii, along with our main factory in Ormond Beach and another in Murray, Kentucky. Our factory in Ireland was the largest on foreign soil.

We opened one there because we received tax credits, which meant the taxes were practically nothing. From there, we would ship the product to Spain, Italy, England and Germany. We always had problems in Germany because the country was controlled by Bayer.

Our growth was astounding. We had to do what it took to keep up with the demand, and the demand was overwhelming. We soon employed about two thousand people around the world, including about seven hundred fifty at our Daytona Beach headquarters.

It had grown to gigantic proportions; I think largely because of our marketing approach.

One year in the early 2000s, I attended the NACDS in Palm Beach when this Coppertone representative approached me.

"I know you never knew this, but Coppertone actually fired three different sets of managers years ago because of you," he told me. "They just couldn't figure out how to compete with all of your marketing ideas."

I had to smile.

I always knew that Hawaiian Tropic pretty much ran Sea & Ski out of any substantial business by the 1980s—it had been number two to Coppertone for several years before we came along, but I never really realized the effect we had on Coppertone, if any. I am honest when I say that I just didn't care where we were ranked as far as sales. I knew what our sales were each year and I was very happy with it and that's all that mattered to me.

We handled all the marketing by the seat of our pants, and I am proud of that, because I had no real advertising background or training. And I never worried about the competition or how they were marketing and advertising their products. My philosophy was just to go full speed ahead and not care about what anybody else was doing at the time.

At the various conventions when I did bump into the Coppertone guys, I always joked to them about their main ad that featured a dog pulling down a little girl's bikini bottom.

"Look, you guys are sick with that ad," I would say. "You are featuring animal abuse and child pornography."

They really got mad when I said things like that. That was their prized ad and they did not like anybody criticizing it, especially their chief competitor, I guess. For several years, one of their largest billboards was at the intersection of 163rd Street in North Miami. Every few years, some prankster would unscrew the screws that held up the little girl's bathing suit and it would fall off the billboard. Then there would be a story in the newspaper about it, with a headline like, "The dog finally got that girl's bathing suit," which would get even more publicity. I always wondered if a Coppertone employee was doing it just to generate another story.

The truth is, I believe that Coppertone ad really was a great idea. It was highly effective—and I can admit that all these years later.

But I still think our approach was better.

We tried to spray the name "Hawaiian Tropic" everywhere throughout the world, using auto races to concerts to long-distance swimmers to billboards and airplane banners to product placement programs and especially to national magazine ads.

It was what was called "Guerrilla Marketing" and it worked for us.

It all added up to name recognition and tremendous sales. Yet, in the early 1980s, I still wondered if we were reaching all demographics and walks of life.

I figured we were appealing to only half the market, so one of the best marketing tools in American business history was about to be created.

Chapter Eight

GIRLS, GIRLS, GIRLS

Growing up, I was not only shy around girls, as I said earlier, but sometimes they scared me to death. But fortunately, I gradually grew out of it and then dated my fair share of girls in high school and into college.

As I said, one of them, Maria Fletcher, happened to become Miss North Carolina and then Miss America in 1962, four years after we graduated and while I was still trying to find my way to a college education.

Maria and I stayed in touch over the years and knowing her and her experiences was my first exposure to the beauty pageant world, its operation, and how the pageants were managed.

What I noticed most was the media attention paid to them and the exposure they generated for their sponsors.

When Hawaiian Tropic became a well-established success

by the mid-1970s, it opened doors for me, too. And because of that, I was invited to judge a Miss Georgia pageant one weekend in 1981. During that weekend, I met all the people who ran the pageants at the state level, such as the MC and promoter Jim Gibson, and that led to even more pageant connections.

By the end of the following year, I had judged fourteen state pageants all over the country. Can you imagine taking fourteen weekends out of the year to travel somewhere to judge beauty pageants while also running a thriving company?

I am sure many of my employees wondered about it, but I enjoyed it. It did turn out to be too much for my schedule at the time, so I cut back to seven the following year.

And by then, I was well versed in the pageant business.

I thought, *"Hell, if they can do this well on the state level, I could do this on a national level."*

A driving factor in my thinking was that I realized we had not been marketing to half of our potential customers with our sponsorship ventures into various sporting events, especially auto racing.

I started to brainstorm again . . .

What if we created our own Hawaiian Tropic beauty pageant?

If it worked, I thought, we will attract women *and* men to buy our product. So, I went ahead with my plans and created it on a lark, really.

Initially we held some small pageants in Florida with local girls, and they went off smoothly and did a good job putting our name out there even more, but I wanted to try something bigger, something that would attract girls from all over the country. My staff and I started making calls to our sales reps to hold some preliminary pageants leading up to our very first

U.S. pageant in August 1983, at a development called Pelican Bay in Daytona Beach.

We flew girls in from every part of the world. I think we had 120 girls that first year, eighty from the preliminary pageants and forty picked from photos that had been sent in. We had placed ads in many magazines promoting the pageant and asking girls to send us photos if they wanted to be considered.

That weekend, we had many of them sleeping on air mattresses around my beach house. We crowned four winners that night, all of whom would head to Hawaii to compete in the first Miss Hawaiian Tropic International the following spring. And before even the first winner was crowned that night, I already knew this new idea would become a huge success.

We had caught magic in a bottle. Absolute magic.

The event became the biggest thing in town that weekend and was well-covered by the local media and it generated huge publicity for us.

I sat there in the audience, looking up at the stage that night and already figured that this thing had no limits. It was just mind-boggling to me that all those beautiful girls from every corner of the globe had flown or driven to Daytona.

We conducted it just like any other pageant: The girls would walk across the stage and each answer a few standard questions about their hometown, their interests and background and where they went to school, etc. We had two categories—swimsuit and evening gown—but never a talent segment as other pageants did.

As I watched that night, I figured a blonde girl by the name of Teresa Blake from Alabama would be in the top four and she was, although she never placed in the international pageant the following year. It jump-started her career before she went on to act in *All My Children.*

The first pageant had turned out so well, as I said, that I knew that it was just the beginning.

Then I went to work and decided to spend more than four million dollars on the second Miss Hawaiian Tropic International pageant the following year. We held it in Honolulu at Kapiolani Park near Diamond Head. We announced that we would pay more than $100,000 in cash and prizes for the winner.

We instantly benefitted from widespread media coverage in Hawaii and had the pageant televised all over the world. It just became a massive promotion for Hawaiian Tropic, a type of advertising I couldn't buy anywhere else. And the best part was it was great fun, albeit a lot of hard work, too.

Allan Carr, the film producer, was one of our judges and he invited us all to his house at the foot of Diamond Head for dinner one night. At the entrance to his house stood about a ten-foot replica of an Oscar and his home looked out at the ocean. It would be the beginning of lavish parties the pageants would generate for the next twenty-five years or so.

As the pageants were taking off, I decided we should hire the cream of the crop each year as Hawaiian Tropic models. We had some models promote the product for us going as far back as the mid-1970s, but we weren't as organized as it could have been.

I was working late one night at the factory when this girl walked in the front door. Me and a few of the other staffers went out to greet her and she took off her coat, revealing a brown bikini with Hawaiian Tropic crochet on the butt. Her name was Jerri Nix and she told us her mother made it.

Immediately, we all fell in love with that suit and the idea of using it for promotions, so we had her mother start making them for us.

And from then on, our Hawaiian Tropic models wore them everywhere—to auto races, to the beach, to just about any event we knew there would be a lot of people.

The pageants and our models would go hand-in-hand of promoting the brand.

Soon enough, as the attention grew, the pageants started attracting major celebrities.

And one would become one of my all-time favorites. I first met Julio Iglesias at the mall in Washington, D.C., when he performed at the same concert as the Beach Boys one year. That day, it did not take Julio long to fall in love with a couple of our models—Bitsy Harrison and Mary Jane Thomas—and he wanted to fly them to Las Vegas for a shopping spree. They asked me if it was okay if they left with him.

I walked over to Julio and started talking to him, feeling him out about his intentions. Finally, I trusted Julio that he would not do anything stupid enough to mess up his reputation in the U.S., so I gave him the go-ahead. Because of the language barrier, he was not sure if I had agreed or not at first, and I could tell he was about to put up an argument. Then when he realized I had given him approval, he grabbed me and started kissing me.

A few days later, these two girls arrived back to Daytona carrying dozens of boxes—filled with clothes, shoes, hats, stuffed animals, just about anything they had wanted. Julio must have spent $20,000 on each girl.

That began our long relationship with him. He became a frequent visitor to our pageants and always acted in a first-class manner.

Of course, he wasn't the only celebrity attracted to the girls.

During a pageant in Panama City in 1985, one of our contestants seemed to be eager to meet a wealthy man. She had driven all night from North Georgia to arrive in time. This certain contestant made it obvious to me that this weekend she wanted to meet a man with money, but she really was not my type and I was with someone that weekend anyway.

But she did end up winning that pageant.

Her name was Marla Maples.

Marla had been hitting on me during that pageant and told me, "I sure wish you hadn't brought a girl here with you."

Sometime after that pageant, several of my buddies, such as Jim Gibson, Tom McMillen, a prominent attorney in D.C. by the name of Jeff Gordon, and Jerry Argovitz, were headed to New York for a party Donald Trump was hosting. I had talked to Marla some at the pageant and I knew she wanted to meet a rich man.

I had Marla's home phone number, so I called her.

"Marla, if you want to meet one of the richest guys in the world, my friends are going to this party at Trump Tower, here are their numbers, call one of them to get you into it," I told her.

I gave her the phone numbers of those four guys to somehow meet up with her. I never did hear the details of what happened, but it obviously worked, because they met that weekend somehow—Marla and Donald started dating behind the scenes, even though he was married at the time.

I am not sure how long they kept it a secret, but eventually the entire world must have heard something about Marla and Trump and also the fact she had won the Panama City pageant earlier, because our company phone lines were lighting up with calls from various newspaper and tabloid outlets.

"Do you have any pictures of this girl, Marla Maples?" they were asking me just as soon as I picked up the phone.

I had some of my assistants search for one, and sure enough, we had a picture of Marla with a Hawaiian Tropic sash across her tan bathing suit. I could not release that photo fast enough. Within two days, I think it appeared in publications all over the world.

I knew it would be great publicity. I picked up the phone one day after that picture hit all the papers and it was my sales rep in Israel.

"What is going on over there?" he asked. "I can't keep up with the sales."

He had no idea what was happening, but it all was because that photo was so widely distributed.

Trump had started coming to a lot of our pageants in the 1980s and seemed to enjoy himself. He was usually so busy with his business that I figured that he did not have much of a social life, outside of his marriage to Ivana at the time. He seemed a little awkward around the girls at first, but that may have been due to being married or knowing that so many cameras were always aimed at him, as well as at the girls.

Now, some thirty years or more later, Marla's the ex-wife of a U.S. president—and their daughter Tiffany is in her twenties—and it all started at a Hawaiian Tropic pageant.

Besides beautiful girls, the second ingredient of what made our pageants so successful is that we decided not to settle for local politicians or city council members or small market TV anchors as judges. We aimed higher. Much higher.

Our celebrity judges were professional athletes, TV stars, movie stars, and well-known comedians mostly.

Over the years, we had NFL quarterback Jim Kelly, Mickey Rooney, Robin Leach, Leslie Neilsen, Jane Russell, Dolph Lundgren, Alan Thicke, O.J. Simpson and Benny Hill, just to name a few who served as judges.

I always took an active role in putting together the list, aiming to host the most impressive and most high-profile people I could find. It didn't matter how A-list they were; I gave it a shot.

Sometimes it worked and sometimes it didn't.

One Sunday, I read an article in the newspaper about Benny, the British comedian. I always watched Benny's show and loved his type of humor. I thought, *Man, I would love to get Benny involved our pageants. He would be perfect.* The article mentioned he had been staying in a certain hotel in the south of France and I just happened to have an important contact in the south of France.

A girl by the name of Hedwige Sluss had been our Miss France a few years earlier and I had a great relationship with her. Her father was an American who had owned nightclubs in Germany and her mother was French. When laser lightshows became fashionable in nightclubs, she would fly to California, buy a lot of lasers and then stop in Florida to see me before heading back to Germany to deliver them to her father (I even bought one from her for my own disco I had built by my indoor pool).

Anyway, I called Hedwige and told her, "I am going to give

you a very important job. Go to this hotel, find Benny Hill and sell him on being a judge for us."

"Oh no," she told me. "I don't think I can do that."

I gave her the dates of the upcoming pageant and told her, "Listen Hedwige, you can do it! We will get you two first-class tickets and you act as his assistant on the trip. Get him over here!"

Sure enough, she went to the hotel, met Benny and charmed him. He became smitten with her. I think she speaks about seven languages and she's incredibly beautiful to begin with. They flew to Florida with a producer and director of Benny's show. I took care of getting them all nice hotel rooms on the beach and made sure Benny was taken care of.

And fortunately, Benny had a blast while he was in town. He loved spending time at my place, so he asked me if he could film one of his shows on my patio on the beach.

"Of course!" I told him.

Benny had more energy in person than he even displayed on TV if that were possible. When he finished judging that first pageant, he told me, "I can't wait to come back and do another one. "

He judged our pageants for four consecutive years and would perform skits on stage during our pageants, wearing his little cap and letting all the girls kiss him on the cheek at once while he made that lovable goofy face that he pulled off so well. When it came time for him to fly over for his fifth pageant, he became ill. I talked to him on the phone a few times and he told me he still wanted to come, but his doctors had forbidden him from making the trip.

Soon after, on April 20, 1992, he died alone at his London

apartment.

His death really hit me hard. He was always the perfect gentleman around the girls and everybody in our organization loved him, none more than I did.

There came a time where I seriously began to think I was a jinx when it came to celebrities.

I had read one day about Malcolm Forbes, the creator of *Forbes Magazine* among other businesses, and his extravagant lifestyle and how he once had chartered three or four jumbo jets just to take Elizabeth Taylor and all of his friends to Morocco. He put everybody up in first-class hotels in Marrakesh and threw a massive party, spending a couple of million dollars in one week.

That intrigued me, so I found his number and called his house in California in February of 1990, and introduced myself, described our pageants and the judging process and simply asked, "Would you like to be a judge?"

He immediately accepted.

"Can I also bring my son, Steve?" he asked.

"No problem," I told him. "We would be glad to have you both."

Then what did he do? He died just a few days later.

One night in 1994, I was watching the *Tonight Show* when one of Jay Leno's guests, Doctor Linus Pauling, perhaps the country's most-famous chemist, was advocating using massive doses of Vitamin C, claiming it was the key to long-lasting life.

I remember Leno had asked him that night, "Doctor Pauling, doesn't all that Vitamin C give you diarrhea?'

"Yes," he answered, "but consider the alternative."

He was ninety-three at the time, with silver hair and blue

eyes and he just radiated energy. And I agreed with much of his theory on Vitamin C—orange juice always worked for me, if you remember how I got healthy after that trip to New Orleans in my early twenties. So, I started reading about him, he had won not one, but two Nobel Prizes—one for chemistry in 1954 and the Nobel Peace Prize ten years later. Few people on this earth were as accomplished as he was.

I discovered he lived in Big Sur, California, so I looked up his name, found his telephone number and called him. Just like I did with Forbes, I told him all about our pageants and how the judging system worked. I told him I would pay for his first-class airfare to come to Florida.

"I would love to do it," he said.

We scheduled his flight, and just like with Malcolm Forbes, I couldn't wait to meet him.

A month later, on August 19, 1994, he died.

It was then that I decided I had better stop calling celebrities out of the blue, for fear that I was somehow killing them off.

Through the pageants, Alan Thicke became a good friend over the years and in fact, I introduced him to his last wife, Tanya Callau. Tanya was a model for us who happened to be a former Miss Bolivia. His first wife, Gina Tolleson, also was in one of our pageants. Alan always loved tall girls. (Alan and Tanya's wedding in 2005 at Santa Barbara was one of the few I have attended over the years. As I said, I never loved attending weddings or funerals for that matter.)

But for every Benny Hill and Alan Thicke whom everybody loved to be around, as they did most of our celebrity judges, we did invite a few who turned out to be assholes, too.

British actor Oliver Reed comes to mind.

He had done *Oliver Twist* and I loved that movie, so I thought he would be great, especially since he was British, and we had so much fun being around Benny.

But within a day after he had arrived, I knew we had made a huge mistake. When he had a few drinks, he always wanted to arm-wrestle everybody to prove how strong he was. He was just a real mess. And he was drunk most of the time. He was, by far, the most difficult judge we ever had to deal with. Of course, he judged one pageant, he flew home, and we never spoke to him again.

Only two people ever turned me down when I asked them if they would consider being a judge. Once I was at Derek Jeter's Super Bowl party in San Diego in January of 2003, and I knew I was losing Jim Kelly after ten years, so I thought it would be perfect to replace him with another NFL quarterback.

I was talking to Jeter a long time when I noticed Tom Brady and walked over to him, made some small talk and told him who I was. I explained our pageants and the concept and how much Jim had enjoyed the experience.

"Would you consider being a judge, if your schedule permits it?" I asked him.

"No, that type of stuff is beneath me," he said.

Beneath him?

It's not like we were sponsoring nude mud fights on Bourbon Street. I always thought we had a first-class pageant much like the Miss America pageants.

But *beneath* him?

I had heard that line before. It came from a guy who I also considered a big jerk once I was around him a few times—*Seinfeld* co-creator Larry David. I called him and told him about the annual calendar we produced for charity. They included pictures of the girls with celebrities and we sold them for twenty dollars, but we had to receive permission first from each celebrity who was pictured in it.

Since it all went to charity, ninety-nine percent of them agreed.

"No way—that's *beneath* me," David told me.

So, we had to take the time to remove his picture.

And I reached out to people you would never think of.

One time I met a man by the name of Adnan Khashoggi in France. He turned out to be a prominent Saudi businessman who was a billionaire. And when I did my research on him, I learned he was one of the world's most prominent arms dealers.

When I explained our pageants and what we do, he suggested two of his sons as judges. As it turned out, I loved his son Hussein. He fit right in with everyone at Hawaiian Tropic and treated everybody with respect. The other son, Mohamad, not so much. He was just a total jerk and we sent him packing after a day or two.

Our pageants and various sponsorships of others never stopped me from still lending my time as a judge elsewhere, either. I knew it still was a wise thing to keep up the connections in the pageant business.

In fact, in 1983, I was invited to judge the Miss California pageant in Oxnard, California. There was a beautiful brunette contestant by the name of Mariska and when I learned her identity, I had a flashback to my adolescence.

When I was about fifteen years old and my brother was twenty-one, we were at a camp in White Plains, New York, and he had been dating this girl for a while. She happened to have a younger sister about my age, and they both were very pretty girls, so we all double dated. The girls' father gave my father the keys to a nice convertible and handed him sixty-five dollars and said, "Go down to the city and have a good time."

It was 1955 and I was a sophomore in high school, seeing the bright lights of New York City for the first time.

We went to the fighter Jack Dempsey's restaurant and there he stood at the entrance shaking everyone's hands. I remember that he had massive hands. I must have looked older than I was because the waiter let me order a drink—my first drink ever. It hit me so hard and so fast and I was completely drunk. On one drink. Probably because I was as skinny as a rail.

After dinner, the drink wore off and we all went to the Broadway play *Will Success Spoil Rock Hunter?*

The lead actress in it was Jayne Mansfield.

I will never forget her performance from that night and was shocked twelve years later when I read about her dying in a terrible car crash in Louisiana. In the backseat were her three kids, one of which was three-year-old Mariska Hargitay, whose father was actor and body-builder Mickey Hargitay.

Anyway, all these years later, I was judging Jayne Mansfield's daughter in a beauty pageant.

Mariska finished as the fourth runner-up that night to Julie Hayek, who went on to win Miss USA.

When they held the Miss USA Florida pageant in Daytona, our office received a call. The organizers wanted samples of our product for the contestants. No problem, I said. Whatever you want.

I hired a woman named Mary West to run our pageants in Louisiana. She was a beautiful blonde herself, a former Miss

America pageant contestant, and she really had an eye for beauty. She always brought us some of the most beautiful girls you could ever imagine.

Her husband, Peter Winters, was a hypnotist and a magician and he managed the Bourbon-Orleans Hotel right on Bourbon Street. He always saved me a two-level, corner suite overlooking Bourbon Street when we hosted pageants there. I would take the top level and we filled the bottom level with air mattresses for all the girls to sleep on before every upcoming pageant.

We used to film little skits as a joke and then play them at our parties. One night, we did one in that suite when I walked into the bathroom and was supposedly wondering out loud where all the girls had gone. Suddenly, the shower curtain opened and about thirteen girls came running out of the bathtub real fast—all topless. I was filming this scene when one of the girls from Jacksonville who was very ample up top stopped in front of the camera and asked, "What do you think about these, big boy?" as she squeezed them together, before walking out of the bathroom.

That proved very helpful as time went by.

When the pageant was over, I had given her a suitcase just to carry all her Mardi Gras beads back home. She had collected a massive number of beads. I told her, "Don't forget to send that bag back once you get home."

Anyway, she never sent the bag and I decided to hold her paycheck until we received it. The next thing I knew, she had filed a sexual harassment lawsuit against me over what happened in the bathroom. She made up some story of something I did, which wasn't true. It had no merit whatsoever and I reminded her and her lawyer of the little film I had of her squeezing her assets together and talking crudely to the camera.

That was the end of her lawsuit.

She sent my bag back and I sent her the final paycheck and I never heard from her again. But it really was a good thing I had my video camera with me that day, or there would have been no proof that I was telling the truth and she apparently had forgotten I was filming everything.

Some crazy things would happen when we put all the girls together in a sleeping situation like that, but it would have cost a fortune to get hotel rooms for each of them. Sandy DiSilver from Orlando was our sixth or seventh national pageant winner and we happened to be attending a debutante ball at the Superdome in New Orleans one night. At the end of the night, this other girl was trying her best to get Sandy away from us to go out with her in New Orleans.

I was with Wink and we knew we couldn't let anything happen to our queen, so we decided to follow them around. We were like spies trailing the two of them down the back streets of the French Quarter. We just had a feeling this girl, whom we didn't know too well, was up to no good. Finally, we managed to separate them, and everybody eventually ended up in the suite.

By the end of the night, the other girl ended up hooking up with another contestant, having oral sex underneath a bunch of blankets on an air mattress. It was then we knew she just wanted to seduce Cindy.

Those were the type of things we had to watch.

I noticed one trend: Most of these girls had boyfriends chasing them with diamond rings, wanting them to drop out of our pageants. Many of them were scared to death their girls would win and then they would lose them to bigger things or stardom. Then when girls didn't win, many of them would go back home and tell their boyfriends, "Okay, I'll take that diamond ring now. It's time to get engaged."

Of course, our pageants and employing our models led to a lot of meetings and marriages. And many divorces, too, for that matter.

I got to know Dick Van Patten and most of his family from first meeting him at a celebrity charity event in Hawaii. His sons Vince, Nels and Jimmy became judges and sure enough, Jimmy started dating one of our models, Shana Hiatt, and they were married for a while (Years later, the Van Pattens invited me to play in one of their celebrity poker tournaments in Palm Springs and being the worst poker player ever, I was the first one out of the tournament, which wasn't a bad thing, since I had the rest of the day to explore Palm Springs).

And we always encountered a number of stalking incidents besides the serial killer that stalked my secretary.

Another time, we discovered one creep who was trying to meet our girls at several pageants and his weapon was the date-rape drug. He would try to get close to them just as they had a drink in their hand. We had pictures of him distributed everywhere and I had security guards prepped to watch his every move if he showed up, and instructions to keep him far away from any of the girls.

But he succeeded once, getting a date rape drug into one of our girl's drinks. Fortunately, I had a doctor with me at the time and he revived her after she had passed out walking down the hallway of the hotel. I really think he may have saved her life.

I really credit one of our top models, Linda Mitchell, with the stalker's identification. She could have been a detective because she was so good at spotting the stalker.

That is one reason we moved our international pageant to Turtle Bay on the North Shore of Oahu in the 1990s. It was more contained, and we took all the rooms so there were none for any fans or hangers-on to stay. The hotel had their own security and I would hire six or seven extra security guys to watch all the rooms and the girls.

My inner circle and I could usually spot guys who were up to no good, hanging around the pageants and hotels just to meet one or more of them. We always used a code to identify hangers-on who just wanted to be around the girls, names such as "Cliff," "Coat" and "Pot"—anything which could naturally precede "hanger" in a sentence.

We were at the Country Music Awards one night and I walked up to the bar where all my vice-presidents were already seated, indulging in a few drinks.

There was one guy in the group who I didn't know.

"Ron, this is our buddy 'Cliff,'" Darby said to me.

Immediately, I knew what he meant.

"Hi Cliff," I said. "Great to meet you."

"MY NAME ISN'T CLIFF!" the guy blurted.

We basically acted as if we didn't hear him and as our friends and some of the girls met us throughout the night, we all took turns introducing this guy as Cliff. They would hear that and know it was our code to stay away from him.

By the end of the night, this guy finally said, "Okay, I give up . . . call me Cliff," but he never figured out our inside joke.

When we held pageants in Daytona, we called those "Rice

Resort Weekends" and invited all the girls to stay at my main house and also at my two guest houses. We would throw down air mattresses everywhere, stock the places with food and let them relax and use the pool.

That always led to some issues, too, by having that many girls in the house at once.

One time, Asa Ankerbrink, a very pretty blonde from Sweden who used to lay on the deck nude all the time, as most Swedish girls do, locked herself out when nobody else was home.

The beach was so crowded that day that she didn't want to climb down to the bottom level to open an unlocked door because the towel she had was too small to cover anything up. As she yelled and waved for help, guys who were playing golf across the street started waving back. Finally, she enticed some guy from the beach to do it, and when the other girls came back home, he happened to be standing in the house. That led to a call to the police and they almost had the guy arrested until Asa told them the entire story.

One time, we even held a pageant on a seven-day Caribbean cruise out of the Port of Miami. We hosted 120 contestants and I had eleven judges who were from the world of basketball, mostly collegiate coaches such as Louisville's Denny Crum.

Everyone had a blast and I will never forget this one old guy approaching me that final night in the cruise ship's disco. I was talking to one of the judges when he tapped me on the shoulder. He had a toupee which was off-center, and he was sweating profusely. But he had a big smile on his face.

"I am so happy you brought all these girls on this cruise," he said. "I have a pretty boring life and just sell used cars back home. I have probably been on sixty cruises in my life and never experienced anything like this. You know what? I think I have danced with every one of your girls. They have been so nice to me, and I cannot thank you enough."

During all of our pageants, I would sit in the front row and try to be accessible to anyone. I was technically the head of each pageant and made all the crucial decisions, but I never once got involved in the judging. With so much money and prizes at stake, I wanted to make sure everything was on the up-and-up and there was no pollution in the judging system.

And if our celebrity judges ended up dating contestants, which happened, I wanted to make sure it didn't occur until after a pageant was conducted and judged.

That's how I got to know Jim Kelly so well. One night after a pageant, he and I sat at a bar firing down double Stoli Seabreezes while one contestant, named Julie Murdoch from Oklahoma, sat between us at the bar. We were each telling her our respective histories, asking her questions along the way and we must have had six or seven drinks each.

Finally, she got up and walked away and neither of us ended up with her. I later hired her as a model, which turned out to be a disaster that I'll get to later.

The funny thing is, I could never pick a winner. As I watched a pageant and figured to myself who would win, they never did. The judges always had different ideas than I did. My three vice-presidents would collect the judges' ballots and take them to a secure location to count them and I never got involved in any of that, other than to oversee it that it was all done legitimately.

People have asked me over the years about fixing contests so girls would win because they possessed certain skin tones.

After all, our product was a suncare product that promoted tanning.

The fact is, I never put any parameters on any part of our contestants. We never turned down girls because of their skin tone, even if they were fair-skinned, or because they were married. (Back then, we also could use self-tanners that gave lighter-skin contestants some color. We developed a self-tanner much later).

We didn't even have age restrictions and I know we had several contestants over the years that were not yet eighteen and also some who were in their early forties.

But the end result is that we always ended up with the cream of the crop when it came to pure beauty. I wasn't going for a collection of brain surgeons or girls who could solve world hunger. I wanted the most-beautiful girls that could be found anywhere in the world.

Hosting a beauty pageant took a ton of planning, executing and like everything else, just hard work. That is one reason I delegated so much authority to all my employees at the factory. I did not want to be bothered with making decisions on all of the day-to-day small stuff that came along.

One day, a junior executive in marketing by the name of Rick Ferritto, a Florida State boy, came to my office door. I happened to be having a terrible day anyway, and he held his arms out, holding a stack of papers that extended from his chin to his waist.

"We have got to make some decisions," he said.

"Rick . . . if 'we' have got to make decisions, then I don't need you!" I responded.

He said, "Thank you very much," turned around and walked

Our family was close, hard-working and proud. (Top right clockwise) my beloved Grandma Grace; our family in the late 1940s; Barbara and me after a productive day fishing; Lewis Rice, a World War II hero and the bomber pilot, holding me with Crosby next to him; and Mom and Dad soon after having met.

I worked hard to help Dad build his dream house on top of the mountain near Asheville. As you can tell, I loved to fish long before I was a proud Lee Edwards High grad. (Bottom) With Mom and sister Barbara sometime in the 1980s.

I loved my football coaching days. (Top left) We look over a gameplan. (Top right, clockwise) With two of my closest high school buddies from Asheville, David Rickman and Kent Lominac; With the famous $4 garbage can that started it all; the infamous "Round House" where it all started; with first wife Linda and "Skinny von Weiner."

With Pam Dymic and the original beach buggy; My first Hawaiian Tropic ad shoot, and the first advertising photo taken ever taken by yours truly, as models Patsy Burgess and Bob Bowers wore themselves out on Waikiki Beach; my first sales hut during the "Tropic Tan" days.

Our first ads were quite a hit—and had an instant impact on sales. (Bottom) literally, the original famous brown suits worn by the Hawaiian Tropic models. All I can say is "Wow!" I now see why that ad worked.

I jumped into sponsoring auto racing on a whim and it worked for us. Neil Bonnett (top left) always held a special place in my heart. The IndyCar (mid right) wasn't a success, but the highlight of it all was Paul Newman winning the 24 Hours of Le Mans in 1979 in the HT-sponsored car; (Bottom) The crowds for our Beach Boys July 4, D.C. concerts were overwhelming.

As I always described them, our pageants were "magic' from the start. (Top left) Cathy Lee Crosby and John Davidson hosting; Benny Hill (mid right), who became a close friend, judged for several years. His death crushed me. A certain future President, along with Steelers' great Franco Harris, Lakers' owner Jerry Buss and Sterling, chip in to hold up winner Jennifer England in 1998.

I often was compared to Hugh Hefner but never thought that was fair to Hugh. I admired the guy immensely and he became a good friend, often hosting us at the Playboy Mansion; Shana Hiatt on cover of "Girls of Hawaiian Tropic" issue; Sandra Hubby holds her issue; but we had to cover Sandra Nilsson in this shot!

When the Princess Sterling (top right) sailed, the fun began. My other toys included "The Rice Rocket" and the black Lamborghini I often drove down the Ormond-Daytona beach. And of course, I attached our famous HT logo to them all as part of my "Guerilla Marketing" approach—and often sailed a catamaran up and down the beach just for the exposure.

From the time I spotted the dark-skinned Darcy LaPier, Miss Oregon, at our national pageant in 1987, I was smitten. We married Sept. 15, 1990, at the event of the year in Daytona, but it didn't last (and really wasn't legal anyway)—although we remained very close over the years. Most of all, we had Sterling together.

I loved basketball, mostly NCAA basketball, and made many close friends in the game, especially former Celtics' great John Havlicek (top right, clockwise), with N.C. State Coach Jim Valvano; imitating UNLV Coach Jerry Tarkanian and his famous towel bite; with buddy Wink in front of Denny Crum and the legendary John Wooden at a Final Four; with Roy Williams; and with Larry Bird.

Jackie Gleason was so much fun to be around, here on the set of "Smokey and the Bandit II" with Melanie Kerr and Lynn Blythe; (Bottom right) with Janette Webb and good friend and stuntman/director Hal Needham; and with Christopher Reeve, one of the bravest men I ever knew.

With Ken "Snake" Stabler (top right, clockwise); with Dolphins' legend Don Shula and CNN's Larry King; with Franco Harris; Jim Kelly became a close friend of ours by judging our pageants for many years; and Sterling with the "Greatest of All Time," Muhammad Ali, on the slopes of Aspen.

During appearances at various charity events, the A-list was never far away. (Top right, clockwise) Charlton Heston and HT's Linda Kramer; with supermodel Cheryl Tiegs, Peter Beard and Princess Caroline; with friend Michael Douglas, Tonya Batson at Cannes; with Angie Dickinson; Priscilla Presley; Richard Branson, comedian Chris Farley, Cher in a photo-shy mood; Robert Mitchum; Sly Stallone; Hulk Hogan; Raquel Welch; Michael and Whoopi; and with the legendary Jimmy Stewart, wife Gloria and my date Marie Sutej.

I was always drawn to comedians and here I am with four legendary men of comedy. The great Rodney Dangerfield cuts a rug; Mickey Rooney cutting me up; Jerry attended my parties and we became friends long before "Seinfeld" became a thing. He paid me back by placing me next to George Costanza at a movie in the "Puerto Rican Day" episode of the show's final season in 1998; with comedian/movie star Eddie Murphy.

One of the greatest honors I ever received was being inducted into the Myrtle Beach "Walk of Fame" and being honored at the Sun Fun Festival parade in 1997 while riding high with Sterling by my side. (Bottom) A rare shot alone of me in a buttoned-down shirt, at the 2011 NCAA Final Four in Houston.

back to his office.

That huge stack of papers represented issues and problems that had built up and he wanted me to do the work for him. And I was getting a lot of that.

That's the very day in 1985 that I decided to stop coming to the office and start working out of my house. I had to get away from the day-to-day headaches. I wanted to focus on my strength, which was the pageants and making sure our name was getting out there to help sales.

And when it came to the pageants, there was a never a shortage of workers from our office who wanted to travel to some exotic location, usually Hawaii, on the company dime to do the work associated with hosting them, either.

I always had a problem when some of our female workers inside our company office wanted to be models. They saw the glamorous life, the runways, the perks and the celebrities that flocked to them. I usually hand-picked everyone into two categories—the "worker-bees" and the "honeybees," as we called them. The honeybees got to travel to exotic places and do some modeling. The worker-bees stayed behind and worked.

Unlike the pageant winners, I personally was involved in choosing a small, select group of models to represent the company, during charity events or modeling jobs. These girls made up our promotion teams. I picked the best-looking and the smartest as well as the girls I knew would represent the company in a professional manner. We dressed them in evening gowns at night and bathing suits during the day.

In their minds, becoming a Hawaiian Tropic model may have been their entrée to big-time Hollywood and stardom. They would meet stars along the way, maybe become actresses, appear on TV or movies, or appear in *Playboy*.

As it turned out, dozens of them just did all of the above.

We would take dozens of girls every year to France and bounce from the International Movie Festival in Cannes in May to Le Mans in early June, sometimes making it into one long working vacation in the South of France. It was a prime assignment for the girls; one that generated great competition. We always tried to take those who best represented our brand.

We had no real official capacity, or duty, or anything to do with the movies, I would take a select group of company models there and just walk around, mingle and attend many of the parties. The exposure was unbelievable, and no doubt helped our brand awareness, and ultimately, sales.

At first, people over there—the so-called Hollywood elites—wondered what the hell we were doing there.

I would just tell them, "Promoting our product."

Nobody wanted us at their parties, thinking it was all beneath them. It didn't take long for that to change, however. We soon got invited to most of the parties, simply because our models were so beautiful and such an attraction.

Or when they asked, "What are you doing over here? You don't have a movie to promote!" I would deliver a stock answer every time. "It doesn't matter," I would say. "We are just here to party with you!"

It usually worked and they laughed and accepted us. Who wouldn't want ten to fifteen beautiful women at their party? We got invited to just about every party, solely because the hosts wanted the girls there. I knew it wasn't to have me be a guest, but me and our top employees and the girls were a package deal.

When *Basic Instinct* premiered at Cannes in 1992, we were invited to attend a party with stars Michael Douglas and Sharon Stone. It was at a five-star restaurant and we arrived at the exact time that Shep Gordon, a friend of Michael's who was in the music business, had told us to be there.

My girls were dressed to the max, wearing long, elegant gowns, as we walked through the middle of this fancy restaurant all the way to the back, where the *Basic Instinct* people were, and we immediately realized all the stars and movie people were still dining.

We had no choice but to turn around and walk all the way back to the exit.

Just as I walked through the door while leaving, I felt a hand on my shoulder. I turned to see Michael Douglas.

"That's the greatest entrance I have ever seen," he said. "You get these girls back in here right now!"

So, we all walked back into the restaurant again and Michael told our models to spread out and sit at various tables. He and I became friends right then and there. And we have been good friends ever since.

Of course, there were times we weren't always so well-received, or at least I wasn't.

One night in Cannes, we were in a bar called Palm Beach and we had our own private area lined with white sofas. I had a dozen or more of our top girls and my head of advertising, Jeff Lalanne, whom we called "Abdul," and we were being served this powerful blue liquor called America.

I also had noticed the actor, Mickey Rourke, sitting in another area when four skinny guys walked in. They immediately stood at the back of a sofa so they could scan the entire dance floor.

A fifth guy who was with them was much larger and wore a suit with an open shirt. He stood behind us closely watching those guys.

I had gone over to talk to Mickey with one of my models, Lara Howarth, for a while and I was headed back to our area. I returned when one of the little, skinny guys stopped me. He wouldn't let me pass through. I just lightly pushed on by him and all of a sudden, I found myself in a headlock and I was being pulled sideways.

It turned out to be the big guy with the suit and open shirt, who was the bodyguard for the four skinny guys who were big time arms dealers.

I finally regained my footing and stood up to see him staring at me. I then worked up the hardest punch I could muster and popped him square in the face. My mistake was that I didn't follow it up and he came rushing at me as Abdul stepped between us, and the three of us ended up rolling all over the floor. Somehow, I lost one of my shoes, so I was crawling around looking for my shoe by the time the bouncers pulled everybody apart.

One of the skinny guys then approached me and apologized for the fight.

By the time I reached the parking lot, somebody from the bar came running out claiming I owed $50,000 for the twenty-five bottles of champagne that those four skinny guys had ordered.

"Wasn't my bill!" I claimed.

I met this wealthy jewelry dealer there and he always gave us a great deal on rental of a large house in Cannes. Then I rented a big van, called it the "Rolls Rice," and we loaded up the girls and bounced around town.

During the day, I gave them time to go shopping and walk around the streets of Cannes.

Within a few years, people got used to seeing us and we were not only welcomed but invited to just about every party. TV crews would follow us to film the girls and it soon became a great and productive trip each year.

As for the girls, they loved it. They were well-paid, ate great food, enjoyed all the parties, often met movie stars and got a free trip to France out of it.

One time, we drove from Cannes toward Nice to take in the nightlife at a place called the Hotel du Cap. It was about thirty minutes from Cannes, and we had to take a road up into the mountains to reach it.

I think a glass of orange juice cost about fourteen dollars there and I had thirteen of our models with me, so I told them, "Do your best to mingle and let the celebrities buy your drinks."

One of the girls, Krista Frazier, who was Miss Hawaiian Tropic in 1995, always had a crush on the actor Hugh Grant. Well, who happened to be there that night but Hugh Grant? Unfortunately for Krista, his wife Elizabeth Hurley was with him that night so she couldn't make her move.

The next morning, we were at an event in Cannes and Hugh was there, too, promoting a movie. He just happened to see Krista standing there and told one of his assistants, "Please get her number for me."

I don't think they ever did get to meet, but it wasn't too long after that when he got arrested for being in a car with a prostitute in California. When that happened, I joked to Krista, "See, all you had to do was stand on the corner of Hollywood and Vine and you would have been solicited by Hugh . . ."

Each year after Cannes, we would fly home and then fly back to Paris three weeks later. We then would drive to Le Mans, which was held each June, since we sponsored a race car in the 24-hour race.

Through the years, I also took many of my friends along with the models.

One time, Tom McMillen, the former NBA player who would later become a U.S. Congressman from Maryland, and I almost didn't make it home.

I was driving one day from Paris to Le Mans in a rented Renault station wagon and Tom and his six-foot-ten frame was in the passenger seat sleeping, as were a few of our models in the backseat. I must have been going about 140 kph when a truck pulled out to pass another truck and then cut us off. I had no choice but to slam on the brakes and Tom instinctively grabbed the steering wheel as soon as he woke. Luggage flew up into the backseat hitting the girls in the back of the head as we skidded along

When we finally came to a stop, the nose of the station wagon actually was under the rear of that truck. That was a close call—an extremely close call that could have left Tom and I decapitated if we hadn't stopped just in time. (Tom was a great guy with a great sense of humor. When he was a member of Congress, he would call me and say, "Turn to CSPAN right now and look in the background." There he would be, behind whoever was speaking, making a funny face or sticking his tongue out.)

Once, during one of those trips, my head of marketing, Bill Darby, and I had to visit South Africa to meet with a sales rep.

We had a good deal on a rental, so we left the girls to themselves in Cannes for about five or six days.

I quickly learned it was very difficult to keep that many girls happy in France for such a long period of time.

When we returned, I was informed they had been fighting like cats and dogs the entire time we were gone. They were all ready to kill each other and two of them were leading a coup against me, for some reason. The two, Julie Murdoch and Terry English, apparently had gone room-to-room, trying to talk the other girls into making demands to rise up against me. They were being paid well, but they wanted even more money, if I remember correctly.

When I returned, I had overheard them complaining to Melanie Kerr, who was a trusted employee somewhat in charge of the girls. Melanie just listened patiently and finally said, "Murdoch, just how long have you been with Hawaiian Tropic?" Since Julie was a new girl, she had made her point.

I sent Murdoch home to the U.S. the following day. That night, I took all the girls shopping and bought them dresses, except for Terry English.

"Terry, you are off the deep end and cannot be saved," I told her. "All these other girls are going to a big party tonight wearing their new dresses. You are going home."

Then I put her on a flight home.

I hated insubordination, especially from employees who were paid well and treated well. But for some, it seemed it was never enough.

In addition to Le Mans, all of the major auto races—such as the Indy 500, the 12 Hours of Sebring and the Daytona 500 and sportscar races on downtown streets of Miami and Palm

Beach—provided the perfect venues to show off our models. They would parade around the pits and track in their Hawaiian Tropic swimsuits and photographers swarmed them like locusts.

One year at Indy, we had heard that the owners of the track, led by one of the relatives of the owners, the George family, a woman by the name of Gloria, didn't want our girls anywhere near the Indianapolis Motor Speedway. I happened to be skiing in Aspen that day, but they described it to me in great detail: We had several models ready to go and they were covered in heavy raincoats as they showed their credentials to get through the gates. Then as they got closer to the track, off came the raincoats as they continued walking down pit lane in nothing but their bikinis. I heard that the track owners were going crazy mad, screaming at the girls as the fans were going crazy happy as photographers snapped away.

We also took them places such as the Grammy Awards and often to the Playboy Mansion. After I discovered "Sun Fun," Myrtle Beach's festival which kicked off the arrival of every summer, we also made sure Hawaiian Tropic had a big presence there and often sponsored the entire event. We always placed the models on their own float for the parade they held down the boardwalk and obviously it paid us back in huge numbers each year because our sales in the Myrtle Beach area were as strong as anywhere as the years passed.

The attractiveness of the girls, not to mention we always had so many of them in one place, always made our events the place to be for men, whether they be rich and famous or just average guys with little money hoping to get lucky. Incredibly lucky.

And some meetings were just out of the blue.

One time, we flew into Lima, for the Miss Universe pageant, which we had sponsored. We would donate a ton of our products toward the gift bags for all the contestants and then attend the event mostly for the parties and the publicity that comes with being a sponsor.

We always took some of our models with us and after we landed, many of them found a bar that afternoon and ordered something called Inca Pisco, which is similar to fruity-tasting brandy. It tasted like fruit punch to me, but I learned very quickly how powerful it was.

Six of our girls each ordered this tall drink in a bamboo container, with a big straw coming out of each. They all took one sip and hated it.

"Okay, we are not wasting these. I'll drink them!" I told them.

The bar was somewhere just on the outskirts of town and there was a big, grassy area where there were llamas. I soon found myself in a spitting contest with a llama, at least that is what they told me later, but I don't remember much. Too much of that stuff could make a person crazy. We had one of our staffers who wanted to fly off a hotel balcony that night.

When we finally made it back to the hotel, and as all six girls hopped out and ran inside, I stumbled my way toward the door.

Melanie Kerr just loved magic and was a pretty good magician. As she jumped out and headed inside, she ran smack into David Copperfield, who was there to be a pageant judge. He was her idol. And she was beautiful. He took one look at Melanie and that was that.

As for me, I had llama spit all over me so I told them, "I am headed to my room to change clothes and I will see you in the bar." But as soon as I saw my bed, I flopped into it, thinking I would take a five-minute nap and then grab a shower. Next thing I knew it was four in the morning.

When I went downstairs in the morning for breakfast, everybody asked what happened to me.

"Copperfield made him disappear!" one of the girls joked.

When we were on the road with the girls, it just seemed there was always adventure in one form or another. For example, me and a couple of the girls took my airplane down to the Cayman Islands for an advertising photo shoot one time. My pilot was a young kid by the name of Mike from Cuba, probably in his twenties who was always hitting on the girls, but he was a great pilot.

One night we pulled the rental van into a gas station and I ran inside to buy some beer. I was walking from the store to the back of the van carrying two cases of bottled beer when all of a sudden, this guy, with a black eye and bloody nose, approaches me from behind and started screaming at me in a language I didn't understand. He then kicked me in the ribs. I was trying my best to set the beer down without breaking any bottles just as he kicked me again.

As this was happening, another guy who was older was trying to get into the van to grab the girls. Then the guy attacking me came back for a third kick. I grabbed his foot, twisted it and punched him in the ear. I ran back to the van and shoved the other guy down, hopped in and we drove off—and I left the two cases of beer sitting there.

It was never, ever boring.

I've always been one to give nicknames to people, sometimes even when they didn't know about it. But they became part of our culture at Hawaiian Tropic and the girls picked up on it and sometimes provided their own contributions to our various collection.

There was Nichole Bennett, who became "Sunny Butt." She was so vain that she thought the sun would rise and set on her butt. Nobody calls her Nicole anymore—and she still works for me in a sense, watching over my Malibu house.

Sunny had the perfect personality and loved practical jokes just like I did. I remember once we had a pageant winner by the name of Jennifer Campbell, who was a bit prudish. At least prudish by our standards. She wanted to make things happen for her in L.A. for her career as a lot of girls do, so I let her stay at the Malibu house for a little while.

One day I called out there and Jennifer happened to be out jogging, so I had Sonny describe her bedroom in great detail. Where were the towels located? What color? Where was her luggage, etc.? What color was her bathing suit? There also happened to be a video camera sitting in the open.

"When she comes back from jogging, call me and let it ring once, then I will call back and you let her answer the phone," I instructed Sonny.

It happened just that way.

"Jennifer, I am so glad I got you," I started. "You have to go to that cabinet by your bedroom door and adjust the camera. That is the main camera for the porn channel that we have a deal with. Also, there's been some complaints about your green bathing suit. Try another color. Also, walk into the bathroom and move that big bottle of pink lotion. It is blocking camera number eight . . ."

As I continued, she started to seriously freak out.

"WHAT? WHAT?" she started to scream.

"Don't worry Jennifer," I said. "The porn channel will still pay you royalties. They have to. We have a contract. We just have to adjust some things."

She was about to have a serious meltdown, so I had to break out laughing and calm her down.

You can see how some girls just didn't get my sense of humor.

They all probably never realized how large a part of my life they were. But I want to make sure they know after reading this. I owe them a debt of gratitude and I will never forget them.

What I learned was that every girl had a story. They were all unique in their own way, with different backgrounds, beliefs, goals and family histories. And I grew close to many of them in a father-daughter sort of way, offering advice when they needed it.

There are so many of the models and pageant winners that became a big part of the company's success who I want to thank right here, right now. I saw dozens of them grow from immature young girls who needed guidance, to mature wives and mothers, and even grandmothers, by now.

The bottom line is that I am proud of them all and hope they enjoyed the experience of being a Hawaiian Tropic model or participating in one of our pageants as much as I did employing them and watching them thrive—either on a stage in front of thousands, representing our brand or in life in general.

All I know is that the idea of hosting pageants and using models worked beyond my wildest imagination and helped make Hawaiian Tropic a household name.

And I like to think we did it all in a classy way.

We had hundreds of thousands of amazing, beautiful girls from all around the world over the thirty years of our pageants, which had branched out through our distributors and sales reps, and yet we never had any big scandals. We had a clean reputation and the Hawaiian Tropic models not only generated a lot of sales but became well-known around the world.

And I am enormously proud of that.

Chapter Nine

THE SALESMEN

I have explained how the guerrilla marketing, seat-of-my-pants advertising, beauty pageants and our models helped build the brand and increase sales, but the salespeople and reps for Hawaiian Tropic who were on the front lines all over the world were a huge factor in our success.

We produced and supplied them a quality product to sell and if they did their job, it was just a matter of time before most of them became wealthy.

Early on, going back to the days of Tropic Tan, I always looked for potential salespeople who had little or no money but did have a lot of time and ambition. I did not want to hire people who had money in the bank. Those were the types who were satisfied, perhaps lazy and not as hungry.

I wanted salespeople who were literally starving to make a living.

Once they convinced me of that, then I sent them all over

the world.

I always thought I had a great ability to pick the right people for the right job at the right time.

I told my salespeople: "If you work for this product, this product will work for you. Just get it into the stores and the product will sell on its own merits. It will make you rich while you are sleeping."

And it did.

After I had hired Elton Brunty in South Carolina, Gene Perkins, and a man named Skip Moore in my Tropic Tan days, they naturally stayed on when I changed the name in 1969. And I soon started adding many, many others—such as Bill Quinlan—as the years progressed.

Bill had been the athletic director at the junior high school where I taught, and I put him in charge of sales in the Daytona and Central Florida area. Another local guy, Ed Kelley, eventually served as my main sales rep in all of Europe. He lived in London most of the time and oversaw the development of our largest factory, in Dublin, Ireland.

With great salespeople like them, our sales figures were like a snowball rolling downhill.

And it wasn't very difficult to find people who wanted to sell the product full-time.

When it came to distribution in those early days, I always thought of Coors beer and how it was marketed and sold in limitation. I would notice airline stewardesses walking through airports carrying cases of Coors, because it was not sold east of the Mississippi back then. I always thought that was a very smart strategy because the company's approach made their beer popular.

And at times over the years, I realized in retrospect that I was way too liberal on the terms I offered for salespeople.

Many of them were old friends from my lifeguarding days.

Such as a man named Don Langer.

Don was a fellow lifeguard on the pool decks and when it came time to get the product sold in Hawaii, I chose him to go over there and run the operation. We had to ship it from Jacksonville at the beginning, through the Panama Canal into the Pacific and all the way to Honolulu.

After only one year of that and sometimes shipping containers on commercial flights, I knew it was time to open a plant in Hawaii. After all, I never forgot the name of the product and where I first saw those native girls rubbing coconut oil all over their bodies.

Hawaiian Tropic was meant to be produced in Hawaii.

Thus, my goal was to open a small manufacturing plant somewhere on the islands, so Don and I did some scouting and eventually found a warehouse to share with another company owner on Waimanu Street, in downtown Honolulu. I remember that the businessman who used the other half of the warehouse was deaf, but he could read lips very well and we later became good friends.

At that time, we could purchase the mineral oils in Hawaii, but we still had to ship the lotions there in those fifty-five-gallon drums.

Anyway, on one of our flights to Hawaii, sometime in 1972, I could tell that Don was worried about his job security for some reason. At the time, I liked Don very much. I noticed a letter-sized envelope in the seatback, so I took it out and wrote this:

"Let it be known that . . . In case of the sale of Hawaiian Tropic, Don Langer will receive 10% of the gross proceeds of the sale, if he is still living in Hawaii, working for Hawaiian Tropic, and meeting all of the above requirements of this Agreement."

I had included some other required details such as him not selling competing products, but I did want to make sure he lived in Hawaii.

And I signed it.

It was a stupid thing to do, a really stupid thing to do.

But I had meant my note to be for a term over the next few years rather than indefinitely, fully knowing I had no intention to sell. I thought it would put his mind at ease and it would be of no consequence whatsoever with me having no desire to sell in the first place.

And in my mind, I wanted Hawaii to be our showcase to the buying world. I really did not care if we made big profits there, or any profit at all, because we were making money everywhere else in the world. I just knew Hawaiian Tropic had to have a manufacturing plant somewhere in the islands, among all of our other factories that would open around the world, and we accomplished that.

Therefore, Don had gotten the sweetheart deal of all sweetheart deals from me in the first place, because I let him take all the profits in Hawaii—after costs of the product, of course.

In other parts of the world, for example the Pacific Rim and Australia, the company took twenty percent of all sales.

My plan was that there had to be two places I just knew we had to make inroads with the product. One was in Hawaii, naturally, so I basically had determined earlier that I would make it very easy and profitable for whoever I was going to set up there. The other was in Israel and it did not take long to do well in sales in both areas.

Later, Don also took Australia as his territory and then hired a guy from Florida State named Dan Cleary. We set up a factory Down Under and we were really doing great for the first several years, but Don and Dan got into a big dispute over something and Cleary pulled out of the arrangement.

In the end, I think Langer owed the Australian government about $300,000 in back taxes and that was the end of that. We ended up going dormant there.

Langer got more and more greedy as time wore on. He would fly into Daytona for company meetings when he needed to be there and start creating trouble with other sales reps. He just wanted more and more profit. He wanted more control and more power, but I had no choice but to keep him on since he was locked in contractually as far as Hawaii and he had all the contacts there. He really became a constant thorn in my side for years, but I really thought I had no choice but to put up with him.

We were so dominant in Hawaii that I just looked the other way regarding his shenanigans.

As I said earlier, we worked hard to get Hawaiian Tropic in all parts of the world, but one of my failings was trying to figure out how to get it sold in Russia. I knew we could make a fortune if we ever succeeded, since it was such a massive market.

One of our top models, Monica Soares, who grew up on the Big Island of Hawaii, whom I was very, very close with over the years, had been chased for years by a guy named Pat Rogers. Pat happened to know the actor, Chuck Norris, who was spending fifty million dollars to buy a casino-nightclub in Moscow.

Rogers and Chuck called me one day to pitch a "Miss Hawaiian Tropic-Russia" pageant. I was intrigued by the idea, so I flew to Moscow at Norris' expense to discuss it. I was dating Monica at the time, so I took her with me. We ended up having dinner at the house of the former head of the KGB which they both knew.

They spoke Russian throughout the night, and we all drank these little glasses of vodka. They would toast in Russian, drink the vodka and throw the glasses over their shoulders. So, at the end of each toast, I started doing it, too. Since I didn't understand a word of Russian, all I heard was "Blah, blah, blah . . . and Monica!" They would then take a drink and glasses would crash. "Blah, blah, blah . . . and Monica!" Take a drink and glasses would crash. And that is about all I remember from that night.

Eventually, we held one pageant there, at Casino Beverly Hills and it went great; it was a huge success and I thought I finally would get the product into the U.S.S.R. There were so many pretty Russian girls in that pageant, it was unbelievable to me. Soon after that, however, the Russian government screwed Chuck and somehow took his invested money and his casino-nightclub, too. There had been one hundred casinos in Moscow and the government shut down fifty of them, including Chuck's.

The lesson for me was "don't ever try to deal with Russia." If something went wrong, as Chuck discovered, you cannot sue the government. The only way to deal with them at all was to trade product-for-product—and how was I going to sell large shipments of vodka in America anyway?

So, obviously, we never got Hawaiian Tropic's products sold in Russia.

I did make a few mistakes in picking salesmen from time to time, or maybe I was just too trusting at other times.

I had hired one salesman in 1977 for the Miami area by the name of Clyde Walton "Bill" Cobb. As it turned out, his sales business was nothing but a front for his drug operation. He was bringing in drugs from Jamaica and distributing them in South Florida, as he sold Hawaiian Tropic on the side.

Bill was a skinny, little guy who looked like Blackbeard the Pirate. He did have a great personality, though, and was bringing in millions of dollars in sales for the product—the legitimate product, that is.

But he was also doing the same for the illegal stuff.

Another guy had worked for Bill and I really liked this guy once I got to know him. I learned later how their operation worked: They would fly two private jets into Jamaica. The other guy would be in the first one and hand over a briefcase containing at times up to one million dollars in cash. Then another guy who worked for Bill would land in the second airplane, pick up the drugs and head back to Florida. He would make the drop somewhere over the Everglades, dealing with two Mafia-type guys out of Miami who would pick it up.

And just like in the movie *Scarface,* Bill had maintained a little hotel room just for his drug dealings. Well, one day, some bad guys had met him at his hotel room, grabbed Bill against his will and threw him and his money into the backseat of a car. They had their orders to take him out to a remote area to kill him.

As I said, just like *Scarface*.

As they drove, Bill began talking.

He was at his best when talking sales and he was now doing it with his life on the line. He told the bad guys what was going to happen to them after he was dead. He told them that they surely would be caught, tried, convicted and sentenced to die in "Old Sparky," which was another name for the electric chair in Florida.

The more they drove, the more Bill talked. Finally, while they had stopped at a traffic light, Bill hopped out of the car and started running for his life. Two cars behind them in traffic happened to be a police car, which Bill promptly flagged down.

They quickly caught the bad guys, thanks to Bill closing the deal on the ultimate sale when it mattered most—and it saved his own life.

But when I discovered what was going on, I called Bill to come to an important meeting in Daytona. Of course, I did not give him a clue what it was about.

We had been supplying him and he had a big warehouse in South Florida, completely full of Hawaiian Tropic products at the time, so I had arranged for a few of my employees to drive a large truck to Miami and wait outside of his warehouse.

Just as Bill left to drive for Daytona for our meeting, they made their move. As he was making the four-hour drive north to see me, my guys started cleaning out his warehouse.

When Bill was sitting across from me at my desk, they called me and told me, "We're all done. Got it all and we're on the way back."

I had to be smiling as I informed him of what I knew he had been doing illegally. Then I told him about the operation that had just concluded at his warehouse. I have to admit that seeing the look on his face was priceless. Of course, that was the end of our relationship.

As it turned out, Bill soon was busted in a federal operation labeled "Operation Sunburn." His case made national news and I immediately knew how the feds came up with the name.

"Operation Sunburn" made headlines and put Hawaiian Tropic's name in the news for all the wrong reasons.

The IRS then came down hard on Bill and he had to pay back millions for unreported income. He also was convicted of several crimes and spent some time at a minimum security prison in North Florida. He also became a star witness for the government, and as part of his plea bargain, he was allowed to use drug profits to pay off his IRS debt.

I had never heard of that arrangement before.

I later read all the accounts of the operation and the federal authorities believed there was two hundred million dollars still unaccounted for. Who knows? If that is true, that money may still be in some offshore account or perhaps in the Caymans or a Latin American bank somewhere today, since Bill died in 2010.

Still, I kept Charlie, his assistant, on with us after that fiasco. He was a Vietnam vet and just following the orders of his boss by flying where he wanted to fly, the way I looked at it.

There were several others who looked out only for themselves, such as the former London cab driver by the name of Simonson who sold Hawaiian Tropic in Spain and on all those islands off of Spain.

He made a ton of money and then took manufactured loads of product from Spain, where it is supposed to remain, to the

European market to sell on his own. We got wind of it and turned him in to the authorities. When the U.K. police closed in on him, they found it and destroyed it all at the boat docks in London, just so he couldn't sell it.

As far as my own employees, especially salesmen, I had one more simple philosophy: Loose lips sink ships.

I told them all, "Don't get drunk and start telling our company secrets. Be discreet. Always be discreet."

It wasn't always easy.

I always realized that if a key person, say one of my vice-presidents, said the wrong thing to the wrong person in business, it could always come back to haunt us later. I learned that you always had to be incredibly careful what was said to people outside the company. Today they may be an associate and tomorrow they may be a competitor, or worse, your business rival.

When I was first starting the business, selling products to the lifeguards, I went out of my way never to burn those bridges. Little things, like never stealing someone's girlfriend, etc., or screwing them out of money when they rightfully deserved it.

And I tried to make sure that all of my employees operated the same way.

Not that we did not have fun along the way. We were cutting up and playing practical jokes all the time on one another. We would take all my key people—vice-presidents, etc., and directors of certain departments—and travel to events all over the world. Sometimes, just for the fun of it.

After we made inroads in the department stores, buyers would invite us to attend a lot of functions in New York.

And we usually acted like a bunch of outsiders, not really trying or worrying one bit if we fit in.

I remember the first Beauty Ball we were invited to at the Waldorf-Astoria: My entire team walked in wearing different-colored tuxedos. I wore burgundy. Somebody else wore blue. Another wore brown, and so on. We all had beautiful dates. Then we looked around the ballroom and every other man in the room wore a black tux and black tie. It was just like in the movie "Dumb and Dumber."

They all thought we were making fun of them, but we weren't—that is just the way we acted in those days.

One time we were all in Hawaii, hanging out at the pool and we all had been drinking, naturally. One of our leading sales reps had invited a top salesman by the name of Scott Schrepple and he had spent most of the day hitting on this one girl. He never got out of the pool and he looked like a prune.

Finally, Bill Darby had noticed and worked up a scheme with one of our models, Vickie Foley, who promptly marched over to Scott and declared, "SCOTT! Come on, the kids are waiting on you!"

Hearing that, the girl he had spent the entire day hitting on just swam away from him like Mark Spitz.

One of the sales reps I liked very much was Gene Perkins, whom am I still good friends with to this day.

Gene started selling in the New England area, west to Ohio and north to Canada. We always fronted the merchandise and would be reimbursed as it sold.

Gene looked like Kenny Rogers and talked a great game, and he was the first salesman to get us a substantial, major account. He had arranged a meeting with the buyer from Macy's, so one day, he and I walked down Fifth Avenue in New York carrying this giant Styrofoam display that contained six products. We were wearing leisure suits and must have looked so out of place. The buyer was located in the basement, about five levels below street level, and by the time we went all the way down there, we just about had to crawl over pipes to get to his office.

Anyway, the guy liked us for some reason and placed a big order right there and then.

Once Macy's carried our product, it seemed everyone else wanted to follow. We soon were in Woodward & Lothrop, which was a huge department store chain in the 1960s and '70s headquartered in D.C., as well as Gimbels, Lazarus and Broadway stores.

Once buyers and customers realized we were not just another fly-by-night company, the product flew off the shelves.

Eventually, we added K-Mart and Walgreens, but we could not produce the product fast enough to satisfy the demand. At least that is what we told them. We did not like the retailers like K-Mart discounting our products below the factory suggested price. However, the Sherman-Antitrust Law basically forced us to continue to sell to them, no matter where they priced it.

One other thing I learned: If you are one of the top-selling brands, stores allowed you to determine where your product was placed on the shelves—and that determined where your competitors were placed as well. I walked into drugstores around town frequently to see where Hawaiian Tropic was being placed.

And I made sure our salesmen often pushed to have it placed in the best locations inside each store.

Another reason we jumped quickly to number two in the

world behind Coppertone: We had all the small beach stores and gift shops and even the so-called mom-and-pop stores, too, carrying our products—places where Coppertone didn't want to be sold.

I always looked at our competition with Coppertone this way: They cared way more about what we were doing than I cared about them. The fact is, I never wasted any time thinking about Coppertone, how it was marketed, advertised, or sold for that matter.

Having said that, I am sure that my vice-presidents and salespeople were concerned with the competition, but I know I did not give a flip.

It was clear that our product's success ultimately got into their heads, as their sales reps had admitted to me.

And I also knew that Coppertone did not always play fair.

As we were making marketing waves and rising in sales, they sent some lawyers down to Brazil to register our trademark before we could. I am sure they paid some judges under the table to make it stick, which it did, and we were basically shut out of the entire country.

My South Carolina sales rep, Elton, had asked me if he could take a knockoff product, Waikiki Tan, down there to try and sell it. I gave him the go-ahead. Everything in it was the same as Hawaiian Tropic but the name, but it did not work and would not sell. People just wouldn't buy it without the name recognition, not knowing if it was a quality product or a bad product.

Every time we had somebody try to get our product into Brazil, Coppertone had to put up more money into the legal fight to keep us out. Finally, their reps approached me about wanting to sell Hawaiian Tropic there and I shut them down.

"No, that's not going to happen," I said.

When the U.S. went into a recession in 1973 and the Arab countries exportation of oil resulted in an oil embargo on the U.S., according to the law, we could acquire only half as much as what we had consumed the year before. I had been buying from Chevron before the embargo and now we faced a big problem.

There was a startup suntan company in Daytona called "Sub Tropic," which I thought accurately described their product, but they had one advantage over us now. They had no "year before," so they could acquire as much oil as they wanted. So, during that period, we were facing a disadvantage.

One day I got on the phone with all of my sales reps across the country.

"Go out and buy up every drum of oil you can find," I told them.

Perkins took my order to heart: He found one massive yard somewhere in New England that was full of mineral oil, our base product. I wrote that company a big check and they arranged to have the oil shipped to us.

There had been a guy from some company in Georgia who had tried to sell me oil for years and I kept turning him down, since I had a relationship with Chevron, and he couldn't beat their price. Then when the embargo hit, and after we discovered that stockpile in New England, this guy happened to strut into our office with a big smile on his face.

"You need me now, don't you?" he asked.

"Nope," I said. "Got all the oil we need. But thanks for asking . . ."

He walked out in a huff. I had all of these big blue drums full of oil sitting behind our factory. After he walked out, I went out back and saw him peering through the fence, writing down numbers. I knew he was trying to discover where I found all of that oil.

Anyway, sales reps like Elton could well afford to leave coaching—just as I did years earlier—after just a short time of selling Hawaiian Tropic. He worked his way up the sales ladder to have our sales rights all the way from Virginia to the Georgia border.

And he ended up becoming a very rich man.

He was not the only one. Our product made millionaires out of dozens of salespeople. It basically sold itself and our marketing and advertising usually worked, so if they were willing to hustle and work hard, they all succeeded beyond what they ever expected when they started.

Not that long ago, I was talking to Cleary about the old days. He had put together a sales team that was second to none. They really moved the product over the years.

Anyway, he confided in me, and said, "We lived like jet-setters and partied like rock stars."

I already knew that was true for the most part, and I let them do their thing as long as they produced and represented the company well. And most of them did that. Some of them happened to spend too much or squander what millions they made, because although they were good salespeople, they were lousy money-managers.

Or they had too many expensive vices, like gambling or overspending on boats, cars, diamonds and houses. I will get to the ramifications of that much later.

But the salesmen who became rich and stayed rich happened to be—just like me to some extent—at the right place at the right time.

And it changed their lives forever.

Chapter Ten

THE WORLD OF CELEBRITY

It did not take long to see that my idea of operating our own beauty pageants would pay huge dividends for the company.

My original intention, from a sales and marketing standpoint, was to generate immense publicity and a widespread buzz about the name Hawaiian Tropic. Name recognition is everything in business and what the pageants and models created was beyond what anything I had first imagined in my wildest dreams.

And I could dream wildly.

The girls in those bathing suits, racing suits and evening gowns who bore the company's name soon became part of Americana and with the overwhelming publicity they generated, largely from the number of cameramen that followed them everywhere. They were a large part of boosting our sales and making our products, our logo and name familiar to people around the world.

What I guess I never saw coming is that the girls collectively would have their own fans and admirers and it seemed everybody wanted to be around them and meet them.

Especially athletes.

And celebrities.

And comedians.

And musicians.

And . . . well, you get the picture.

I soon knew how Hugh Hefner felt when all the single, and some married, athletes, TV stars and movie stars flocked to the Playboy Mansion just to be in the presence of his Playmates.

Many of the same people flocked to our beauty pageants, and to the parties I hosted, and as far as I was concerned, they were more than welcome, because I realized they also helped push the name Hawaiian Tropic to the buying public's attention.

Frequently, they would call the office wanting to become pageant judges or to get invitations to our parties.

Most male celebrities were already rich to begin with and would have wanted to be a part of our pageants and parties just for the exposure to the girls, whom I always considered the most beautiful in the world.

So, it was only natural that men loved being around them.

And that, along with having a successful company and now the financial ability to travel and attend celebrity charity events and donate to all those good causes, opened the door to the world of celebrity.

As I sit here, and look at the various pictures around my home to jar my memory, these are a few of the people I met over the years: Bob Hope, Dean Martin, Frank Sinatra, Robert

Mitchum, Michael Douglas, Gregory Peck, Priscilla Presley, Gene Hackman, Jimmy Stewart, Charlton Heston, Kevin Costner, Ron Howard, Rodney Dangerfield, Burt Reynolds, Lee Majors, Spike Lee, Cher, Leslie Nielsen, O.J. Simpson, Christopher Reeve, Robin Williams, all the Beach Boys, Sylvester Stallone, Jay Leno, John Denver, Alan Thicke, Benny Hill, Sam Kinison, Paul McCartney, Robin Leach, Pierce Brosnan, Ricky Nelson, Pat Boone, Alice Cooper, Fabio, Jerry Lee Lewis, James Brown, Jim Belushi, Dan Aykroyd, Larry King, Marlo Thomas, Phil Donahue, Charlie Sheen, Drew Carey, Jim Carrey, David Hasselhoff, Bruce Willis, Chris Farley, Lloyd Bridges, Sonny Bono, Raquel Welch, Jerry Seinfeld, Larry David, James Garner, Al Gore, Roger Moore, Timothy Dalton, too many professional athletes and coaches to mention and Presidents Carter, Reagan, Gerald Ford and of course, Trump.

There were so many others, but I cannot remember them all.

Out of this group, many of them became good friends and we saw each other or talked often. I also worked with Burt Reynolds, Jim Carrey, Lloyd Bridges and Roger Moore on movie sets. I sponsored President Ford's charity ski event. Many of the others became repeat judges for our pageants. James Brown and Jerry Lee Lewis came and performed at my parties at my Florida home.

I had met Elvis as a kid and saw one of his final performances in Las Vegas two months before he died. It was almost uncanny, because I was with Ricky Nelson only two weeks before his airplane crashed. And after reaching out to Malcolm Forbes and Doctor Pauling, at times I really wondered if I jinxed people's immediate future.

My buddy Wink and I had been invited to our other buddy's nightclub in Orlando in December of 1985. Ricky had been on tour and performed that night.

He sat with us after he played that night and I remember us talking about his parents, Ozzie and Harriett. To me, they were the All-American family. Ricky told us about his upcoming schedule: He had to fly to another concert in Georgia, and then to Mississippi, to Alabama and then to Texas for a New Year's Eve concert and then he said goodbye and walked out the door that night. His airplane crashed that New Year's Eve in De Kalb, Texas, and although I met him only one time, I never believed all those claims that he was freebasing cocaine in the airplane that night.

And John Denver . . . well, I will get to him later.

I really think I probably became closer to singer Julio Iglesias than just about anyone.

When I first met Julio, he didn't speak much English and I didn't speak any Spanish, but we somehow learned how to communicate.

As I said, he had fallen for one of our models, Bitsy Harrison, who lived in Tampa with her mother, who apparently once had a brief fling with Elvis. That is what she told everyone anyway. She also told many people that she believed Bitsy was Elvis' daughter. At least that is what she told me once.

Bitsy lived in a tough area of Tampa and I once told her mother to call me if she ever had any problems. She soon took me up on it, wanting Bitsy to live somewhere safe. I made the arrangements to move her over to one of my beach houses in Daytona and then I put her through school.

Anyway, Julio loved blond haired, blue-eyed girls and Bitsy

was all of that. Once his English got a little better through the years, he told me one day that he wanted a blond haired, blue-eyed baby.

"Julio, if that is the case, you had better go to an adoption agency," I told him.

Julio judged our pageants for several years and became a really good friend. He always treated the girls with respect, and as an example, during one pageant at the Plaza Hotel in Daytona, he had 160 dozen red roses delivered—a dozen for each girl in the pageant. That had to be a hell of a florist bill.

Julio was a sun worshiper unlike anybody I had ever seen, and he had the dark skin to get away with it. Therefore, our products were a natural for him and yet another reason we bonded. We once were in Ibiza, a tiny island off Barcelona, which is a marvelous vacation spot for only the very, very wealthy.

He would lie in the sun every day, get as dark as he possibly could, and he would go to any length when the weather did not cooperate, too.

On one cloudy day there, the phone in my room rang.

"Come to my door now, Ron," he told me. "We fly to sun today."

Sure enough, we took his airplane and flew to Madrid where the sun was shining. He lay in the sun all day, getting even more tan and then we met for dinner and flew back that night. When my late friend Robin Leach had his show, *Lifestyles of the Rich and Famous*, I think he had that kind of day in mind.

He always had an entourage, which included his backup singers among other people. When we traveled with enough people that we had to take two private planes, Julio insisted everyone draw numbers out of a hat to see which plane they were assigned. He wanted to leave it to fate and did not want to feel guilty for the rest of his life if one of them crashed. That was just how his mind worked.

I traveled with him all over the world for years and saw many of his concerts. Before one in Germany, he had thousands of posters to sign, and no time to do it, so me and a few others pitched in. We studied his signature and sat backstage signing away with a Sharpie.

One time in 1989, he invited me to sit at his table at an event honoring Bette Davis at the Beverly Hilton Hotel. Julio, it seemed, knew everyone in Hollywood, and he introduced me around that night.

"Come on, you have to meet Roberto Mee-chim," he said in his thick, Spanish accent.

Roberto MEE-CHIM?

We approached the legendary Robert Mitchum at his table.

After we shook hands, Mitchum said, "Meet my wife . . . she hates everybody."

He was pointing to his wife Dorothy, and I thought it was strange, but I had no idea what he was talking about unless they were not getting along that night. I proceeded to tell him all about skipping high school several times as a junior to watch him film *Thunder Road* in Asheville. He loved that story and we talked a little about my hometown.

Then he invited Julio and me to sit down and join him, so we did.

We were having fun listening to him tell stories, when my date for the night who was one of our models, Cheryl Gentry, came running over to our table.

"Ron, I have been having a great time talking to Lucille Ball for the past half an hour," she told me. "Come on over with me and meet her and I want you to take a picture of us together."

I grabbed my camera and we walked over to Lucy's table. Cheryl introduced me and Lucy looked puzzled. She had no idea what Cheryl was doing. She acted as if she did not even remember her from the previous minutes she had spent at her table. And she was really rude and obnoxious about it, too.

Cheryl, whom everyone called "Ostrich" because she had such long, thin legs, was shocked.

"I was just with her!" she said. "How can she not remember me?"

Sadly, Lucille and Bette Davis both died soon after that night.

It was always fun being around Julio and he did teach me a little something that I continued for my entire life. We were sitting at Tom Selleck's restaurant, the Black Orchid, in Honolulu, drinking champagne one night.

A lot of champagne.

So much champagne that I feared the next sunrise.

"If you stir bubbles . . . no headache later," he instructed.

I had never heard that before, but I did it. He turned out to be right and I never had a champagne hangover once I started doing it.

In addition to the famous, we hosted those who would someday become *infamous*.

One frequent judge for us was none other than O.J. Simpson, the retired NFL star turned sportscaster-actor. I have to admit that I liked O.J. from the start. He had a great personality and he was easy-going around the girls, and as far as I knew, very respectful. We never had any problem with him.

When we met, he was dating a lot of girls at the time, as was his lifestyle and we quickly became good friends. He would bring his oldest son, Jason, and introduce him around to a bunch of the models and looking back, I am sure that may have been his motive sometimes. Jason was the same age then as most of our pageant girls and models.

One night after I started to date Darcy LaPier, whom I will get to later, we agreed to attend a Luther Vandross concert in Los Angeles with O.J., and he brought a new girlfriend.

Her name was Nicole Brown.

Nicole was very polite and shy when I first met her, but I could tell right away that O.J. was taken with her. I also could tell she scrutinized me and my motives since I always had a lot of pretty girls around me, and maybe she also was worried about O.J. hanging around me because of those girls.

But after that night, we double dated often when I was in Los Angeles.

On December 31, 1988, O.J., Nicole, Darcy and I attended film producer Peter Locke's New Year's Eve party together.

That party had been relaxing and I never noticed one cross word between O.J. and Nicole. There were no arguments and no fights that I witnessed. It was just a typical, fun New Year's Eve. Usually when we were with the both of them, O.J. did all the talking and Nicole never said too much.

When I read later that happened to be the night in which he had beaten her to the point that she had to call 911, after they had returned home, I was completely shocked.

Of course, everything that came out of the double murder the night of June 12, 1994, shocked me—and anyone else who knew O.J.

I happened to be in Hawaii at the time for a charity event near Fort DeRussy on Waikiki Beach. The media was in a frenzy over the murders and were covering the story around the clock. One of the national networks learned that I knew O.J. and had requested an interview. I really did not think it through or what I would possibly say beforehand, but I immediately agreed to it, so they hooked me up with a camera through a satellite feed.

I verbally shot from the hip, saying something like, "I never saw that in him. I couldn't believe he really would do something like that. I really don't believe it was him."

Well, most everybody who followed the case closely knew more than I did. They knew enough to believe he was guilty. The police obviously thought it, too, given the mountain of evidence that linked him to the crime, as I learned later. But in the immediate aftermath, I had no idea.

Understandably, the backlash from my comments on national TV was immediate.

My accountant called me from Florida the following night, asking, "Ron, what are you doing? People are calling here planning to boycott the product and put you out of business. You are going to cost us millions in sales!"

I just felt the same as many of O.J.'s friends during this time. I admired the guy and just never saw that side of him, but I never should have opened my mouth in the first place, not knowing the facts of the case.

Obviously, I knew that I had to do a second interview to try to fix things. The next day, I backtracked to the media and tried to wash my hands of the entire mess by saying something like I would not support O.J. during his trial.

Soon after the not guilty verdict more than a year later, I was in Snow Mass walking around an outdoor mall after a day of skiing, when I heard somebody yell my name.

"Ron! Hey Ron!"

I turned to see O.J. with a guy I did not recognize. He greeted me and we made some small talk but the trial or murder did not come up and I did not bring it up.

And that was the last time I ever saw him.

He never called me in those thirteen years after his acquittal to the time he was convicted of robbery in Las Vegas, so I doubt he would ever call me now that he is out of prison. (One of his trial lawyers, Robert Shapiro, would play a small role in my life in the years to come, which I will explain later).

Of all the A-listers I had met, one of the highlights was being seated at the same table as Jimmy Stewart at one event and we hit it off really well. By the end of the night, he tore off this huge piece of the paper table-covering and started to draw something with a black magic marker. When he finished, he signed the bottom of it and handed it to me.

It was a large drawing of Harvey the Rabbit.

Somebody took a picture that night of him handing it to me and I had the portrait framed and placed that small snapshot in the corner of the frame. It is on the wall in my upstairs hallway today.

Mickey Rooney also once did a painting and gave it to me, too.

And after our first meeting that night in Cannes, it seemed that I bumped into Michael Douglas a lot over the years. We were at a party together in Dallas before a Super Bowl once and he took me over to meet Harrison Ford.

Almost every celebrity, no matter how rich they were or how famous, outside of Frank Sinatra who acted like a jerk every time I was around him, were very nice people and great to me. I once attended a party at Bob Hope's Palm Springs house (that looked like a spaceship) and Sinatra and Gregory Peck were there. Everyone in the room was very welcoming and nice, but Sinatra was rude and demanding of anybody in his path.

And then there was the biggest jerk I ever met, or worked with for that matter, a curmudgeon by the name of Henry John Duetschendorf Junior.

You may know him by his stage name as a singer—John Denver.

Skiing always was a big part of my life and we soon sponsored celebrity-driven charity skiing events in Vail, Lake Tahoe and Aspen and even in places like Chateau Lake Louise in Alberta, Canada, and in Banff, Canada, almost every year. These events lasted three or four days and attracted many big-name celebrities.

Because of these various sponsorships, Hawaiian Tropic had to work with Denver for seven consecutive years on an annual TV special that aired before Christmas. We became the main sponsor of the show he hosted that was filmed in Aspen.

For the show, I would arrange to bring in some of the top skiers in the world, such as Andre Arnold, Franz Klammer, Franz Weber, Billy Kidd and Yvonne Blackburn while John brought in other mainstream celebrities.

But for some reason, he didn't like me from the start of our business relationship. I quickly realized he had a drinking problem and he acted as a total jerk to a lot of people, not just to me, and I didn't like him, either.

Over the years, I am sure that a lot of guys didn't like me, without knowing me, because they figured I was being intimate with our models and pageant contestants. That, of course, was total bullshit. But I did not owe any of them an explanation of how I treated the models and certainly didn't have to explain my personal life.

One night, I was sitting in a booth in a bar in Aspen, surrounded by six or seven of our girls. We were laughing and drinking and having a great time and I happened to look at the booth above us on the second floor. There was John, sitting by himself, just staring at me with an angry face. He looked absolutely miserable.

I chalked that up to simple math: I had six or seven girls with me and he had zero. That had to piss him off, I guess.

He became so hated around Aspen for the way he treated people that the locals started contributing to a fund to send John to the moon on the space shuttle. The common joke was, *"I will give to it, only if it's a one-way trip."*

He was not happy with life and he was not happy with himself and that became obvious to all of us who worked around him or knew him. During that time, I really believed his goal was to make everyone around him as miserable as possible.

One time, for some reason, he wanted me to fly with him as he piloted his experimental plane from Aspen somewhere for a promotion. I was scared to death and not liking to be around him anyway; I turned him down.

I finally pulled Hawaiian Tropic out of Denver's Aspen show, mainly because I just couldn't stand to be around the guy anymore. The organizers replaced us with English Leather as the main sponsor. In our final show together, John wanted to feature blind skiers. It wasn't long after that, in 1997, when he crashed his airplane in Monterey Bay and died.

I always wondered if he had killed himself on purpose because he was such an unhappy, tortured soul. As I look back on that now, I thank my lucky stars that I never agreed to fly with him, because I still wonder if he had an ulterior motive because he didn't like me either.

I was a decent skier in my day. Spending winter days on the slopes in Colorado or in Lake Tahoe became commonplace for me and several of my employees. We took ski company trips to Aspen as often as most other CEOs took golfing trips.

And on those slopes, I bumped into—sometimes literally—tons of celebrities.

One day, I went whizzing down a straight, smooth slope at Lake Tahoe and I must have hit seventy miles per hour. When I reached the bottom, a guy skied up to me and he did not mince words.

"You're crazy!" he said. "I couldn't believe how fast you were going."

It was Sonny Bono.

Sonny was right. If I had fallen on that particular slope at that speed, I probably would have had a broken leg or two.

Sonny was a great guy. When I first met him, he was with Cher at a charity event at Turnberry Isle in Miami. The event provided me with a nice big suite. Then after I checked in, the front desk called up to the room and said, "Sorry, Mister Rice, but we need your suite."

They took it away from me and gave it to Dinah Shore.

One night at dinner during the event, my head of marketing, Bill Darby, had gotten so drunk that he stumbled up to a table and put his face right down in a plate. It wasn't his seat to begin with and it just happened to be Sonny's seat. Somebody told me about it, so I sent somebody over to the table to pick Darby up and get him out of there. They had to get a new plate just so Sonny could sit down and eat.

As the years went by, I saw him often in Cannes, after he remarried and became a U.S. congressman. And later, he and his wife Mary invited me to their house in Palm Springs. He was a great guy with a great personality, and I liked him very much.

I was crushed when I heard the news in 1998 that he died after hitting a tree while skiing. It happened to be on the exact same slope in Lake Tahoe where he had called me crazy. I certainly hoped he was not trying to imitate what I had done years earlier.

But aside from Denver, I met so many nice people through those skiing events, such as Patty Hearst, Joey "Pants" Pantoliano and Cheech Marin of Cheech and Chong.

Patty became a good friend. She invited me and my daughter Sterling and our nanny to stay at the famous Hearst Castle near San Simeon for one weekend in the 1990s. It had been built by her grandfather William Randolph Hearst, the publishing billionaire, back in the 1920s and had hosted all of Hollywood's top actors as well as Charles Lindbergh and several presidents over the years. The way Patty explained it, each Hearst daughter got to use the castle for two weeks out of the year.

We stayed in one of the many guest houses down by the river and it was very lavish. Bernie Shaw, who had been her bodyguard and then married her, was always with her when we were there and they were very gracious hosts. We had a great time that week and I enjoyed being around them.

In the early 1990s, I was spending so much time in Los Angeles that I decided I was tired of staying in hotels when I had to be on the West Coast, so I bought a second house on a hill in Malibu for one million dollars which overlooked the Pacific. Ironically, a few years after Denver's fatal plane crash, there was a brief time in which I had put the house up for sale. One day, a real pretty girl happened to be walking her dog out front.

She stopped and asked me, "Is your house for sale?"

I gave her a brochure and told her a little bit about it. It turned out that she was John's ex-wife, Cassandra Delaney, who had divorced him the year before he crashed his plane.

Fortunately, I never sold that house, took it off the market and I still own it. One of my Malibu neighbors for years had been actor Gary Busey, who always told me he wanted to be a pageant judge. So finally, I bought two first-class tickets for him and his agent to come to Las Vegas for our national pageant one year.

But he never showed up.

A few months later, while he was getting his mail, he noticed me getting into my car in the driveway and he came running over carrying a package.

"Ron! Ron!" he screamed.

He was carrying a few packages.

"How you doing? These are tapes of movies I have to watch and then vote for the Academy Awards," he said.

"Open them up," I said. "Let's see what movies are up this year."

One of them was the movie *The Man Who Wasn't There*, which was nominated for best cinematography in 2002.

Obviously, I was still pissed off that he never showed up in Las Vegas after we had made the arrangements as he asked, so I blurted out, "Gary, that movie is about YOU!"

It took him a minute to get the joke, if he did get it at all, forgetting he had blown off the pageant without calling me. But that was typical Gary, often goofy and clueless.

When I was sponsoring stock car racing, one of the guys who I stuck up a friendship with was Hal Needham, who was a film director and stuntman. Hal loved NASCAR racing and he also was considered the top stuntman in Hollywood at one time and that is how he broke into the movie business. Then he partnered with Burt Reynolds to make several movies.

I was invited to the sets of all of those movies, starting with *Smokey and the Bandit*, which became a huge hit in 1977. I would bring models with me and Hal and Burt would try to use them in background scenes whenever they could.

Although he had never finished high school, Hal was very, very intelligent and knew what he was doing in the movie business. We had a lot of fun on his film sets—*Smokey and the Bandit, Smokey and the Bandit II, The Cannonball Run* and *Stroker Ace*, as well as being around the great Jackie Gleason who was Sheriff Buford T. Justice. Burt was always a class guy and we soon became good friends. He loved being around the girls.

During the filming of *The Cannonball Run*, which also starred Farrah Fawcett, in June 1980, a freak thing happened that began Hal's downfall in Hollywood.

An actress named Heidi von Beltz was the stunt double

for Farrah in the film. She was only twenty-four at the time and she was very nice, very tall and slender. I got to know her a little bit on the movie set and I learned she was a former championship skier, so we had our love of skiing to talk about in between takes when they needed her.

Hal was directing this scene in Las Vegas, which called for two speeding cars to have a near miss. He just could not get it quite the way he wanted it, so he put a new driver in one of the cars and they continued filming with another take. As they re-shot the scene, the Aston Martin in which Heidi was riding in the passenger seat collided head-on with a van. She was trapped inside, and emergency workers had to tear off the roof to get her out to rush her to the hospital in time to save her life. They saved her life, but she was paralyzed from the neck down.

It turned out there were no seat belts in the car, and it had other defects and she sued Hal and the other companies involved, winning almost seven million dollars. The crash and her severe injuries also led to several changes in safety requirements regarding movie stunts.

Heidi spent the rest of her life in a wheelchair before she died in 2015 at the age of fifty-nine.

I thought about her and that terrible crash often over the years.

The best was yet to come for us in the movie business.

At one party, I had met a Hollywood producer by the name of Brad Krevoy and we had hit it off, becoming good friends.

Brad started working on a movie about two dimwitted characters and we began talking seriously about somehow getting the Hawaiian Tropic models involved in the script. He and the lead actor, Jim Carrey, loved the idea, so they just had to figure a way to write them into the script. They worked and worked on the idea and finally one night in a three-way telephone call, we hashed it out and agreed to all the details.

I had no idea what a sensation it would become, but if you watch the final scene of *Dumb and Dumber*, you will understand what I am talking about.

Near the end of the movie, Carrey's and Jeff Daniels' characters were walking along a highway after their car had broken down, when a bus full of Hawaiian Tropic girls pulled up and stopped. Our name and logo were displayed in huge letters on the side of the bus. One of our models, Samantha Carpel, opened the bus door and told Carrey's and Daniels' characters, "Hi guys. We are going on a national bikini tour and we are looking for two oil boys who can grease us up before each competition . . ."

"You are in luck!" Daniels' character says, "There is a town about three miles that way. I am sure you will find a couple of guys there."

The bus door closed, and it pulled off, as Carrey then grabbed Daniels by the face and screamed, "Do you realize what you have done?"

They started running after the bus. It stopped again, the door opened, and Carrey said, "You have to forgive my friend. He is a little slow. The town is back *that way!*"

I thought the ending was perfect and it was pure magic for us once again. Originally, we thought it would be a funny little movie, but we had no idea it would become a box-office hit, and with every viewing, I think our sales increased.

Several of our girls also appeared in a movie in 2002 called

Boat Trip, with Cuba Gooding and Roger Moore. After I met Roger, I could say that I met every James Bond but Daniel Craig. In fact, Pierce Brosnan became a good friend and I just saw him recently as I write this.

The product placement thing was so big that we continued to field frequent calls from Hollywood, wanting us to pay a fee to place our product in movies.

When we had sponsored that comedy showcase in Daytona in 1984, I had thrown a party at my house. A little-known comedian was performing in it, so he came to the party. That night, he walked up to me, stuck his hand out and said, "Hi, I am Jerry Seinfeld."

"I know who you are," I said.

I had seen him perform and liked his act, and this was way before he made TV history with *Seinfeld.*

"I love your comedy," I told him.

Fast forward to 1998 and Jerry allowed me to be an extra in one of the final episodes of the final season of the show, titled "The Puerto Rican Day." I knew it would be huge if I could somehow get our logo or our name shown on the episode, but I also knew his producing partner Larry David, who was such a jerk and had turned me down on that promotional calendar, would not allow me to wear anything with the company logo.

Before filming began, one of my rich friends heard me talking about what I was scheming to do and he said, "There is no way they will let you wear a Hawaiian Tropic shirt or get that logo on the show."

I was so confident that I could do that, I bet him $10,000.

I had a black coat that had a small Hawaiian Tropic logo on the left side near the zipper and I was scheduled to appear in a scene in which George Costanza is watching a movie in a theater as someone shoots a red laser pointer in his face. I was sitting about two seats on the other side of George, and in between takes, I made sure that my coat was opened enough so that the logo was covered up and nobody could see it.

Then when filming began, I just pulled the front of my coat back enough so it could be seen. And sure enough, it was visible when the show was broadcast, but neither David nor Jerry ever said a word to me, if they even noticed.

And I collected my $10,000 bet.

That would have qualified for "product placement," as they call it in Hollywood.

Product placement has been a big part of the film and TV industry for more than fifty years. While viewing a show or movie, you may never realize that a company, such as PepsiCo for example, has paid big bucks to have that Pepsi can sitting on the counter in the background as two characters talk in the foreground.

Once I learned about how it worked, I decided to start my own product placement company.

I hired two girls from another similar company and opened the business in Los Angeles, and within a short period of time, we had forty employees and two big warehouses full of products. I learned that the key was to develop relationships with prop masters on all the movie sets around Hollywood. Companies paid us anywhere from $20,000 to $100,000 each to get their products placed in films and TV shows.

We also had people reading scripts to learn location shoots and they would add something like, "Okay, put a box of Keebler Cookies over there, or a Nissan car in the background over here and a typewriter right there."

Then we made overtures to the all the prop managers in Hollywood and arranged for them to receive free goods to place the products of the companies that paid us around the set. It really was a very small price to pay for companies who wanted their products seen by millions of movie-watchers around the world.

At one point we figured a Hawaiian Tropic product was in a movie or TV show once every three days, or in more than 120 movies or separate TV episodes in each calendar year.

After a few years, the two girls running my company could not get along, so I flew to Los Angeles to mediate. I had already given each of them a one-third stake in the company.

"Now listen, I don't have the time to run this company in addition to running Hawaiian Tropic," I told them. "So, work it out."

They could not agree and rather than buy them out, I just sold the company to a guy named Norm Marshall for one million dollars.

Some of my celebrity interactions happened totally by accident. One year I was with several of the models at the National Association of Chain Drug Stores trade show in Hawaii, wandering around when we walked into this small building, following the noises of what was an obvious party in full throttle.

It was a party that we hadn't been invited to.

I noticed dozens of Revlon gift bags sitting on a table.

Then my models noticed Cindy Crawford and Claudia Schiffer and wanted their pictures taken with them. Fortunately, Ron Pearlman, the CEO of Revlon, just happened to be a friend of mine. He saw us and invited me to the party after dinner—Kenny Loggins was performing that night. Ron then told all my girls to go grab a Revlon gift bag on their way out.

I took a couple of our girls to the dance floor and was trying to arrange a picture with Kenny Loggins in the background. All these people were dancing around us, and all of a sudden, I took either a knee or sharp elbow to the ribs. I slumped to the dance floor and my face fell directly into Claudia Schiffer's crotch.

As I was on my knees, Cindy Crawford stood there screaming, "You are not part of Revlon! You are not part of Revlon!"

I immediately knew who hit me in the ribs. I regained my balance to finish taking the picture, and then—she did it again. If she had been a man, I swear I would have knocked her out with a right cross. I just sneered at her but did not say much. On the other hand, Claudia was as nice as could be and she later became a judge in our pageants from that first dance floor meeting. As far as Cindy, I think she hates me to this day.

And to be honest, I am not too fond of her, either.

Whenever my ribs ache a bit, I still think of Cindy.

I could relate to other CEOs and bosses like Ron Pearlman and how he ran a big business, but the one man on earth who possibly could understand my life at this point, running a successful business while surrounded by dozens of the most beautiful women in the world—and often dating some—was Hugh Hefner.

Hef invited us often to visit the Playboy Mansion often and he never seemed even a tad competitive as far as our girls and his girls. Or him and me. In fact, he was always the perfect host and gentleman and we soon became good friends. When we visited the mansion, I would bring several of our models and you never would imagine so many of the prettiest girls in the world in one house at one time.

Over time, media people would ask me about Hef or compare me to him and I never liked it much, but not because it wasn't flattering. I just think his life and work stood on its own and I did not want to take away from that in any way.

One day in the 1990s, a guy who had a television variety show called *Having a Beer with Mike*, came to my house to film me in a feature in his one-hour show.

One problem: He forgot to bring any beer.

I had one of the girls grab us a few bottles from the bar and as I sipped my beer as a prop, he looked around my house like a hungry dog eyeing a pork chop. Four or five of the models were bouncing around on trampolines laughing at the time. That was their way to stay in shape. They were wearing virtually nothing at the time and when the show appeared, the producers had to blur the shot just below their waists.

"You know, you are just like the Hugh Hefner of the East Coast—and this is the Playboy Mansion of the East," Mike said.

I smiled but inside I cringed. I knew I had to play down that comparison, because I never wanted to slight Hugh Hefner.

"No, no, I don't think so," I said. "Hugh is a really good friend of mine. He's a great guy and I have no desire to steal any of his thunder. What we have in common to a point is that we are surrounded by beautiful girls."

After the guy left, I started thinking about Hugh. He really changed the way America thought and the way we live. I really still do not think he received enough credit for opening up peoples' minds.

I think Hefner did more to change our way of living than anybody in the last one-hundred years, and that includes Thomas Edison, Alexander Graham Bell and any president I can think of. Who had a bigger impact on our country and the way we live?

Of course, I am not thinking of any invention that makes life easier when I say this, I am talking about the morals and the level of acceptable decency of how we live and how we think.

One time I was at the Staples Center in Los Angeles to watch a Lakers game with several of our models when Hef walked in. He had a photographer following him for a feature. By the end of the night, that photographer had spent all of his time getting the addresses and phone numbers of all of our girls.

I thought it made perfect sense to cross-promote, and *Playboy* and Hawaiian Tropic developed a great relationship. The magazine featured the "Girls of Hawaiian Tropic" three times over the years.

We were together a lot over the years, but Hef and I never had any conversations about our lifestyles or if we were indeed similar. He was very private in that way and never revealed much, at least not to me, and I purposely did not ask him much. But he always was very inviting and gracious. He was comfortable in his own skin and I was always very careful not to step on his toes when I took girls to the Playboy Mansion.

I never created a magazine that changed the masses' outlook or entertained millions, but as I look back on our lives, we did have a lot in common. I did know what it was like to live Hef's lifestyle.

Guys like Hef and Ted Turner seemed to have respect for me, whether it was the fact we all loved surrounding ourselves with pretty girls, or the fact we all started companies from scratch and they ultimately became successful, I don't know which.

But I liked them both.

When I was judging the Miss Georgia pageant once, talking to a judge who happened to be a former Miss Georgia, who happened to be dating Ted at the time, he walked over.

"I am really impressed with what you have done," he told me.

He invited me to appear on one of his business shows on WTBS or TNT, which was hosted by the former Miss America Debbie Shook, and a few years later I was at a party at the Georgia governor's mansion, before the 1993 Super Bowl. I had several of our models with me that night, such as Linda Mitchell with whom I am still very close, and by then he had married Jane Fonda.

And that night while watching Jane, I knew she was comfortable in her own skin. She walked into the place late and made a beeline straight for the models, Linda Mitchell and Suzanne Stokes, and started talking to them. I had never noticed any other pretty women who did that over the years. Most of them always felt threatened by someone else's beauty.

Besides Cannes, and because of our involvement with movies and the product-placement company, we often received invitations to movie premieres and awards shows such as the Grammys.

One time, I attended the Grammys with four of our girls, but I had only four tickets. Five of us. Four tickets. You do the math.

La Gena Lookabill, one of our very first models and pageant

winners who would turn out to be one of my all-time favorite people in the world, was with us. La Gena was a petite blonde, no taller than five-foot-two, and very pretty. She also was one of the most intelligent people I ever knew. She concocted a scheme where I would hold up the four tickets as we entered and she would scoot through the entry point just as I distracted the security people by waving around the tickets and asking them a few questions.

After we all got in, I must have been feeling my oats because I went back stage, grabbed a pink sheet of paper out of a trash can and pulled out a pencil, standing next to the stage entrance as if I were checking people off on a script.

Some of the performers or presenters that night approached me and asked, "Is it time for me to go on yet?"

"Not quite," I would answer.

A few of the Beach Boys noticed what I was doing. They knew my personality and sense of humor and just stood there laughing, as I checked people off of my fake list and told them it was not their time to go on stage.

"Ron, when you are done with your duties for the night, we are hosting a party," one of them said.

"We'll be there!" I answered.

Anyway, I always feel great remorse when I think of La Gena, because I was the one who introduced her to the auto racer Tim Richmond. We had sponsored Tim's car in the 1980 Indianapolis 500, and I initially liked him. He was a good-looking guy and had a great personality but fame soon went to his head.

But unknown to anyone, he had contracted AIDS.

Of course, he never told anyone and continued doing what

he was doing, and he gave it to several women through the years. And one of them was La Gena. He infected her on the night he proposed to her in 1986 and then she never heard from him again.

I will always regret the day I introduced them because she was one of the finest people I ever met.

The great thing about this story is that La Gena, who married actor Danny Greene in 1990 and became a successful actress herself, is still living today thanks to the advanced HIV-fighting medicines that were developed, much similar to Magic Johnson's survival after being diagnosed at about the same time. She carries it to this day, still alive thanks to modern medicine. But her life living with the disease has been tough and trying.

We often had La Gena talk to our models and pageant participants over the years. She would tell them her sad story and warn them about the danger of contracting AIDS and the perils of falling for the wrong men.

Her talks obviously worked, because I had several guys—mostly the "hangers-on"—say something to me like, "Can you stop having her come to talk to these girls about this . . ."

Today, she lives in Charlotte and devotes herself to AIDS Awareness speeches and education.

And Richmond?

He died of the disease in 1989 and several of the women he had sex with soon followed him to a grave and I have nothing much good to say about him.

Another thing I learned is that once you have money, athletes like Billie Jean King and NASCAR teams may have needed sponsorships to compete, but so did politicians, who wanted donations.

I was never very political when running the company, but I did meet several politicians and tried to help the ones I liked or believed in.

I was friends with a local lawyer by the name of Bill Crotty, a democrat who was very involved in politics. He asked me if I would host a fundraiser for an up-and-coming then thirty-nine-year-old senator from Tennessee and I gladly said I would.

And that is how I met Al Gore in 1987.

I hosted a big fundraiser at my house and Bill arranged most of it, including the guest list and donors, etc., and Al and I bonded from the time we met. It was a big success and we raised a lot of money for him. He asked for my phone number—and within a few minutes of leaving, he called from the phone in his limo.

"Ron . . . ah . . . I think we are lost!" he said. "How do I find Bill Crotty's office?"

The following day, Al announced he was running in the presidential primary.

Of course, it did not work out for him, but we stayed in touch even when he became part of the ticket with Bill Clinton a few years later, defeating incumbent President George H.W. Bush. Before he became vice-president, Al once invited me to a party at his house in Georgetown. I got out of the car that night and his little ten-year-old daughter Sarah was greeting all the guests.

"Hello Mister Rice!" she said. "Happy you could come!"

I stood there with my mouth open, completely taken aback that she knew my name and was so mature for a little girl.

I must have lingered and appeared clueless of what do next,

because she promptly demanded, "Excuse me, Mister Rice, you must proceed inside because we have many more guests to greet here."

I walked inside dumbfounded with my mouth still open. I wondered, *Is that girl really ten, or an ambassador in a child's body?*

In the middle of the party, Al whispered to me, "Come up to my bedroom, I have something to show you!"

So, I followed him upstairs.

"Okay," he said. "Sit down on the edge of the bed there."

I did, not having a clue of what he was getting to or what he wanted to talk about.

All of a sudden, he walked behind a curtain and then wheeled out a stand holding a nineteen-inch TV.

"I wanted you to see my one and only TV!" he said.

He was joking, contrasting his bedroom to mine.

I always arranged a bank of TVs in one place at my house to form one large media center. I usually had nine nine-inch TVs and one big screen TV. This may sound somewhat strange, but I actually hired a girl in the early 1980s to do nothing but sit around and tape news shows or business shows for me on my two VCRs. She also was supposed to read various magazines and newspapers and cut out business stories, anything that may be of interest to me or may help me running the business. I do not remember exactly what I paid her, but I know I paid her well. Then when I came home that night, she had a list ready for me of what to watch and what to read.

One day she told me, "Ron, we need to order more Kahlua for the bar." I wondered what the heck she was talking about since I did not drink it, but I learned that she was turning into an alcoholic sitting around at my house all day, so I had to let her go.

Anyway, my self-made media centers often grabbed people's curiosity. I can explain it simply by saying I wanted to be in touch with the outside world (I still have this arrangement to this day—with ten TVs—and the TVs are always on). But I never ever watched sitcoms or soap operas or mindless stuff.

Anyway, Al had noticed it that night at my house during the fund-raiser, but never mentioned it.

When Clinton and Al were being inaugurated in January of 1993, he invited me to attend. I had been in Hawaii and I was dating Heather Hays, who was the reigning Miss Hawaii at the time (she now is a news broadcaster for the Fox affiliate in Dallas), so I brought her with me.

We had passes for three parties in successive days. I brought one suitcase that was nothing but dirty clothes from Hawaii and I happened to leave it in one of the limos that first night. It was the same limo and driver who was supposed to pick us up at the hotel and take us to the D.C. airport following the inauguration.

But he didn't show up that morning and finally, we had no choice but to hop into a cab to make our flight.

I called the limo company when we got back to Florida and was told, "The driver stole the limo and drove it to California. We are trying to track him down now."

They eventually found him because they shipped my suitcase full of dirty laundry to me a few weeks later.

And to balance the political scale, one of the highlights of my life was sitting and talking to Ronald Reagan one day after he left office.

One time in Los Angeles, we had sons of two legends—Kyle Eastwood and Chad McQueen—as judges for a pageant. I got along great with those two and they called me before the pageant and invited me to go meet Reagan with them.

We walked into his office on the top floor of the U.S. Secret Service offices in Century City and they led us into his empty conference room. There were no seats or chairs but there were plenty of pictures of his life scattered on a few tables. Kyle, Chad and I walked around the room for a while looking at those pictures before he walked in.

Immediately, he had asked me what I did when I was younger and I told him I was a lifeguard. From that moment, we really hit it off.

He took me over to a picture of a river in Illinois.

"I was a lifeguard right there on that river," he told me. "In fact, I still hold the record for the fastest lap across that river."

I must have stood there talking to him for at least an hour, and he was one of the nicest guys I had ever met. When I walked out of that room, I thought, "That is the most secure person I have ever met."

Another time, just by happenstance, I met another president.

I was sitting with my daughter Sterling in first-class helping her with her homework on a flight from Los Angeles to Atlanta when she was about six years old when somebody tapped me on the shoulder. I turned to see former President Jimmy Carter.

"I just wanted to introduce myself," he said.

It was not because he knew my name or anything like that—he had taken the time to walk down the aisle of the airplane, meeting and greeting every passenger. When he finally sat down, he was directly across the aisle from us, sitting next to Rosalyn. Sterling went over to see him and we got a nice picture of her sitting on his lap.

Meeting presidents and getting to know movie stars provided a lot of great times and memories, but I always said over the years that I gravitated more to comedians and musicians. I guess I could relate to them more.

Anyway, it all was special for a kid from the mountains of Asheville.

Chapter Eleven

HAVING FUN WHILE FIGHTING OFF THE VULTURES

Once Hawaiian Tropic's name became a commercial success, generating millions from sales annually from all the products we manufactured, a bunch of large corporations started contacting us, as early as the late 1970s.

And that continued for the next thirty years or so.

I counted once and there had been over twenty attempts by some company or corporation to buy it from my company, Tanning Research Laboratories Inc., which owned the brand Hawaiian Tropic.

Rather than shoot them all down initially, I always took advantage of these overtures as a way to learn something by either touring their own factories to see what I could learn from to them to use for our company, even if I had no intent to sell.

They just did not know it.

Throughout the 1970s and '80s, our sales were going crazy and we were growing like crazy. We were expanding almost everywhere and I soon had thirteen factories around the world. So, I knew it was very premature to pull the trigger on selling it.

However, I still went through the listening process a few times.

The one thing I learned early on in business is that by playing up the poor, ol' country boy routine, I could use it to my advantage. Other people in business, either competitors or those I negotiated with, or even those trying to buy my company, probably thought I was some dumb hick from the backroads of North Carolina.

In other words, they thought I was someone that they could take advantage of.

In reality, I thought I was smart like a fox.

One of the first overtures was from Alberto-Culver which owned VO5 products. The company's owner, Leonard Lavin, invited me to fly to Chicago to discuss it. I stayed at his house and then toured their factory with him. They produced almost everything but sun-care products, so it was natural that they wanted their own line.

Then Lavin made the offer: Twenty million dollars. It was a ridiculously low offer and I never would consider it, so I thanked him for his interest and caught the next flight back to Florida.

Another was from Revlon.

A guy by the name of Marty Fox was Revlon's CEO.

I gathered my main group of key people—about eight at that time—and we flew to New York to meet with Marty.

I included them in this process to let them know I would never do anything behind their backs. I wanted to gain loyalty from them, too. It was the honest thing to do and I wanted them involved in the process and I wanted them to know that I would take care of them financially if I ever did sell.

We stayed at a downtown Holiday Inn, the cheapest place we could find. Within a few hours, it was as if I was hosting a frat party.

We all had connecting rooms on the fourteenth floor and we got pretty drunk that first night. That is when someone started a water fight, which turned into a giant water fight. Bill Darby carried around this large bucket of water, looking to get somebody. That is when Don Faughn, our most prominent sales rep, who had started our operation in Murray, Kentucky, climbed out on the ledge to get away from him—fourteen floors above certain death.

Darby did not care: He reached out the window with that bucket and doused him. Don carefully crawled back in the window, covered in water and pigeon shit. I remember one of our reps, Gene Perkins, got locked outside of my room in his underwear and was trying to hide behind the soda machine in the hallway when some lady walked by with her two little girls. The moment she spotted him she started screaming, thinking there was a rapist loose in the hotel.

We all survived the night and made it to Revlon's building the next morning, somewhat hungover. We did not check our baggage with the bellman at our hotel and chose to lug it up to Revlon's offices on the fiftieth floor, since we had flights scheduled in the afternoon.

After we got off the elevator, all of us carrying our

luggage, we instantly noticed the long red carpet, gold-framed paintings, and the opulence of their offices. We approached the receptionist, who was situated about thirty yards down the red carpet from the entrance, I asked, "Is this the Revlon Hotel?"

As the guys behind me started cracking up, some of them still half-drunk, I am sure, she said, "No, no . . . you have to go back downstairs. . . ."

As she started explaining where to find the hotel, the guys started piling all of their luggage around her desk. Within a minute, I could barely see the top of her head because of our luggage stacked around her desk.

She had no idea what we were doing, but finally I leveled with her and she directed us to Marty's office.

The first thing I noticed was Marty was a little guy and he liked to wheel around his office on a secretary's chair, rather than a big firm reclining office chair you normally see CEOs or presidents use. After we made some small talk, he got up and walked to the window and just started laughing.

"What's so funny Marty?" I asked him.

"Well, every day I walk over here and look down at Avon's offices. They are two floors below us!" he said.

I could tell the guy was a nut. He actually thought his company was better than a competitor because it was located higher than Avon's offices in the building next door. I learned later that Revlon rented the fiftieth floor of the office building we were in at the time, which was actually *owned* by Avon.

Subsequently, Revlon's offer was better than Alberto-Culver's, but it was not near enough, either, so I passed on it, too, and that trip was nothing more than a fun road trip for me and my guys.

I always thought of Hawaiian Tropic as a family company and I worked hard to develop that atmosphere.

Or you can also say I played hard to develop that atmosphere.

I regarded all of our employees as one large family and I created a fun-loving atmosphere where there was not the usual high pressure on everyone to perform to the point that they were miserable.

That is why about every three months we held games and outings where we competed against each other and blew off steam. We played tennis, racquetball, and golf together. We had our own softball team. Heck, there was even a pinball machine, ping-pong table and pool table in a game room outside my office.

What other CEO or president or company would have that?

My team of executives that I relied so much on and grew to think of as family included: Bill Darby, director of marketing; Larry Adams, my main attorney; Bill Jennings, my accountant; Jeff Lalanne, head of advertising; Corky Surrette, who later became my director of marketing after Darby left the company; Dan Foster, assistant director of marketing; and Dan Daugherty, who also was in marketing.

Some of those guys may have thought that I had the perfect "I don't give a shit" attitude to deal with the so-called vultures, or rude people, or so-called jackasses we dealt with throughout the years.

I was never politically correct to begin with and I loved nothing better than to play practical jokes on those I was close with—and even those I did not know at all.

One time we were in Hawaii on a photo shoot and we had brought along Johnny Johnson, one of our top photographers.

Johnny was an older guy who loved to call the shots and be in charge, right down to what restaurant in which we ate every night.

We were at a nice resort on Kauai not too far from the airport. On our last night, I called what I thought was his room to say goodbye and chat a little.

"FUCK OFF!" the man who answered the phone told me.

Then one of our models told me that Johnny had been forced to change rooms because some spoiled jerk who checked in would not stay there unless he had that certain room. It had been eating at me all night. First, he had kicked Johnny out of his room and then he insulted me.

And for some reason, I kept thinking about this guy and his rudeness.

So, as soon as we reached the lobby early that next morning, it was no later than about six a.m. I noticed a house phone and I could not resist.

I called his room.

"WHAT?" the guy answered.

"This is your 'Good morning fuck off' call!" I said.

I held the receiver about a foot from my ear and I could hear him screaming, "WHO IS THIS? WHO IS THIS?"

As we headed to the airport laughing about it, Darby suggested, "Let's get his name and address from the hotel and track down his home number and call him every year on this date and scream, "THIS IS YOUR MORNING 'FUCK OFF' CALL!"

I thought it was a great idea, my kind of idea, but I do not remember any of us following up on it.

Darby always had that mischievous side and maybe that is why I liked him so much. Plus, he was a darned good and loyal employee.

It is true that as we grew, Hawaiian Tropic became like a family to me, because of my employees, how well we got along, and especially because of how much fun we had, either at home, at the pageants or on the road for business.

It was never drudgery or boring or tedious, at least not to me, and I am fairly sure they all would agree. They were all having a blast in the enjoyable work atmosphere I created, making a ton of money, as was I, so why should I break up a good thing by selling it?

We were just having too much fun.

Like I said, I was not looking to sell the company anyway, but I thought it was foolish not to listen—and not to learn from it. And what if somebody offered one hundred million dollars? That is why I figured I had to go through the song and dance of visiting their respective offices and listening to what they had to say.

And there was not one time I did not pick up something that helped us going forward.

A representative from the 3M Company in Minnesota called me one day in 1980, also wanting to buy Hawaiian Tropic.

"No, I don't think so," I told the guy.

"Listen, if you don't sell to us, we are going to create our own sun-care product and put you out of business!" he then told me.

"Go right ahead and try," I said. "I am just not interested in selling to you. Good luck!"

I laughed at him, which I am sure did not go over well. I knew he was probably a junior executive in his big leather chair who was being told what to do and what to say by some vice-president in a bigger office.

I hung up the telephone, imagining their executives sitting in their office thinking, "Okay, how do we develop a sunscreen? What goes in it? And what are we going to name it?"

The 3M Company developed one alright, spending fifteen million dollars and they named it, "Mmm!—What a Tan!"

It was a miserable failure and with a name like that, how could it not be?

But as the years wore on, and sales continued to increase through the 1990s, there was just no reason to sell. I was still relatively young and enjoyed running the beauty pageants and traveling with the models all over the world every year.

No matter what offer would make me happy enough to accept it, if I sold Hawaiian Tropic, I really had no idea how I would spend my time.

Chapter Twelve

BACHELOR LIFE

Since I focused mostly on marketing the Hawaiian Tropic brand, overseeing the pageants, promotions and models, while I allowed my vice-presidents to run the day-to-day operation of the company, I still found time to date.

I traveled with our models on promotional trips throughout the world each year, including annual trips to Cannes, Le Mans, Aspen, Hawaii, Los Angeles, Indianapolis and many other places.

That meant I was almost constantly surrounded by some of the most-beautiful girls in the world, and it was no secret that I dated some of them, but I always respected the fact that I still was the boss and never took advantage of that position.

And no matter what my image or reputation was around the Daytona area, I know I did not sleep with as many girls as Hugh Hefner did or Wilt Chamberlain claimed.

I have a good story about Wilt, by the way. It was the only time I ever met or talked to him.

As background, the University of North Carolina Tar Heels have always been my team and Dean Smith was always my coach. Before the 1957 season, they had played a scrimmage in my high school gymnasium, at good ol' Lee Edwards High in Asheville. And then they won thirty-two games in a row and beat Kansas and "Wilt the Stilt" in the national championship game. The star of that team was named Lennie Rosenbluth, who also was named the College Player of the Year over Chamberlain.

Anyway, Wilt happened to be staying at the Daytona Hilton during the week of one of our pageants one year. I happened to be sitting on a couch in the lobby, waiting on one of the girls. My good friend, John Havlicek, whose Celtics won many NBA titles over Chamberlain's Lakers, had just spent the previous night at my house. As I waited, Wilt and one of his buddies sat down nearby and started talking really loudly.

For some reason, he turned and gave me a dirty look and I guess he must have thought I was eavesdropping because he then made some snide comment to me.

I ignored it and told him that Havlicek was in town, too.

He stood up and said, "Well, I don't keep up with John Havlicek!" and he stormed off.

But before he got out of range, I asked, "Well, do you keep up with Lennie Rosenbluth?"

He turned his head slightly, and I know he heard me, but he continued on walking.

And that was my brush with the guy who claimed to have slept with 20,000 women. I did the math—it was impossible.

Anyway, I was always asked why I did not settle down and get married.

I usually answered, "I don't have the time for that. I am too busy being married to Hawaiian Tropic."

And it is true that the ones I wanted didn't want me—and I didn't want the ones who wanted me. I have used that line for decades.

Over the years, I would be asked, "Do you prefer blondes, brunettes or redheads?"

I would always answer, "All of the above!"

I loved attractive girls, intelligent girls, and girls with great personalities who weren't full of themselves (And when I say "girls," of course I mean women of age).

I loved the girls who took care of themselves and never used drugs. I was never a drug-user and didn't stand for it with any girls in the pageant or in my company, although most of us consumed a decent amount of alcohol over the years.

I hated smokers, too. I tried a cigarette when I was ten years old, took a few puffs, and about choked to death. I swore, never again. I didn't even like to be around people who smoked. I ran from them, even if it happened to a beautiful girl. If she had a cigarette hanging off her lips, she wasn't for me. And I didn't like it if we had a model who smoked around the other girls, and the others usually didn't like it, either.

I would never get into all the details of what my sex life was like back then, but let's just say that there were nights when I was glad that I was alive.

Even nights when I did silly things like injure myself.

One night in the 1980s, seven of the models were staying at my house and we had been invited a to a party a local nightclub called Finky's Country Showplace. The Chippendales performed that night and the girls got all riled up and we all ended up having a lot to drink. When we went to leave the club, there was a line of guys trying to get into that van as all the girls climbed in somewhat inebriated.

Not one of the guys made it in.

Once we were back at the house, one of the girls just blurted out, "Let's watch porn!"

I was never into porn, and said, "I don't have any."

Then I realized I had once brought an old Beta porn tape back from Japan, but never had watched it. I dug up this old Beta tape player and headed toward an outlet in the floor. As soon as I inserted the plug, flames shot out of it and my hand was on fire.

I stood there screaming in pain, trying to figure out what to do next. I ran into the kitchen and found a giant oven mitt and a knife and then ran outside and cut an aloe plant with my other hand. I took a section of the plant and poured the oozing aloe into the mitt and then stuck my hand inside of it. Then I took some duct tape and wrapped it around the top of the mitt, so the Aloe wouldn't seep out.

Somehow that did not damper the girls' mood at all, probably because we all were very drunk, so I eventually got the machine working on another outlet.

I stuck that tape in there and all the girls gathered around to watch it.

It wasn't too long until I was in the center of my bed, surrounded by every one of those girls. I had one hand to work with as I held the other, covered in a giant oven mitt, above my head. And I wasn't feeling much pain at all despite what was a severe burn.

It was a crazy night, but that is just the way it was back in the day.

I really was lucky that I didn't electrocute myself that night. The next morning, I woke up—surrounded by seven or eight of the most beautiful girls in the world—got out of bed and called an electrician.

And there were plenty of girls whom I dated who became very special to me over the years, some I met through Hawaiian Tropic and some by pure happenstance.

I dated my first assistant when I created Tropic Tan, Karen Streichert, the one who purposely closed the garage door on the county code inspectors at the Round House; and the first model for our magazine ads, Patsy Burgess, who was from the backside of Oahu. They were special girls to me, and they both marked the early days of the product line.

Patsy had a look to her that was unbelievable. When she pulled her hair back, she looked like a cobra and I loved it. They were the first of all the girls who would come and go throughout my life with first Tropic Tan and then Hawaiian Tropic . . .

Rick Webb had been a basketball coach at New Smyrna Beach High when I taught and coached football and we became very close and remain so to this day. We partied together and were pretty much best friends. He looked a lot like Burt Reynolds, especially when he wore a cowboy hat like Burt did during his *Smokey and the Bandit* days.

My long-time maid was an African American lady by the name of Virginia Smith. Over the years, Virginia became like a member of my family. All my friends loved her like I did and she would come and go from the house every day. And she got somewhat used to all the traffic and goings-on at my home.

Anyway, one night Rick and I had brought a few girls back to the house and the next morning they happened to be lying in bed naked, the doors open, as Virginia walked by the bedrooms to get to the room she had designated as her "ironing room."

She immediately noticed he girls and suddenly announced loudly in her Southern twang, "There sure is a lot of foolishness going on around here today!"

That soon became one of our catchphrases.

It was a fact: *We always had a lot of foolishness going on around here.*

Virginia had a habit of taking off her diamond ring before she began to work and then she would hide it somewhere in the house. At the end of the day, she would go retrieve it and then head outside to catch her ride home. I guess she just didn't want to wear it as she worked. She never drove, but somebody would drop her off and pick her up each day.

Problem was, she constantly forgot where she hid that ring. And it became a normal routine for her to get home and then call me.

"Misser Rice . . . can you go find my ring?" she would ask.

She would have me search the entire house day after day. I must have looked for that little diamond ring a thousand times over the years. Anyway, she was very special to me. When she died, Rick and I with some others attended her funeral and there must have been a thousand mourners there. That symbolized a life well-lived.

When Rick left coaching, he worked for me for several years, including some time in our marketing department and in Mexico as our sales rep there.

One time in the early 1980s I think it was, I was driving down the beach when I saw a powder blue car, and a real pretty blonde getting out of it. I pulled over (remember you can drive cars on the beaches here) and within minutes I had a date that night. Apparently, when she left the beach she had headed straight to the mall.

I got a call from Rick later and I told him, "I met a great girl on beach today," and I started to describe her.

He said, "Wow. You won't believe it. I met a great girl at the mall today."

It turned out to be Janette Vostrejs, the same girl.

He didn't get a date with her, but I dated her for a few years and she even worked some as one of our models, and during this time, I figured Rick probably still liked her from that first meeting and from being around her so much while she dated me.

One time while he was working for us in Mexico, I had to fly to Spain on business for at least two weeks. He then flew back to Daytona and stole her away from me. But I admit that it really was the best thing that ever happened, especially for her, because I was not ready to get married and she probably knew that.

And Rick is a great guy.

It is ironic because I knew both Lee Majors and Farrah Fawcett and their story of how Lee's buddy Ryan O'Neal fell for her is so similar.

Today, Rick and Janette Webb are still happily married with two grown kids and I am still close with them.

I admit I fell for a beautiful Hawaiian girl named Monica

Soares, a petite brunette, whom I had taken to Russia on that trip to try to get the product there. She was from a middle-class family on the Big Island and we dated and traveled together for years, but she ultimately married that Rodgers guy who had been chasing her the time we had gone to Russia and then later divorced him.

Monica always wore a collection of gold bracelets and you could hear her coming because she jingled.

I remember one year when we were all in a van driving in the country somewhere outside of Le Mans, France, either before or after the 24-hour race. One of my top employees, Jeff Lalanne, whom we all called "Abdul," noticed some cows roaming in a field by the road.

"Okay girls, whoever can get out and touch a cow first gets this one-hundred-dollar bill," Abdul said, holding up the cash.

I pulled over, stopped the van, as several girls rushed out and took off running down this hill toward the cows.

Monica got out of the van last basically just to stretch her legs, because she apparently didn't hear Abdul's offer.

"What are they doing?" she asked me.

I said, "They are trying to be the first girl to touch a cow to win a hundred dollars."

She looked to the left and took off running down the road, cut over to the fence and arrived at the same time as the other girls. She then stuck her arm through the fence and shook her wrist, jingling all of her bracelets. Those cows walked right up to her, she patted one on the nose and turned around and asked, "Okay, where's my hundred dollars?"

Today, she lives in Hawaii and is married to the national radio host, George Noory, who works out of Los Angeles. Monica continued working for us as one of our top models and she and George remain close to me. . . .

Jennifer Yon, a tall blonde who grew up in the Panama City, came to us one year in our U.S. finals pageant. We started to date right after the pageant, and I took her everywhere. I still always considered her very elusive and intriguing, but she was as striking as any girl I ever saw.

One year, I took her to a fundraiser in North Carolina for the "Jimmy V Foundation" to raise funds to fight cancer—Jim Valvano, like a lot of top NCAA basketball coaches, was a good friend who died of brain cancer in 1993—and we happened to be standing under a tree when a foursome of celebrities teed off about one-hundred yards away from us.

"That looks like Kevin Costner up there," Jennifer told me.

I noticed Bobby Cremins, the head coach at Georgia Tech, was waving for me to come to the tee box. So, Jennifer and I walked up there, and it turned out it was Costner, who was the guest celebrity for the fund-raiser that year. This was just a few years after he had made *Dances with Wolves*, and he was at the height of his popularity.

It turned out that Costner had noticed Jennifer standing under the tree and asked Cremins if he knew her.

"No, but whoever she is, she is with Ron Rice," Bobby told him.

"Well, get them up here! I want to meet her!" Costner said.

From the moment he saw Jennifer, he was in love with her and he tried that entire weekend to steal her away from me. He didn't get anywhere, because as I said, she was very elusive, even with a top movie star.

I later took her to Atlanta for the 1996 Summer Olympics

and we attended the *Sports Illustrated* party where we joined NBA legend John Havlicek and Al Joyner, who was the 1984 gold medalist in the triple jump. John had been one of my good friends for years and Al was one of the nicest guys I ever knew. Anyway, John and Al both were scheduled to be in Hawaii to judge our Miss International pageant a few weeks later, and ironically, Jennifer was scheduled to compete in it.

But, by the end of the night, she would have no chance if either of those guys had a big sway in the vote.

Al started bringing her glasses of wine that night. Prince Albert of Monaco walked up to our table and I had known him from our many trips to Cannes. But as the night wore on, she continued to drink all that wine Al was bringing and she could not handle it on an empty stomach. She had eaten nothing at the table but some carrots and was getting very drunk.

At the end of the party, John and Al did not want to ride back to the hotel on the celebrity bus the sponsors had provided, so they asked me for a ride. As soon as we walked outside, Jennifer barfed. We finally got her into the car, as John and Al climbed into the backseat. We were east of Atlanta on the freeway headed to their hotel when she suddenly rolled down her window and hung her head out. I knew what was coming, but I could not pull the car over in time, or even slow down.

Sure enough, she barfed out the window as I was driving about seventy-five miles per hour, and all the remnants of those carrots flew into the back seat and landed all over John's face and glasses.

"Man, Jennifer!" I said with a full laugh. "With that move, you just blew your chances of winning that pageant in Hawaii!"

I am not sure that John, his face covered in barfed-up

carrots, was laughing, however.

I really don't remember where Jennifer finished in that pageant in Hawaii, but I know she didn't win.

We later traveled together to Los Angeles and attended one of Hef's parties at the Playboy Mansion. That night at the party, I bumped into a frequent nemesis of mine by the name of John Rockwell, who was always there since he was good friends with both Hef and Los Angeles Lakers' owner Jerry Buss. Jerry, who also became a good friend because he loved hanging around the models, always came to our pageants in California and I got Lakers' tickets from him whenever we needed them.

That night, Rockwell did all he could to snake Jennifer away from me. I spent the night protecting Jennifer from him, but she drank a lot again.

After the party, we returned to my Malibu house and Jennifer went straight to bed. It was late on a Saturday night. On Sunday, Monday and Tuesday, I would crack the bedroom door and check on her, but she wouldn't get out of bed to eat or drink anything. She slept 24 hours a day. Finally, on Wednesday, she got up and opened her eyes.

When I looked into them, I saw nothing but hate.

I guess she hated me for allowing her to get that drunk, but I couldn't control her. I never saw anything like it.

And that was the end of our dating, although we still remain friends to this day. Nicole Collins, who entered one of our pageants in Daytona in the early 1990s, was from Oklahoma and was a real doll. I think her face had to be one of the most beautiful faces I ever saw. She now lives in Pasadena, California

Another time in the mid-1980s I was invited to be a judge for the Los Angeles Rams' cheerleader tryouts, along with their star running back Eric Dickerson. The tryouts were being held at the Angels' baseball stadium in Anaheim where the Rams also played at the time.

The Rams also had asked me to donate one-thousand gift bags of products.

About 500 of the girls arrived, grabbed those gift bags and left without even trying out. I looked over the other 500 who stayed, and one tall blonde girl's face just jumped out at me. She was by far the most beautiful girl there that day.

I told Eric, "My God . . . that girl is just unbelievable!"

He thought the same thing and obviously she was going to make the squad. She was just so beautiful. I had made friends with two bartenders from the Westwood Marquis from a party I had hosted there every year and one of them, a guy by the name of Tom Meserby, was with me that day.

I told Tom, "Go get that girl's name, address and phone number. She is going to become a Hawaiian Tropic model."

We were headed to a party later—some guy they knew who owned a tugboat was throwing a big party on it near Balboa Island, which was right offshore by Newport Beach. Tom got her information—her name was Shawn Weekly—and then after the tryouts concluded, we just happened to notice her getting into her car.

I approached her, introduced myself invited her to come with us that night to the party.

She thought it was a great idea. After we boarded the tugboat and headed out to the island, I was talking to the captain and did not notice that she had disappeared. I looked everywhere on that boat and couldn't find her. I then went down toward the bow below deck and noticed two small bedrooms. I opened one door and there she was, sitting on the bed kissing some guy.

I grabbed him from behind and threw him out of that bedroom and then locked the door.

And then, I took his place.

Anyway, she became one of models over the next few years. Her nickname was "Wedge," and when I asked her how she got it, she said it was because she had a reputation for wedging herself into every situation.

Today, she is an airline stewardess for United, but I think she may have gotten laid off during the Coronavirus spring of 2020.

Lynn Blythe won a small pageant we held in Jacksonville, and from the time I saw her I thought she was the best thing since sliced bread, and we soon started dating. She was a pretty blonde who later became secretary for my attorney, Larry Adams. I remember when I took her home to Asheville for my thirty-fifth-class reunion, my high school buddies couldn't believe I was seeing someone so beautiful.

Linda Mitchell, one of our models for a long time, always has been one of the more special girls in my life. She loved sports as much as I did and she always went with me to the NCAA Final Four each year (Through my friendship with Denny Crum and some other coaches, I never had problems getting tickets right down near the court and that is one of the trips I never missed).

One year, Wink and I were sitting in front of Denny and his mentor, former UCLA coach John Wooden, when the CBS cameras aired a shot of the four of us. The TV announcer said, "Now those two gentlemen know a lot about basketball . . ."

Some of my friends were watching and I got a lot of calls

the next day with comments like, "I had no idea that you and Wink knew so much about basketball!"

When Linda got married in 2018 where she resides in Pittsburgh, she asked me to walk her down the aisle, since her father had died. And I don't do many weddings, as I said earlier, but I would do anything for Linda. She married a great guy who already had three sons.

One day, I was sitting in the office when I heard my secretary pick up the phone and ask "Ross Clark?" There was a Ross Clark from high school that I once knew really well, so I picked up the phone.

"Ross?" I asked.

"No, my name is Kim Jones," the voice said. "My sister is good friends with Ross and he told me if I ever was in Daytona to call Ron Rice. I am here for Spring Break with my friends."

Ross had moved to St. Louis and I hadn't seen him since we had graduated.

She told me where she was staying on the south end of the beach. I told her I couldn't come there today, but that I would be there the following afternoon. I rolled up there to the parking lot and leaned out of my car, noticing five pretty girls lying together on the beach.

"Okay, which one of you is Kim from St. Louis?" I asked.

"There's no Kim here, but there are some girls from St. Louis up on the pool deck," one of them said.

I soon found her and she immediately reminded me of a young Sally Field. She looked just like her and had the same personality. And as we started to talk, that really pissed off the lifeguard, because he had been trying his best to hook up with her. From the minute I saw her and the more we talked, Kim and I hit it off.

I went home, showered and hopped into the delivery van, taking her and her friends out that night to Big Daddy's, buying all of them dinner and drinks. And I did that the next night at another restaurant, and so on throughout the week, knowing they were on spring break, didn't have much money and were all crammed into one tiny hotel room.

After that week, Kim and I started dating long distance and became close.

I took Kim to our Beach Boys concert in D.C., and Long Beach we had sponsored, to France, to Spain, and a few other places. She still was living in St. Louis, but I was getting very serious about her. Then on one trip, we got stuck in Spain when I overslept and we missed our flight back to the U.S., forcing us to wait two more days. She was starting to get homesick and she was so pissed off at me for oversleeping that day, causing us to miss our flight. And when we returned home, she was still mad at me.

That was the last time I ever saw her and I later heard she had married her high school sweetheart.

And I never did see Ross Clark again, but I owed him big time. I heard he died at a young age and I regret never having called him for thanking him for telling Kim to contact me.

It seemed everybody who met Krista Frazier, a very pretty girl from Texas, wanted her the minute they saw her. And I was no different, but she too was very elusive.

I took her to a lot of places, too, like Russia and France. We did end up dating for a while and she was one of the most beautiful girls I ever saw. She was so striking that when I introduced her once to Prince Albert at Cannes, he insisted she sit down next to him. He fell for her instantly. When the film festival was over that year, we flew back home, but he was so smitten that he told his people that he was flying to Texas to do some hunting.

He went hunting alright, but he was hunting Krista. I do not think he ever got anywhere with her, at least not that I heard.

His sister Stephanie joined us often at all those events and I really liked her. She had a great personality and she was beautiful, and like Jane Fonda, she was very secure in her own skin around the girls.

Monica Lange was our pageant winner in Canada and then she won our Miss International Pageant in 1987. We hit it off immediately and started dating right afterward. Her mother Marie was the manager of the West Edmonton Mall, which is the largest mall in North America. The mall housed such displays as actual-size submarines and an indoor water park and large salt-water tanks that included dolphins. Her mother once had a Boeing 747 remodeled to contain a small pool just so they could fly it to Sea World in Orlando to pick up six dolphins they had purchased for their display. I stayed at the hotel inside the mall once when we were dating and was just fascinated by the place.

One day, in the late 1980s, I was driving down the beach and I stopped when I happened to see a few of my friends. As I talked to them, I noticed a girl and guy looking at the Porsche I had just bought. I told my friends, "Wow, I have to go talk to this girl."

She introduced herself and told me she was from Summerville, Georgia, and they were on vacation together. She was a tall, dark-haired girl and as sweet as could be. Her name was Rosanne Woodard. The conversation lasted no more than twenty minutes, because her boyfriend could sense I was hitting on her, so they left. But I figured that I had just enough information to track her down somehow, so in a week or so, I found several Woodards listed in that town and I planned on calling each of them until I found her.

An elderly lady answered the first number I dialed.

"Rosanne?" she asked. "That's my granddaughter!"

For the next twenty minutes, the grandma told me the Rosanne Woodard story. She was a student at Georgia Southern in Statesboro, and by the end of the call, she had given me her phone number. I really think the grandma was just lonely and wanted to talk to anybody, because I really had a hard time getting off the phone.

I called Rosanne at her dorm and started, "You may not remember me, but I am the guy you met on the beach last week."

Before long, she had invited me to Statesboro, and we began dating. She came down to Daytona a few times and I also took her to France on one of our trips there. Then one night, shortly after I started dating Darcy LaPier, I was hosting a company party at a local restaurant called Marker 32.

I was sitting at a table, surrounded by friends and employees, when Rosanne appeared in front of me, happy to see me. Five of her friends stood behind her.

Problem was that Darcy also had come to Daytona unexpectedly a day or so earlier and was somewhere at the party mingling with guests.

I thought, *"Oh oh . . ."*

I suddenly had a terrible choice to make.

"Ah . . . ah . . . Rosanne," I started, searching for the words. "I am so sorry but . . . ."

I do not remember what words came out of my mouth after that, but to this day I can still see her storming off as her friends trailed her to the door. That was an awful experience. And I never saw her again. I really, really liked this girl, but she had a right to be upset.

Michelle Stanford, who graduated from the University of Georgia with a degree in pharmacy, was a tall, dark-haired beauty who won a pageant we held in Jacksonville while the old Gator Bowl was being renovated into the NFL Jaguars' stadium. She also had a blonde friend and they both became Hawaiian Tropic models.

I took her everywhere for a while and she was one of the smartest girls I ever dated. She later became one of Pfizer's top salespeople in California and now is married with two kids living in Los Angeles.

Alicia Rickter was in one of our pageants in California and she looked exactly like Jackie Kennedy. In fact, when they introduced her during the pageant, the announcer said, "And here's a Jackie Kennedy lookalike.' She later went on to act in *Baywatch* and a soap opera. She now is married to retired baseball player Mike Piazza and I recently saw her at a *Baywatch* reunion. . . .

Jennifer Gareis came to us as a pageant contestant from Pennsylvania, where I think she was runner-up Miss Pennsylvania one year. She became one of our top models and we hit it off big-time. I took her to the Cannes Film Festival one year and she later went on to star in the soaps, *The Young and the Restless* and *The Bold and the Beautiful* and now is married with two kids. . . .

Amanda Henkel was from Slidell, Louisiana, and she was beyond beautiful. I remember one night in New Orleans we loaded all the girls, wearing their best evening gowns, into the van and headed to one of the debutante balls we attended each year. When we arrived at the hotel, a crowd of fans and photographers gathered around the van and as each girl exited, there would be slight applause or some "ooh-ing and aah-ing."

Amanda was the last one out and when she stepped down from the van, the crowd just went nuts. She was that beautiful and she became one of our top models for years.

Katrina Ray from Texas also was special to me. When we started dating, me being a huge basketball fan, we flew to Barcelona to watch the 1992 Summer Olympics. That was the first year of the true "Dream Team," in which NBA stars could play in the Olympics. Problem was, I never booked a room before the trip and we went from hotel-to-hotel begging for a room.

We got to a place called the Hotel Presidente' and the front-desk clerk responded, "You are in luck. The Presidential Suite just opened up."

Robert Earl, one of the owners of the Planet Hollywood chain, was opening a restaurant by the ocean and wanted Arnold Schwarzenegger to stay at a hotel close to it, so Arnold had moved out of the suite that opened for us. I don't remember the room rate, but it wasn't cheap. I know it was more than four figures per night. I was in the process of trying to woo Katrina, I admit, but it wasn't going anywhere.

Katrina ended up appearing in *Playboy* under the name of Ashley Allen.

And what can I say about Linda Kramer?

We hired her to work in the national accounts in 1980. At that time, it was my policy to interview all potential office employees, but I was on an extended trip to Europe and when I returned, she was already on the job. We finally met at an event for local lifeguards and we instantly hit it off and started dating. One of the things we had in common was a love of sports, and our first trip together was to a Tennessee football game. I also taught her how to ski and we made many trips to the slopes together.

She later became our assistant promotions director, and then our promotions director, and remained there for more than twenty years. She also worked on the pageants and we dated throughout the eighties.

Today she still works for me handling our archives as well as setting up the warehouse and shipping operations.

Linda was always the one to make things happen. She had a great attitude and would do whatever I asked of her. I would tell Linda to do something and I knew it would get done. I also got her into owning dachshunds, since I always had dachshunds running around the house—and she loves animals like I do.

I have to say here and now that I never pushed myself on any girl at any time in my entire life. I was just enjoying life and enjoyed whoever came my way and I accepted what didn't.

I was sued twice for sexual harassment and both cases were totally bullshit. I just chalked it up to "they come with the territory" when you have money and other people want it the easy way.

There was a girl who worked for me in the late 1980s who looked identical to Bo Derek. Her whole life revolved around being a fan of the band Pearl Jam.

Well, when Roy Orbison died in December of 1988, I was crushed because he had become a good friend of mine. Roy had lived a tough life, but he had an incredible voice and was a wonderful person in my eyes. Naturally, as when any top singer dies, their latest release instantly heads to the top of the billboard charts. His was a song called "You Got It," which he recorded when he made an album with the Traveling Wilburys.

She was listening to the radio and got all upset one day and said, "I can't believe this nobody's music kicked Pearl Jam out of the number one spot on this week's charts!"

Well that pissed me off.

Anyway, her father happened to be the city manager of Holly Hill, a little town nearby where I once taught junior high school, and her mother was very involved in her life and always pushing her. And I think she pushed her right into suing me for an easy buck, although there was no merit to her case. I did nothing inappropriate.

A few of my employees and myself were guilty of only one thing—a few of us sometimes were politically incorrect and we sometimes ribbed each other with crude jokes. It was just part of our culture back then and I guess she started taking notes and collecting data on all of our social infractions.

When it came to the depositions of her lawsuit, my lawyers told me she had enough evidence to win damages, and that I should settle the case.

So, I did.

Big mistake.

Once I did that, a few other girls noticed and thought, *"Now it's payday and it's my turn to cash in!"*

I decided that I would never settle another one if it came my way, no matter how much it cost me in legal fees.

It was not long until a second girl, a girl named Kelli, after hearing about the first settlement, sued me for nothing more than making some jokes.

When that happened, I told the attorney, "There is absolutely no way I am settling this. We are fighting it. If I settle, there will be more and more and more of them—and none of them have a case."

After a short jury trial, they sided with me and her case was dismissed.

When it came to the models or pageants, I gave all the guys who worked for me strict orders: "You can take names and numbers, but don't act on it in the moment. Don't be pushy or you won't be around very long. Just act like a perfect gentleman during the pageants, the modeling jobs and the actual work promoting Hawaiian Tropic. Then when you are on your own time, you can call them or try to date them. If they say no, be polite and back off!"

Is it true that pageant contestants and/or our models came on to me all the time, since I was the boss and they knew I had money? Yes.

Did I turn them all down? No.

There was no reason to turn down many of them. Still, I had my antennae up at all times, worried about some girls who may have been trying to trap me just so they would be financially set for life. As I said, I saw several of them for short periods of time over the years, but I got pretty good at deciphering who was genuine and who was not.

Remember, I would grow older each year, but the girls

coming in were always about the same age as the year before.

I never seriously considered marrying again after my first venture into matrimony flopped in the early 1970s. Why would I? I had a fun life, a purpose to get up every day while running a major company, and plenty of girls available to date.

The truth is, I really wasn't looking to get married. I was always looking to have a good time. There was absolutely no reason to get married. I would pursue some girls, want them close to me—but not too close, if that makes any sense.

I loved my freedom and I never lacked for companionship, so why do it again?

Chapter Thirteen

"MARRIAGE" AND FATHERHOOD

During our national pageant at Daytona in 1987, I could not take my eyes off Miss Oregon. She was striking with an exotic, Indian-like look. She had dark skin and was a cross between Gina Lollobrigida, Sophia Loren and Raquel Welch.

The only thing I did not like was that her hair was extremely short, maybe an inch long. She looked like a rooster the way she had it cut.

The MC that night was Jim Gibson, who had become a good friend over the years. He knew all the pageant girls and I could trust his judgment. I approached him and asked about her and he told me that she was recently divorced.

I referred to her earlier, like the time when Rosanne Woodard showed up at our company party, I had to make a choice between two girls.

Her name was Darcy Lynn LaPier.

I talked to her a little that night and she was very outgoing, very confident and had a great personality. She said she was trying to further her acting career. She did not win the pageant that night, but I did not care. Like I said, my guesses for which contestant would win our pageants never aligned with the judges anyway.

I thought it was love at first sight, at least for me.

I invited her to fly from Oregon to one of our parties at the Westwood Marquis in Los Angeles. In the meantime, one of the Beach Boys—I forget which—told me they had seen Darcy somewhere in Los Angeles and they had been trying to fix her up with the actor John Stamos, who played drums with them from time to time ever since Dennis Wilson had drowned.

We had arranged to meet a few nights before the party and I already had booked a three-bedroom suite at the Marquis. I had my attorney Larry Adams and my buddy, Rick Webb, with me and they each had a bedroom.

On that first date, Darcy and I really hit it off.

I will never forget the date, October 1, 1987, because the most-severe earthquake in about twenty years had shaken L.A. that morning.

Darcy was studying to be an X-ray technician if her acting career did not pan out, and she had landed a role in a movie called the *Young Guns* starring Richard Farnsworth, Lou Diamond Phillips and Emilio Estevez. She had a bit part as a gun moll.

The Westwood Marquis had become my home away from home whenever I was in L.A., and I threw a large party there every summer for four years in a row. We invited everybody we knew in Southern California and many others flew into town just for it.

There was no holiday or particular reason for my parties there—I just wanted to have a party in L.A. every year. We invited guests ranging from ditchdiggers and bartenders to movie stars and professional athletes. It was not your typical Hollywood party. One year, I looked around the room and saw Tony Curtis sitting on a couch next to a plumber.

That was typical.

One night during one of those parties, actress Sybil Danning, who became a good friend, told me, "You know, I go to a lot of Hollywood parties and this is nothing like anything I have seen before. Usually, I walk in and I am handed a glass of champagne and the conversation goes like this: 'How is your dog? How is your Mercedes? How is your Malibu beach house?' Then I finish my champagne, set the glass down and walk out . . ."

After she told me that, our annual invitations read: "You are hereby invited to the 'Annual Hawaiian Tropic Not-So Typical Hollywood Party' . . . as quoted by Sybil Danning."

We would normally go through about sixty bottles of champagne, which would be piled on mounds of ice in each bathtub of the suite. The front-desk staffers at the Marquis would see these people carrying in bags and bags of ice and several large suitcases, which were filled with the champagne, and they had to wonder, but they never really knew what was going on.

Then after the fourth year, I was sent a $15,000 bill from the hotel because the managers claimed the ice had melted and leaked through the floor to a lower room. I thought it was a bullshit claim, but I paid it, and that was the end of our summer L.A. party.

I had to get out of that hotel anyway, and that is when I bought the house in Malibu.

Darcy and I continued dating and things were going great for us. She was pursuing acting on the West Coast and I was running Hawaiian Tropic on the East Coast and we met often somewhere, usually in California.

Then she became pregnant, and on June 12, 1990, I became a father to a baby girl. We named her Sterling.

I then proposed and she accepted.

I was focused on Hawaiian Tropic, so she planned the wedding. Also, I had given Darcy unlimited funds and let her handle the detail—it would be held September 15 in Daytona Beach. Other than perhaps a royal wedding, I think Darcy may have broken some spending records.

She hired some key designers at Disney to turn the Daytona Hilton main ballroom into a castle for the wedding. She invited more than 1,000 people and had her entire family and distant relatives from Oregon fly in for it. Her grandfather, Art, did not fly and took the train from Oregon through Canada, then south to the Orlando area where we picked him up.

The invitations alone cost thirty dollars each. When they were opened, a castle popped out and music played. Darcy's dress was designed by Renee' Strauss of Beverly Hills and cost $20,000. She had three veils that went with it.

As far as I was concerned, getting married again really had nothing to do with Sterling being born. I thought I was in love, but maybe it really was lust. Who knows?

We were married in a small church across the river on the mainland and then we were pulled by a horse-and-buggy a few miles to the Hilton. Darcy had the horse painted pink. The wedding had received so much publicity, that the streets of Daytona were lined with people during our procession from the church to the reception.

When we arrived, we actually rode that thing into this massive ballroom. Wolfman Jack served as the MC and I also had hired David Somerville, the lead singer of the Diamonds, along with the two singers from The Lettermen to perform.

By the time the night concluded, I had spent more than two million dollars for the wedding and the reception; I did not have much say in how it was spent, either.

I guess I did not really care either, because I was happy.

And Darcy seemed happy.

(That same week we were married, I also made a major contribution to the Pentagon. It was during Desert Storm and many of our soldiers were getting burned from the intense desert sun in Iraq, so I donated $500,000 worth of our highest SPF-factor sunscreens. We joked that our stuff smelled so good that we were worried the Iraqis would smell our troops coming from miles away. That donation made the news, but I really was not seeking publicity for it.)

For our honeymoon we flew from Los Angeles to Hong Kong, Australia, and then to Bora Bora. Andy Williams was on our first flight, headed to Hong Kong for an opening of a Conrad Hotel as a guest of the Hilton family. And he invited us to the grand opening. The moment we arrived that night, I noticed Ernest Borgnine outside having his picture taken.

Then when we went inside and headed down the escalator, we met this man, Stanley Ho, who happened to own six casinos on Macau Island, which was just offshore.

Next thing I knew, he invited us to have dinner with him

that night at one of his casinos. After this party, we walked outside with Stanley and there was a gold Rolls Royce waiting, which took us to the dock where we boarded a hovercraft which took us to one of his casinos. By the time the night had finished, we had hit every one of his casinos, and better yet, it seemed that we won money at everything we played that night

By the time we reached shore, he had a limo waiting for us to take us to our hotel. I really felt guilty, having won thousands at this guy's casinos as he took care of us after just meeting us.

From there, we flew on to Australia and then to Bora Bora.

It seemed that Andy Williams and I collided with each other often through our lives. Before Super Bowl XIX in California, between the Dolphins and Forty-Niners, for which Tom McMillen had given me a few tickets, I was with friends in a nice restaurant in San Francisco and I slid my chair back to get up when I bumped it into another chair.

It was Andy's chair. Then as we pulled up to the stadium in a cab before the game, a limo slowly moved along next to us. The window rolled down.

It was Andy.

We worked our way to our seats for the game and guess who I was sitting next to?

It was Andy. It got to be a running joke between us.

When we arrived in Bora Bora, Darcy and I stayed in one of those little huts over the water, where we could see fish swimming in the ocean beneath our hotel room. It was perfect, but they would let us stay there only one night because of the demand.

The wedding had been an amazing event, we had fun on a long honeymoon, and then it was time to return home and get back to everyday life.

But there was a premonition of sorts. It was not too long after that when Darcy and I walked into the Mondrian Hotel on Sunset Boulevard in Hollywood and there was Sylvester Stallone, standing alone by the fish tank. He immediately noticed Darcy.

Then he looked at me.

"That ain't going to last," he said matter-of-factly.

I had never met him at that point, but we later became very good friends through some celebrity events and later even supplied some models for his movie about auto racing called *Driven*.

But Darcy and I were happy in married life, for the first year or so at least. She was getting bit parts in movies and going back and forth to Los Angeles while I was busy running the company. I saw a big future for her, because I thought her unique look would lead to more movie roles. And she had a huge personality, which I thought would help her. We had a nanny tend to Sterling who lived with me in Daytona.

I never was a movie or TV buff because I simply did not have time for it. And I was not always as aware of certain stars as Darcy was.

One night in Los Angeles, we had been invited to the premiere of one of Ron Howard's movies. When we arrived, I noticed the interior of the lobby of the theater was created to look like New York. There was a mini-Empire State Building, a mini-Brooklyn Bridge and so on.

Just as the movie ended, Ron walked right by us to head to the lobby to greet the guests who would be leaving. I watched him and noticed he was suddenly standing alone, waiting for guests to approach him with their reviews of how much they loved the movie.

"Come on, let's go get a picture with Ron," I told Darcy.

We walked over and Darcy said, "I really love your movies," and he smiled and thanked her.

Then as he shook my hand, I stuck my foot in it, big-time.

"You know, Ronny, you and I have a lot in common. I grew up just like your character 'John-Boy,'" I said.

Darcy suddenly bowed her head and stared at the floor. Ron looked at me like I was asking for his wallet, but he never said a word. He just turned and walked by me to greet another guest.

I had not realized that what I said that was offensive.

"THAT'S NOT 'JOHN-BOY!'" Darcy screamed at me when he was out of earshot. "HE WAS 'OPIE!'"

Like I said, I never watched sit-coms or those type of shows like *The Waltons*, but somehow I had gotten the notion in my head that he had been in that show.

Darcy did have a jealous side.

One time we were in Hawaii, at the Ala Moana food court in Waikiki eating lunch at a picnic table. I just happened to catch the back of this girl walking with long, flowing hair down to her waist. I guess I had leaned out to watch her as she walked by us, because suddenly, I got slammed in the side of the face by something heavy.

It was the thud of Darcy's large purse. I swear I saw stars and got dizzy for a moment.

"What was that for?" I asked.

"That's for looking at that girl!" she barked.

That "girl" must have heard our commotion, because she turned around—she was wearing a bushy mustache! It turned out that it was a little guy with long flowing hair. All I could do was laugh out loud. Then BAM!

I got hit again.

"What was that for?" I asked her again, rubbing my face.

"That was for laughing about it!" she said.

That is just how temperamental she was.

And damn if Stallone did not turn out to be a prophet.

While we were attending a charity event in Palm Springs, I talked to Buzz Aldrin and his wife Lois for a while and then I bumped into Jean-Claude Van Damme, who was with his wife, Gladys. I had met him several times at charity events over the years. I then introduced them both to Darcy.

In the weeks after that, our relationship suddenly was becoming stale and it was noticeable to me.

Van Damme happened to come to Daytona for one of our pageants soon after that, and the next thing I knew, he and Darcy had flown off somewhere together. They started an affair immediately behind my back and behind Van Damme's wife's back.

I think from that moment I had introduced them she must have fallen head over heels for him.

Of course, I was pissed off at first.

The more I thought about it as the days passed, the more I thought it was a good thing for me in the long run. Her attitude had changed from the day she had met him; I knew her affair would be my way out of the marriage.

But we still had a two-year-old daughter to care for.

I decided to hire some investigators to check her out. I hired a young guy and a girl who did investigative work in Daytona and I also hired two former lifeguards who had gone into the

Secret Service who did investigative work on the side in Los Angeles. They started following Van Damme and videotaping him and we soon had tape of them together. They also had video of her meeting a friend of mine by the name of Tommy Baker, hugging him outside my Malibu house before they walked inside together.

"Let us use our resources to check her out," one of the L.A. investigators told me.

A few weeks later, after they conducted a background search on Darcy, they called me.

"We got some good news for you," the investigator said.

What do you know? It turned out Darcy had never legally divorced her first husband, a guy from her hometown in Oregon by the name of Larry Robertson. She had filed for divorce and had the papers drawn up in Las Vegas, but neither one of them returned to sign the final divorce decree.

Thus, she was still legally married to him, and our marriage obviously did not legally exist in the first place.

When I heard the news, it became one of the best days of my entire life. I figured it saved me about ten million big ones in alimony from the prenup we had signed before our so-called wedding. I did not even need my attorneys to draw up a settlement.

After all, there was no marriage. No marriage, no settlement.

All these years later, I still do not believe Darcy deceived me on purpose; she just figured her divorce from the first marriage had been final and official. And what I thought was a massive wedding really was nothing more than a two-million-dollar party.

I could have had her nailed with bigamy charges, but I didn't want to be that vindictive to Sterling's mother. And I really must thank my lucky stars I met her, because there would be no Sterling if we had never met.

She eventually did marry Van Damme in 1994 after he divorced his wife and then he and Darcy had a son together. Their marriage did not work out and they divorced three years later. I still cared for her and we talked often because of Sterling and we both loved Sterling to death, so we still had something in common.

Somehow, Darcy became good friends with several members of the al-Fayad family of London which owned Harrods' Department Store—on August 31, 1997, she had taken a trip there. So, when news broke that Dodi al-Fayed and Princess Diana were in a horrific car crash that night in that Paris' tunnel, my mind really started racing. I admit that I was very worried for her throughout the night, until she called and told me she still was alive and well in London—not in Paris.

(Harrod's and Hawaiian Tropic shared a sponsorship one year at Le Mans, and it did not cost me a dime. They wanted to be part of it since they knew the girls would be photographed often with their name and logo. It was a partnership I could not refuse.)

Soon after her divorce, Darcy met Herbalife founder Mark Hughes and while they were dating, they invited me to a party at his beachfront Malibu house, which he had bought from Merv Griffin. Sterling was only nine at the time and I had custody of her at that stage of her life. I was with Krista Frazier that night and I remember Farrah Fawcett being there that night, among other celebrities.

I really liked Hughes from what I knew of him and I thought

he was a decent guy, but he cornered me that night and asked me the toughest question I ever had to answer.

"Ron, Darcy wants to get married," he said. "Be honest . . . should I marry her?"

Talk about putting a guy on the spot.

I had no idea how to answer that one, as I searched for the words, I just blurted out, "Well . . . I did!"

They were married soon after that, on Valentine's Day, 1999.

The only thing Darcy really did above all else that infuriated me, even more than spending the two million dollars for the wedding and then running off with somebody else, was hiring Los Angeles attorney Robert Shapiro, the original attorney for O.J. Simpson during his double murder trial in 1995.

Now that she had a lot of money because of her marriage to Hughes, she wanted to take custody of Sterling and she was able to afford a top attorney, even though I had known Bob from earlier celebrity events and I had considered him a friend.

It was a mistake by her on many fronts, but I knew she could not win in a court case held where I live in Volusia County, Florida. During the trial, held before a judge and not a jury, Shapiro held up one of our annual Hawaiian Tropic calendars and asked me, "Do you think it's a good idea to have her around all of these bikinis all the time?"

He then started flipping through the pages, showing the judge pictures of Sterling, who also was pictured in the calendar.

I had remembered that Bob had been pictured in that certain calendar as well, as many other celebrities were from our events or parties, with his arms wrapped around a few of our models.

It was great ammunition, and I figured he did not realize

it. I then interrupted him and said, "Bob, if you turn two more of those pages, you are going to see *yourself* in that calendar."

The judge saw right through her case and ultimately ruled that it was best that Sterling stay with me. After his verdict, he told me privately, "I already had made my decision about five minutes before his little calendar stunt."

Hughes, whom Darcy had brought to Daytona with her during the trial, was not much of a drinker but the following year as they were celebrating his grandmother's eighty-seventh birthday one night, he drank an entire bottle of wine that night, according to Darcy. Then he took some sleeping pills on top of it. She also told me that they were not sleeping in the same bed because he had snored so loudly.

The next morning, he never came to breakfast, so she walked into his room and found him dead. He was only forty-four.

I walked out of a restaurant on Sunset Boulevard just days after that and was almost tackled by a few reporters, who were asking several questions that made Darcy look like the black widow of L.A. They begged and prodded me to say something bad about her.

"No, she comes from a good family and is a very good mother," I said. "That's all I have to say."

Two years later, she married a guy named Brian Snodgrass, whose family founded and operated the Seven Dees nursery chain. They divorced in 2013.

I had pretty much sole custody of Sterling until she turned eleven, although I made sure Darcy got plenty of visitation. At that point, I decided Sterling needed to learn how to become more of a girl while I had been raising her more like a tomboy.

She had natural ability on the ski slopes and became a really good skier, a real dare devil. I always treated her like an adult and never spanked her, never told her the word 'no.' I know she didn't know what the word 'no' was. But that was the right time to give her to Darcy, who had primary custody of her from that point.

Through it all, I held no grudges against Darcy.

And I still don't.

All these years later, she and I still are close, and we talk quite often. She lives on the horse ranch, which I bought for eight million dollars and still own, in Oregon with Sterling and her other kids.

I wanted to keep the peace and I did not want any of what went on between us to affect Sterling.

After Darcy, and my earlier marriage to Linda which lasted two years, there was never another reason to get married again.

The funny thing is, I still send Linda alimony checks four times each year—some five decades after we divorced. Linda got way more than she deserved for our short marriage and I am sure she realizes that.

A lot of girls came and went through my house between and after both marriages, but I really was married to Hawaiian Tropic. I just did not have time for many serious relationships.

And I loved hanging around our employees for a social life.

On Wednesday nights, for example, we would load up the van with a bunch of guys and head to a Rosie O'Grady's in Orlando for nickel beer night. We would get drunk as skunks and whoever was the soberest would drive us all back to Daytona—and that would be me every single time.

It is a wonder we did not all get killed several times over the years. I got to be the best late-night driver over the years over all the other guys. Most of them were morning people, anyway, and I was a night person.

After Darcy, I returned to my dating ways.

My family, in addition to Sterling, of course, was Hawaiian Tropic and the people who worked for me.

I had tried the marriage thing twice.

It did not work out for me twice.

You live and learn.

And I learned I liked my life just the way it was—as a single man.

Chapter Fourteen

THE PERKS OF BECOMING WEALTHY

"*The difference between men and boys is the price of their toys.*"

That was Robin Leach's line from a segment he produced on me for his popular TV show, *Lifestyles of the Rich and Famous*.

The title of that show was, "Life's a Beach."

And it is true.

I always liked Robin. He was always one of our first pageant judges when he first started holding pageants at the Plaza Hotel in Daytona Beach and he continued to come to my house over the years for our parties and events related to the pageants. He was always great about helping promote the company and he loved being around the models, so I was glad to have him anytime he called.

As for the show, it turned out great. He labeled me "the sultan of suntan," and a "former beach bum who made his pot of gold out of sand," referring to my lifeguarding days when I first created Tropic Tan. And he said, "this story from rags to riches begins in the bottom of a trash can," referring to the four-dollar garbage can I bought to begin mixing Tropic Tan.

They were silly clichés, I suppose, but they were all true.

Robin brought a film crew and they stayed a few days, shooting footage of me at the pool surrounded by dozens of our models, in the hot tub with three girls, toasting champagne with a dozen more, and watching a basketball game with two of them in my media room. He also shot me driving down the road in my black $250,000 Lamborghini.

For the show, I said, "There is more opportunity in America, we have the greatest system in the world if you are willing to work hard. I look at that beach in front of my home where I lifeguarded and think about running out to make rescues. And then after a great idea and a lot of hard work, I was always running to the bank to make deposits."

And as far as his line, "the difference between men and boys is the price of their toys," I guess I did buy a few expensive toys.

Maybe because I had a modest up-bringing—remember Dad limiting me to three sheets of toilet paper? When Hawaiian Tropic's success was generating millions in income, I never went on wild spending sprees like some other guys in my position have over the years.

I still knew the value of a buck and that never changed.

Still, I did purchase an array of sports cars over the years, a large sailboat, three airplanes, several houses, and some commissioned artwork.

If I saw something I really wanted, I bought it.

The fact is, I never took a paycheck from the company. You

know how a lot of CEOs of large companies today are paid in the millions each year? I never did anything like that. If I needed cash, I told our accountant, "Write me a check for $9,999."

Anything $10,000 or above had to be reported to the IRS.

I would cash that check and stick some cash in my pocket and put the rest in my safe in the house to keep for later. And usually, that amount would last me a long, long time. I never used checks or credit cards much at all personally.

And I did not throw around big year-end bonuses, either. If we were doing really well, instead of giving larger paychecks to key employees, I handed out perks.

Once, I bought five Corvettes for me and my vice-presidents, each brown and each identical to the others. Our license plates were "Tropic 1," "Tropic 2" and so on. A few years after those, I bought several Porsche 911s or Carreras for each of us, but I let them pick their colors on those.

And I did drive a beautiful black Lamborghini at one point, which I loaned to Burt Reynolds and Hal Needham to use in *The Cannonball Run*. They insured it through Lloyds of London for two million and when I got it back, I then turned it into a promotional car and had our logo placed on the back of it.

The only Mercedes I ever owned I had kept garaged at the Malibu house, but I was not a big sedan guy. I was more into sports cars. As far as that house, I spent just over one million for it and today, it is probably worth about four times that.

I never was one to collect expensive artwork, either, but I did pay Ralph Cohen, a well-known artist, to commission a few paintings, including one with Sterling sitting on my shoulders. That painting still takes up the middle of one of my living room walls.

And since I always loved the water, I had to have a big boat, too.

My first one was a seventy-one-foot ketch, made entirely of wood, which I bought from the author William F. Buckley. Not long after that, he wanted to use it for a week, so I rented it back to him for $4,000. There was one problem—I employed a terrible captain.

While he rented it, the captain somehow rammed it into another boat on a trip on the Intracoastal Waterway in Fort Lauderdale. My insurance took care of the $50,000 damage on the other boat, but I was out the $4,000 deductible on the repairs, which was exactly what he had rented it for.

I ended up giving that boat to Jacques Cousteau and he took it to Russia on one of his ventures studying how humans survive in sub-zero temperatures. Two years later, I missed having a boat so much that I sent some of my executives out to find another one.

They found one for sale in Cancun, Mexico. The owner had been operating a scuba-diving charter with it, but he had an interesting backstory: He had owed the IRS about two million dollars in back taxes and that is why he had moved to Mexico to live in the first place.

The boat was a beautiful teak seventy-foot ketch with four bedrooms, and worth much more, so I offered him $200,000 for it. He turned down my offer.

Then it was not too long before the guy called me back and said he would take my offer.

"There's one catch," he said. "I can't come any closer than three miles off the coast of Miami."

So, we took a suitcase full of twenty-dollar bills, amounting to the $200,000, in another boat and we met him three miles offshore. I re-named the boat "The Princess Sterling," after my daughter and I adorned it with a huge Hawaiian Tropic logo. Over the years, we had a ton of fun on it and hosted many parties.

I never really had an interest in owning my own airplane, or even thought of it for that matter, until a salesman showed up one day at our offices in the early 1980s. He had a Mitsubishi Marquise to sell.

I told him, "What do I need an airplane for?"

But he was a great salesman and very persistent.

"Tell you what," he said. "Just ride in it one time. We'll fly you and some of your employees over to Cedar Key for lunch."

Cedar Key is a tiny island in Florida on the Gulf of Mexico, about forty-five miles southwest of Gainesville.

I thought, *I am hungry, so why not?*

We grabbed a few of our secretaries and hopped on their airplane. It had nine seats, plus the two pilots' seats, and it was extremely plush. As soon as we got airborne, they poured glasses of champagne for us—we had to drink them fast since we landed about thirteen minutes later, enjoyed a great lunch of crab claws in Cedar Key and then flew back to Daytona.

The whole thing took no more time than if I had hopped in my car and driven to one of my favorite lunch spots in town. And there were no stop lights to wait on and no traffic to fight.

About the time that airplane's wheels touched down in Daytona, I knew I had to have it.

"What the hell? We can afford it," I told one of my vice-presidents

The salesman had to think he had just made the easiest sale

of his career, because I bought a new Mitsubishi Marquise that day after lunch and our fun-quotient was about to be taken up a giant notch.

Suddenly, whenever I got the whim to go somewhere, there was no more calling the commercial airlines or buying tickets. I contracted with two pilots and told them to be on call. We could travel about 1,500 miles in that thing, but I never pushed it that far because of the risk. I named it the "Rice Rocket" and had the Hawaiian Tropic logo painted on the tail.

And when the whim hit me, we flew somewhere just for lunch or dinner. There happened to be a place I loved to eat called the Cherokee Restaurant in Midway, Georgia. It was midway between Savannah and Jacksonville which was owned by the Wilson family who had six restaurants. (Today the place is called Captain Joe's.) I had first eaten there in the 1960s and the food always was awesome.

Over the years, we would fly to this tiny airport near there. The owner of the airport stored an old van he used for a doghouse for his German Shepherd on the property. I got to know him well, so we would borrow his van to drive from the airport to Captain Joe's, where we ate shrimp until it came out of ears and then we would be back at the office in Daytona within two hours.

That airplane was fast, but it cost me more to take off and to land it than the fuel we burned during those short flights to Midway.

We would fly up each year for the "Sun Fun" summer kick off party in Myrtle Beach, which we sponsored for years, just party and get drunk as skunks every night and have a blast. The band Alabama often performed at an oceanfront bar called the Bowery. Those were some good times. (Myrtle Beach had its own Walk of Fame and the city eventually presented me with my own star on it. I was prouder of that than if it were on the Hollywood Walk of Fame.)

My sudden affinity for my new toy led me to another business venture—the air-ambulance business. I soon bought two more airplanes, hired four more pilots, and we started flying patients from New York to Miami and back.

To put it bluntly, there was a large demand for transporting the old and dying people who lived in Miami Beach back to their roots in New York—to die. Or the other way, too. We had no competition in the air-ambulance business on the East Coast and it soon became very profitable. We had six pilots working twenty-four hours a day. And sometimes, we used my private airplane to cross over into the air ambulance business if we needed it.

One time we were about to land in Miami when rescue workers radioed us, saying they needed it to fly a shark-bite victim to Houston. We hit the tarmac, hopped out as quickly as we could as they brought the poor guy aboard. Then they loaded his arm, which was wrapped in a salt water-soaked towel. They never even turned the engines off. They zipped off to Houston, where they re-attached his arm, and last thing I had heard, the surgery had been successful.

We were making tons of money and helping rich people die where they wanted to die, and we were saving lives and limbs. What was better than that?

But one thing I soon noticed while owning three small airplanes—air-traffic controllers had no problem treating us like shit. Directing commercial jets was their No. 1 priority and everybody else had to get the hell out of the way.

One night we were coming into Teterboro, New Jersey, and air-traffic controllers would not give us permission to land. We were in the air in a holding pattern, helpless, waiting on all the jets to land in New York first. It was raining cats and dogs and lightning was everywhere around us. Right behind us in the air happened to be the actor Christopher Reeve on his private plane and he was running low on fuel.

When he finally was allowed to land, I saw Christopher standing on the tarmac, pointing his finger at the tower screaming, "You son of a bitch! You almost killed us all!"

He was Superman at the time, and they all knew who he was because he landed there often, but they still gave the jets preferential treatment, surely because of the number of passengers onboard.

The final time I saw Chris, after his horse jumping accident, he was confined to his wheelchair and I was overwhelmed with sadness for him. Still, he always had a smile on his face, no matter the pain he must have felt for never being able to walk again.

But flying somewhere out of the blue to try a new restaurant or enjoying one of our favorite haunts became almost a hobby for me. I would gather some of the top guys who worked for me and fly just about anywhere on nothing but a whim.

When it came to long trips to Europe or some exotic location, other than that exorbitant honeymoon with Darcy, it had to be related to the company or I did not go. And with that approach, I think I have been to almost all 200 or so countries there are in this world looking for places to sell the product. Or maybe at least to ninety percent of them.

There were a few exceptions to my business rule on travel, but not many.

One day, in the summer of 1976, long before I bought the airplanes, I told a few of my top sales reps, "Let's fly to Montreal to see the Olympics." So, we did. That was the summer in which Bruce Jenner won the decathlon and was then featured on the Wheaties box.

As time went on, I frequently bumped into Bruce at celebrity charity events, and he did me the greatest favor in the world one morning without ever thinking twice about it.

We were all in Mexico for a promotional event and I was eating breakfast with several of the models. I had gone through the buffet line and had piled my plate high with just about everything. I always had a big appetite and weighed about 270 then. All the models next to me had plates with a little bit of this and a little bit of that.

I sat down to eat just as Bruce walked by.

"Half that," he said, motioning to my plate and then he continued walking.

Just two words: "half that."

I knew instantly what he meant. I always figured I needed all that food to give me enough energy to get through each day with my hectic schedule. The more I thought about what he said that morning, the more I knew he was right. From that day, I started eating about half of what I used to eat at one sitting. If I were in a restaurant, I would take the other half home for lunch the following day.

One funny thing I always remembered about Bruce is how he easily could fall asleep in the middle of a party. One time we were at a Super Bowl party, and there was Bruce, America's greatest athlete, sound asleep on a sofa in the middle of the game.

One of the coolest things I ever did came on a trip I took to Egypt one year with Darcy and a few other people. We saw the Pyramids, the Sphinx and I actually sat in King Tut's chair. He had designed the chair to have the images of his two enemies—an Oriental and an Ethiopian carved into the wood on the left and right arm rests where his hands would be. So, when he sat in it, he essentially was holding them down with his hands. At least that is what they told me.

One time, Bill Darby and Jim Nelson and I just took a trip around the world. Literally.

I got us all first-class tickets on Singapore Airlines, and we headed in one direction and kept going. We stopped in Hong Kong, but nothing was open because it happened to be the Chinese New Year. Then we stopped in Bangkok, where we stayed in a fabulous place, but there was one problem, they would not let us bring girls back to our room.

And there were trips to check out other business ventures, too.

Of course, we were always looking for other businesses on the side if they appeared promising. Wise businessmen usually diversify if possible.

One time I had met this guy who looked like a beach bum at the Sun Fun Festival in Myrtle Beach. We happened to sit next to each other on a flight from there to New York. He was wearing flip flops, shorts, and a dirty T-shirt, but during the flight, he lowered his tray table and opened a bag and then poured out the contents.

Suddenly, hundreds of thousands of dollars' worth of

diamonds were lying on his tray table. He said he was taking them to Macy's to sell on a flat-weight basis.

Naturally, I was curious, so he explained that he and his partners owned the rights to a ten-mile stretch of the Ora River near Ciudad Bolivar, the capital of Bolivar state south of Caracas, Venezuela. All the diamonds they mined there were seventy percent gem-quality and thirty percent industrial-quality.

The more he explained how the mining process and the rights to it worked, the more interested I became. And he happened to be looking for an investor.

Darby and I then flew down there just to check it out. When we landed in this tiny airplane right next to the river, all these naked girls came running out to us asking for bolivars, which were the currency in that area. We gave them some and told them to guard our plane. We could tell that it was an extremely poor area.

Then we all climbed into canoes and took about two hours to paddle upstream to reach the mining area. One of our canoes had a hole in it and leaked, just as the guide told us about the river being full of piranhas.

"Don't get out of the canoe and don't tip over," he instructed. "They are vicious creatures and they will eat you!"

When we finally arrived, I noticed a big barge in the water holding a giant vacuum suction pump system. The workers pumped river water and silt through screens and slowly worked their way up and down this ten-mile stretch of river. They hired locals who had long fingernails to pick through the silt to find the diamonds.

When they found one, they put it in their mouths and when they had a mouthful of diamonds, they spit them all into a pouch.

They would do this for eight hours each day. I have to say that it really was an amazing operation.

When we arrived back at the village, I noticed a three-legged dog running around.

"What happened to that dog's missing leg?" I asked.

"Crocodile got it," this guy answered.

Suddenly, I realized there were crocodiles *and* piranhas to battle to get to these diamonds.

Then I heard that another would-be investor before me did not last long. He had been staying in a thatched hut when an earwig—little bugs that lived in the hut—crawled into his ear and caused him all kinds of medical problems. Then he died from it.

I discovered that I was there to replace him.

They wanted me to invest one million dollars to buy another barge and machine, so they could be placed side-by-side as they worked their way up and down the river. I really thought it was a great opportunity and I was considering it, but it was so far away, and in the end, I did not completely trust the people working there. There were people standing everywhere holding machine guns for security at the airport, which told me something.

Not to mention it was illegal to bring diamonds back into the U.S. if they were uncut.

Getting out of that jungle was a miracle. We flew in that little airplane back to an airstrip where my airplane was parked. Then we flew to Caracas, on to Lima and we stopped in Ecuador to refuel. When we first came through there, I had walked by a gift shop where I spotted a poncho through the window. But the shop was closed. There was this little guy running around, asking us for a ride out of there. He wanted to get to America. So, I had given him money to buy the poncho for me when the shop opened.

He was there with my new poncho, and I really would have loved to make his dream come true by smuggling him back to the U.S., but there was no way we would do that. I felt bad for the little guy, leaving him behind as we flew home.

President Reagan later signed a tax bill that really took the profits out of the air-ambulance business. And I also noticed more and more the issue that Reeve complained about. Air-traffic controllers just did not care much for private planes like mine and I started to feel unsafe.

That is when I decided to sell all three airplanes—at a nice profit.

There was nothing I loved more when it came time to spending money than on all the parties we hosted over the years.

Our three annual bashes were spring break, Halloween, and Christmas parties, each held at my oceanfront house in Ormond Beach, for which I had spent five million and five years to build. We would invite just about anybody, from our celebrity judges to comedians to athletes and TV and movie stars, as well as hundreds of locals.

During that "Lifestyles" show, Robin Leach labeled my house "Daytona's party-hearty headquarters."

And if he was right about anything, he was more than right about that description.

I remember one year sometime in the 1980s at one of our spring break parties that coincided with a pageant, I looked around my living room just to soak it all in. Rodney Dangerfield was sitting on the couch by himself. Jerry Lee Lewis was at the piano. Troy Aikman and Jim Kelly were there talking football. Fabio was there. So was Sam Kinison.

"Entertainment Tonight" was in town for the pageant and they had sent a film crew.

In front of the house, Universal Studios had parked this huge vehicle they called "The Shark." Everybody had gathered around it while the driver demonstrated the various sounds the massive thing produced, like fart noises and jet engines. A huge plume of fire shot out of the back of the thing just as Jerry Lee walked out into the driveway.

"*Great balls of fire!*" he screamed.

I followed a lot of comedians who had not yet hit the big-time and I usually bonded with them, just as I did musicians. I related to comedians and musicians and it was much more fun to hang around them, more than any famous politician, movie star or professional athlete.

Jay Leno, Robin Williams, Jerry Seinfeld, Chris Farley, Joan Rivers, Dan Aykroyd, John Goodman, Dangerfield, Kinison were just a few of the comedians I got to know and admired and all of them on that list had been to one of my parties or to my house over the years.

Our Halloween party eventually turned into a big mess. Fights would break out and we had to hire bodyguards for the celebrities. As it grew bigger and bigger each year, it just got out of control. Plus, people were in costume, so we never knew who anyone was, so a lot of uninvited people we did not know crashed it. For our Christmas party, we never had those issues. Everybody dressed up in tuxedos and formal gowns, drank champagne and ate lobster.

And of course, since I had the revenue, I tried to be as charitable as I could, if the cause or the event was a good one and not something where the money was wasted.

Robert F. Kennedy Jr. became a good friend over the years and I always attended his charitable auction. Through this event, I met a man named Marjoe Gortner, who had one of the most fascinating backgrounds of anybody I ever knew.

Marjoe became an ordained minister at the age of five and later won an Academy Award in 1972 for a documentary about his life. In addition to acting and his work as a minister, he also hosted charity auctions and served as the auctioneer. He could do it all.

One year, me and Bruce McNall, the owner of the Los Angeles Kings, got into a bidding war at RFK Jr.'s event over a new Hummer. They had just come out and they were a hot commodity at the time. Anyway, he and I went back and forth, bidding each other up as Marjoe called out the bids. When we reached $75,000, for a car that was worth about $55,000 at the time, he went up another $5,000 to win it at $80,000 and I stopped bidding.

One of Marjoe's methods to raise even more money would be to announce to the audience that both high bidders would win and each would receive that prize. That way, they could double the donation.

And he did it this time, too. McNall would receive a Hummer for $80,000 and I would receive one where I had stopped bidding at $75,000.

I called Marjoe over and told him, "That really is not fair. You have to have my bid the same so I will add $5,000 to match his bid."

In the end, we both got $80,000 Hummers. It was an orange-like color, but I never drove it much.

And through Marjoe, I met Leach, the British writer and entertainer. Those two often appeared together on stage of celebrity-charity events as hosts and auctioneers.

One of the other people I met at those events and continued to see over the years was Priscilla Presley. Let me tell you, she has a heart of gold. One of our pageant reps in Arkansas had called Graceland one year trying to plan a tour there for our pageant contestants, but they were getting nowhere. They finally called me.

"Give me a couple of hours," I told them.

I called Priscilla. She was so gracious. She made a few calls and within an hour somebody from Graceland called me back. They offered one hundred comped tickets, snacks, and drinks for all our contestants. I sent her a large box of Hawaiian Tropic products as a thank you and we became good friends after that. I always knew she was very smart, because of how she turned around Graceland. It really was not making any money until she took it over.

The amazing thing was, in June of 1977, I attended one of Elvis' final concerts at the International Hotel in Las Vegas. Afterward, my date and I were invited backstage to meet him. I never got any one-on-one time with him that night, but I thought back to that youth jamboree twenty-two years earlier in Asheville when Paula Elkins and I met him after his performance of gospel music.

And now I was friends with his ex-wife.

It is amazing how things turn out that way in life sometimes.

Having money and a successful company did have a few downsides, however.

I got hit up by virtually hundreds of moochers wanting money.

Some of them were nice in their approach and some were not. I always hated arrogant people anyway, so any approach that smelled of arrogance immediately turned me off. And I always paid close attention to how my secretaries and receptionists handled people wanting money from me. They never knew it, but I eavesdropped on a lot of their conversations.

One time, we had a new girl answering the phones and I heard her say, "Yes sir. Yes sir. Yes sir . . ." This went on for a few minutes and she finally said, "Well sir, if your company is doing so well and making so much money, why do you need Mister Rice's money?"

I walked over to her and said, "Your logic makes so much sense. You did good."

I made a note to promote that girl.

I had to train all the girls how to handle solicitors, because there just were so many of them. Some of the girls wanted to do every deal or contribute to every charity. If they were reputable charities with good reputations, I usually got involved with them somehow, even if it meant only sending a check.

But I had solicitors walk right up the beach to my house, knowing they could get access from the beach. Finally, I had to put a big gate bordering the beach and mark it with a "Private Property" sign.

I was careful about which to align myself, but I also was partial to the Make-A-Wish Foundation and any animal charities.

Like my disdain for disreputable charities and frivolous quick-cash lawsuits, I grew to hate the scammers and con people that always tried to get something for nothing. Or lied. Or cheated.

Funny thing about having money. It can buy you whatever you want, take you wherever you want to go, but it is true that it can make you a target for scammers.

And besides the shake downs, some women just wanted to be taken care of financially, whether I knew them well or not.

One time after my hometown newspaper in Asheville published a story about me after Hawaiian Tropic made it big, I received a letter from a girl I had dated briefly in high school. I had long forgotten about her and had not talked to her since we had graduated many years earlier.

Her letter simply read: "I am coming down to Florida to live with you."

I never even replied to her.

I also learned that Hollywood is full of fake people looking out only for themselves. As best I could, I tried to tell the scammers from the genuine people who had genuine business deals or genuine charities.

The aftermath of the breakup of my company, The Catalyst Group, proved that I could misjudge people, too. I had sold the company for one million dollars to Norm Marshall, who owned some restaurants and another product placement company, but I really did not want to sell it. I had to because the two girls I had hired to manage it were constantly fighting with each other.

One of them then really took advantage of me. I liked this girl a lot, so I gave her back my share of the sale, which was one-third—$333,333—because she told me she needed it for "start-up costs" to produce a movie. She convinced me she had French investors who would fund the movie, and once I heard all the details, I thought it was a good idea with a good script, and I believed her.

In the end, she lied to me, saying the supposed French investors wanted too much control and it was not going to be made.

Then I learned she had just spent the money on personal stuff.

When I learned the truth, I just said, "You told me a lie."

And this is what got me—this is the line that really hurt.

She simply responded, *"Everybody does that in Hollywood!"*

As if it were perfectly normal and acceptable to lie to your business partner who had given you a job and then been so generous to you. That one really hurt.

And a few times I got burned by bidding on auction items at charitable events.

Then there was an episode with Michael Jackson and the people who ran his Neverland Ranch in Santa Barbara County.

At one of Marjoe's auctions, one of the items I eventually won, with a $30,000 bid, was to have Neverland host children for an entire day, including drinks and food. I bid on it for Sterling and many of her friends, and I think we started out with more than twenty kids on our first attempt to schedule it. But the dates did not work for the people at the ranch.

We had to make all the arrangements for the kids to travel there and it was time-consuming. Getting all of Sterling's friends together at one time was a test in itself. We had to fly everyone in at the same time, but each time we had a date we thought would work for everybody, Jackson's people turned us down. After we had planned, and after each time we tried had failed, our total number of kids dropped. I am sure their parents were getting tired of trying to clear their schedules for it and by the time we made a final attempt, we had only Sterling and five or six other kids.

Jackson's people just continued to avoid fulfilling the auction prize to host us. Every time we found a date we thought would work, we were told, "We can't do it. We can't do it. . . ."

I really think they were trying to wear me out until I gave up and went away, but I was determined and still trying to pull it off until June 25, 2009—the day Jackson died.

And that was the end of it.

I was out the $30,000, but I knew it did go to charity. We just got the kids' hopes up to see Neverland and then they never got to experience it.

One of the best benefits of becoming successful was enjoying the fact that those who doubted me in the beginning suddenly wanted something from me.

Remember all those local banks who turned up their noses at me and refused to loan me money to get it all started?

They came back to me and started begging for my business after Hawaiian Tropic made it.

In fact, I brought NCNB into Daytona Beach from North Carolina. They had never done any business in the area before I came along.

Once Hawaiian Tropic got rolling, I invited some of the NCNB executives down to one of my parties as a way to thank them for being the only bank to invest in me in the beginning. And once they visited Daytona, they all loved it, saw it was a thriving area and decided to locate some branches here in Florida—I was responsible for that, at least indirectly.

Of course, at that time, many of the local bankers came crawling back to me as I figured they someday would.

"Why not deal with us instead of a bank head-quartered out of state?" they would ask.

"Because you wouldn't give me a loan when I needed it most," I would answer every time.

But in the end, NCNB screwed me over, too, when I later asked for another loan, so I came to really hate bankers. Generally, they were two-faced slimes in my book. They only wanted my business when they needed my business when I was doing well.

When I needed them, they were never there for me.

And as time went on, and we entered a new century, unfortunately, I would need them again.

Chapter Fifteen

IT'S TIME TO SELL MY BABY

Remember that I had mentioned that little 9,000-square-foot building in Ormond Beach that Dad helped me negotiate to build for our first factory in 1973?

By the time we had finished our final expansion, that building had blossomed into a 360,500-square-feet complex. We also had a storage building that was approximately 200,000 square feet. At our peak of our production, we also had twelve other factories around the world.

I only wish Dad had been alive to see it.

Hawaiian Tropic had exceeded four billion dollars in sales over some thirty-seven years.

We had more than 2,000 employees, and several, from salespeople to vice-presidents, became rich over the years. Not to mention the independent distributors who sold our products.

Over the years, other than Coppertone, which was a publicly

owned company, our competitors came and went with the wind as we remained the largest privately held suncare company in the world.

Panama Jack never really was a serious competitor. They made more money on hats, shirts and sunglasses than on sun-care products. Sea & Ski had fizzled out for the most part. Coppertone had tried to come up with an oil product similar to ours, but they finally figured out it was just cannibalizing their own brand of lotions that was successful. So, they dropped it.

When Banana Boat came out, developed by a guy named Robert Bell in Miami, I didn't like the name and thought it would fizzle out like all the rest. But they marketed it well and it sold initially and became somewhat of a small competitor to us. Then he sold it to Playtex by 1993.

I was attending the grand opening of our Hawaiian Tropic Zone restaurant at the Planet Hollywood Hotel on the Las Vegas Strip when this guy Bell, whom I had never met, noticed me and came over to our table and started bragging about all the money he had made in the sun-care business. He had been drinking that night and was a mess and I had a hard time getting away from him.

A girl named Billie Summers had worked for me for a few years in the 1980s and I remembered that she had paid close attention to all the details of our operation. She had learned a lot and memorized everything we did except for the actual formula, which as I said, I kept to myself. No employee ever knew that. Even the chemists I had hired knew only portions of it. And if I had somehow died, and taken it to my grave, I do not know what would have happened to the company. I never thought about it because I guess I thought I was indestructible.

Anyway, all she ever talked about around me was hoping someday to move to Eleuthera, but she ended up moving to Miami and worked for Bell, helping Banana Boat become a success, I had heard later through the grapevine.

As Hawaiian Tropic had become successful over the years, as I said earlier, I had resisted all those dozens of offers for me to sell it. The offers were never high enough, I was having a blast running the beauty pageants and I realized we had thousands gainfully employed as well, so I never even seriously considered it.

But things started to change in the late '90s.

I always knew it was important to be nice to the underlings in business, although I should not call them that. I called them "Worker Bees." I knew if I were nice to them, and treat them well, that it would pay the company dividends in a good way. Throughout the years, I saw people in my position—bosses or CEOs who had become rich and somewhat powerful—treat people who worked for them like shit.

And I never wanted to be that person.

As much money as we earned over the years, and as popular as Hawaiian Tropic became, there were always problems in running a big business—small ones and large ones. Just like in any other business, I suppose.

As for the small stuff, I realized there was a lot of theft from the warehouses.

There was so much that I guess I just got used to it.

One year we had manufactured a huge line of Hawaiian Tropic T-shirts. One night I was working late at the office when somebody knocked on the factory door.

I opened it.

"THEY RAN OUT OF T-SHIRTS!" the guy screamed. "THEY ARE OUT OF THE DOLLAR SHIRTS AND I WANT ONE!"

"What dollar shirts are you talking about?" I asked him.

"They were being sold right up there at the Gulf station," he said.

"Well, we are out of them, too. Check back with us in a few days," I said.

I started investigating and it turned out that an employee was stealing them by the boxes and had been selling them for a buck. I caught the culprit in charge of the scheme and promptly fired him.

Theft was a real problem through the years, including theft of the actual products as well.

Another thing I always noticed with the company's hierarchy: It seemed many employees always wanted that job above them instead of focusing on their current one. For example, our housekeepers wanted to be secretaries. Our secretaries wanted to be the models. Our models wanted to be the executives. And maybe some executives wanted to be the president or owner.

It seemed to be a continuous game of fighting with people about what they did not get to do or what they wanted to do, instead of what they did.

But the truth is that we had little turnover over the years, because of the way I ran the company. An employee had to do something really bad to get fired, like steal from us.

You know how I had lectured all my male employees about how to act around the girls? Well, one of my executives failed to obey my orders. He had acted inappropriately, and the girl sued him and she also was getting ready to sue the company.

Then he started coming into the office around two in the afternoon. He was drunk all the time and he would scream at everyone near him. Then he would go into his office and sleep it off, snoring so loudly you could hear it through the walls. He would wake up, come out and scream at everybody one more time and then leave for the day.

I had other employees ready to quit, so I had no choice.

He had been with me a long time and was a great employee and I liked him, but I had no choice but to fire him.

I actually told him, "If you had done nothing more than come into the office every Friday just to get your paycheck, you would have been fine. You still would be with the company. But you have become disruptive and I have no choice."

And today, I still love the guy and we are still friends and I will not embarrass him here by naming him. It was just a bad period in his life and he eventually moved beyond it.

Things like that were troublesome, but not overwhelming to the health of the company.

But then one major issue popped up.

First, let me first explain how getting the product into stores and to the consumer worked back then:

The company, Tanning Research Laboratories, Inc., would sell the various Hawaiian Tropic products to individual distributors or distribution companies, who then would turn around and sell it to retailers such as Walmart, Walgreens or K-Mart and so on.

Everybody in that equation needed a margin to make money. But as the retailers started consolidating, and the government's anti-trust laws allowed them to price the product as low as they wanted, the margins grew smaller.

It became harder and harder to involve that middleman, the distributor, in the larger accounts and it suddenly did not make good business sense. It was smarter to hire my own salespeople for the larger national accounts and go directly to the retailers, similar to the way we did it in the early days, but we continued to handle the gift shops and smaller accounts the same way we always did. Those salespeople had such a big hand in the company's success anyway.

At the same time, our largest distributor got itself into some major financial trouble.

It became a complicated mess, but the crux of the problem was that after we acquired the distribution rights back from this distributor, he was supposed to pay the retailer for the end of season returns for the season just ended. However, contrary to the assurances from the distributor, when the returns started coming back from the retailers, he didn't have the funds necessary to pay for them.

Consequently, since Tanning Research Labs now was selling directly to the retailers that weren't getting paid for the prior year's returns, they told us that if we didn't pay them for those returns, they wouldn't carry Hawaiian Tropic any longer.

This distributor happened to have 45 states. Thus, their sales were huge—and we got stuck paying millions to the retailers for the returns from the prior year for goods that we didn't even sell to them.

By 1999, we had no choice but to buy out the company's distribution rights if we wanted to stay in business, and it was very costly—way beyond eight figures—since it had accumulated a lot of debt to the retailers.

After the deal, the amount owed to retailers for returns

turned out to be much larger than we had anticipated.

And in turn, that forced us to restructure our debt facilities through various lenders.

It never should have been that way, but it was, and I admit the buck stopped with me. I missed it.

It had kept me up at nights for a while and it was something that we never fully recovered from.

Within several years, I had had enough of dealing with all the issues and I knew it was time.

By the end of 2006, I had a sixteen-year-old daughter and I really wondered what would happen to her if something happened to me. She was too young to run a company that was this size.

So, I put Hawaiian Tropic up for sale.

I hired investment bankers to initiate the process and they were in charge of finding interested buyers. The bankers sent out a short teaser including some highlights about the company, which would soon be placed on the sales market.

They received indications or feelers about which companies might be interested in buying and then they selected the particular companies they wanted to follow-up with. At that point, they sent them a much more detailed proposal, something called an "offering memorandum," which took a ton of work by our vice-presidents Larry Adams and Jack "Corky" Surrette.

From that, the bankers pre-qualified the buyers they wanted to bring in for a management presentation, at which time the potential buyers' representatives could ask several questions. These were done individually for each potential buyer. Then, initial bids were offered, and the bankers sifted through them, matching them against each other.

In the end, they picked the buyer they thought they could get to the finish line and a closing of the sale.

We were still going strong in sales and the product itself was not suffering at all just because of the debt we had assumed, so I knew that Hawaiian Tropic would be attractive to many potential buyers. And I was right: There were about fifty companies interested at first, although many of them wanted to make low-ball offers and were never seriously a contender.

Playtex, which had bought Banana Boat fourteen years earlier from that Bell guy, emerged as the frontrunner and I started to meet regularly with the CEO, Neil DeFeo.

I must have had dinner with him about ten times and he asked me a lot of questions.

Because I had placed several of my personal holdings—such as my ranch in Oregon, my house in Malibu, a few other oceanfront properties in the Daytona area, land in North Carolina, some cars, my sailboat and a few more miscellaneous items—under the ownership of the company, my biggest worry is that some of those items would be included in the sale. The process had happened so fast, we didn't have time to restructure those assets.

I would sit and listen to the Playtex CEO say things like, "Well, this is worth this . . . and that is worth that . . . ," and I never agreed with much of what he was saying.

One day, he even asked me, "Why are you selling?"

"Well, it's the right time now," is all that I told him.

There even was a very traumatic three-month period when I did not know if I would even be able to keep my house, which had taken me five years to build with that North Carolina fieldstone I had shipped to Florida. It has been my main house to live in since 1985.

We were renewing our debt terms with the bank for the upcoming few months until the sale would close and the bank strong-armed me to terms that normally would never be acceptable. And then they hit me below the belt and even threatened to foreclose on my main home if I did not agree.

During one of those dinners with the Playtex CEO, he had mentioned to me that he had played in Jackie Gleason's band in Miami for several years.

"You know, while I played in his band, they wouldn't even let us talk to him or get to meet him or even shake his hand," he said.

The next time we met, I brought some pictures of me and the models with Jackie (when he played Sheriff Buford T. Justice) on the movie sets from when we worked with Hal Needham and Burt Reynolds. He was just fascinated by those photos and my stories of being around Jackie.

From that moment, our negotiations improved.

On April 17, 2007, we closed the deal.

And to this day, I really think the Jackie Gleason stories were a determining factor in getting a great price. The final deal was for eighty-three million dollars, but that was not what sold me.

It was the fact that I could keep all the things I had paid for—all my properties, land, cars and sailboat. Playtex didn't want any of it. And once the sale was completed, I no longer had to deal with the unscrupulous bankers that had strong-armed me, either.

In the end, they got the factories that remained in Ormond Beach, Ireland, Jamaica, Singapore, Hawaii and Israel and the most important item, the brand Hawaiian Tropic, as well any other products and brands we manufactured.

And I got to keep everything else.

I was more than happy with that. I knew the land and various houses were the most valuable assets I owned and would have been crushed to give them up by selling Hawaiian Tropic.

I also signed a five-year non-compete clause, so the buyers didn't have to worry about me taking the formula of Hawaiian Tropic and then starting a similar company with a different name.

I had some small debts to pay off first before I invested a lot of that money into government bonds, knowing they were tax-free. I had wanted a safe investment where I could not lose it.

Then another problem popped up.

Remember my sales rep in Hawaii, Don Langer, and that letter-sized envelope on which I had jotted down an informal agreement on a flight together in 1972, stating that he would receive ten percent of the proceeds if I sold it?

Playtex had let him go after the sale, so he promptly sued them and was in the process of winning a five-million-dollar settlement.

And it turned out he had kept that envelope all these years and was now using it as leverage against me to get another big payday.

As I had said, my huge mistake was not including a time frame on that envelope. There was no end date to it, and he knew it. He sued me that July, wanting ten percent of the sales price. He was just one big pain in the ass when he worked for us and now, he was asking for even more money.

My lawyers had gotten the lawsuit thrown out early on, with a summary judgment, but Langer won an appeal reinstating it. I then saw the writing on the wall, so to speak, and was worried about a potential jury case in Hawaii. My lawyers told me I could be on the hook for more than eight million dollars plus interest and that I should settle it. We finally came to a settlement agreement. By the time it was concluded, I also had paid more than one million in legal fees, so it turned out to be a very costly envelope.

It still bothers me. He had been a thorn in my side over the years and he continued even after I was no longer the owner of Hawaiian Tropic.

I needed a vacation once it was done, so I took Sterling and we went to Spain, Italy and France for three weeks and I also flew out to stay at the Malibu house and the Oregon ranch for a while. By the time I got back to Daytona, Playtex had sold its company to Energizer.

After I sold the company, what I missed the most were the pageants and being around the models during promotions. We had developed a worldwide pageant network that sent us girls every year and that suddenly stopped. Hawaiian Tropic had been as synonymous with pretty girls as it was with the suntan lotions and oils.

The new owners had to hold three more years of pageants according to the various existing contracts, and they had invited me to Las Vegas as their guest. I would sit in the front row with Sterling and my friends, but of course it was never the same.

Was I sad about giving up Hawaiian Tropic, the company I had built from the ground up, starting with a four-dollar garbage can in the garage at the old Round House?

Of course, but I tried to look at it this way: Been there, done that.

I had been married to the company since 1969—thirty-eight years of my life.

Hawaiian Tropic was a place and time of my life, but still the most important place and time of my life because of the people that had become like family to me. The people who all worked hard had enjoyed the fruits of their labor and became financially well off.

I also liked to think of the hundreds of their children that were put through college because of it.

By the summer of 2007, soon after the sale, the economy started going to hell. I wanted to hire a realtor to find oceanfront property for me, since the prices were dropping, but I could not find anybody to do it for me. So, I got into my car and drove up and down A1A looking for what I thought were good deals. One thing I knew well was real estate and especially oceanfront real estate in the Daytona area.

I ended up buying a bunch of properties on the ocean, somewhere around twelve or thirteen oceanfront houses. I started renting many of them, knowing they would appreciate in value as the economy turned around.

It gave me something to do and I knew that oceanfront property would always be a good investment.

I was not the type to just sit on the beach or play golf—a game I never played much anyway—like other retirees or do nothing at all.

And the freedom of not having all the responsibility, and all the headaches that came with running a big business, as well as a full schedule, felt very good for a change.

I was now 67 years old. I now had even more money in the bank than ever before. I had plenty of friends, many of whom were now "former" employees. I still was living the dream in the same house I had built on the same beach I loved so much in my adopted hometown of Ormond-Daytona Beach. So, all in all, there was little to complain about.

What was so strange to me is something else I also suddenly had, probably for the first time in my life—plenty of time on my hands.

How would I fill it?

Chapter Sixteen

YESTERDAY, TODAY AND TOMORROW

As I grow older—I turned eighty years old on September 1, 2020—I often think back on my life, my career and I hope I made a difference somehow. I hope I helped make the lives of others, whether it be my friends, family or my many former employees, somehow better.

And I think how often and how close I came so many times to not reaching this age.

There were so many close calls or near-tragic moments when what I consider a wonderful life could have ended in an instant.

You know how they say that your life flashes before your eyes?

My life flashed in front of mine so often, I forgot all my close brushes with death, starting when I was just a kid.

But I do remember a few:

When I was twelve, our family took a trip through Colorado up into Wyoming and we visited Yellowstone Park. As I told you at the beginning of this book, Dad loved to travel, taking us and Mom with him, and he always tried to teach us as much as he could along the way.

On this particular trip, we stayed at this little, log cabin in Yellowstone. Dad always had assigned me various tasks, like getting the fire started and organizing things at the campsite.

One night, the park rangers had delivered a presentation at this small amphitheater and once it finished, my job was to get back to the cabin and get a fire started. I may not have been very big, but I was very fast then. So, the moment the rangers finished talking that night, I took off running, and got way ahead of the rest of the family.

It was as pitch-black, in the middle of the dark of night, when I turned a corner at full throttle, and ran face-first into this big, sturdy, hunk of fur. It seemed just a like a big, furry tree to me. Then I realized what I had run into—a large bear. I believed it was a grizzly, even though as soon as I hit it with my face, it took off running.

Many bear experts have told me over the years that a grizzly would not have taken off running as if it was scared. It would have either swiped my head off with its massive claws or eaten me like an appetizer right on the spot. They have also said it probably would have smelled me coming, but I am telling you that I was running so fast at the time, I got there before my smell.

So, maybe it was a black bear. All I know is that when I hit it face-first, it was standing upright on its back paws and it was a lot taller than me. Whether it was a grizzly or a black bear, I know another thing for certain: I was lucky that I had scared it as much as it scared me.

I guess it just was not my time to die by being devoured by a bear as a young boy.

My next brush with mortality occurred on that long trip that Steve Santoro and I took to New Orleans in my early twenties. My car spun out of control on a wet road somewhere in the Smokey Mountains soon after we left Asheville, and by the time it came to rest, we were facing the opposite direction overhanging a cliff. There was no guardrail in sight.

As I noticed the one hundred foot drop next to our car, my heart pounded out of my chest.

It was not my time to die by driving off a cliff, either.

It wasn't too long after that when I went on a scuba diving trip to see the underwater caves in Lake Mack near Orlando with a few of my friends, even though I had a cold and had taken a lot of cold medicine that day. We did not have much money then and we had rented scuba gear and taken some hot dogs to cook over an open fire near this small sandy beach.

My friends went ahead of me and were already diving in the caves by the time I started down from the surface. I got lightheaded almost instantly, maybe from the medicine. Just as I started to enter a cave, I thought, *If I go in there I may just pass out and drown.*

But as a lifeguard, I always had the confidence that I could swim my way out of danger, so I tried my best to reach the surface. Problem was, I had let water get into the mouthpiece of my apparatus, which was the old double hose regulator divers used in those days. I also was afraid if blew a big breath of air into the mouthpiece to try to clear it, I would pass out. So, I had no choice but to swim for it, but the weight of the tank and all my gear was pushing me to the bottom of the middle of the lake.

My mind flashed to the next day's headline in the local newspaper: "North Carolina man drowns in Florida Lake."

I could have dropped the scuba tank, too, but I knew if I did that, if I did survive, I would have to pay for it since there would be no way to find it at the bottom of this lake. I continued to swim for my life, but the weight of it all was just making it too difficult. I had on total frog gear from head to toe. Finally, I had dropped to the bottom of the lake and had no choice but to crawl toward the shore.

Before I had entered the water, I noticed a couple of little kids playing by that small beach area. I crawled along the bottom, holding my breath along the way, and I finally made my way to shore, emerging directly in front of those kids. As I came out of the water and tried to stand wearing all that black frog gear, I must have looked just like the creature from the black lagoon, because those kids ran away screaming at the top of their lungs.

I collapsed right there, half of my body in and half out it of the water. I was so exhausted that I passed out, but fortunately, my head was out of the water.

My friends later surfaced, spotted me, but I was always such a prankster, they figured I was goofing off again. Finally, after about an hour they walked down the hill to see what I was doing, as I tried to explain what had happened.

That was not my time to die of drowning, either.

You would not think I would go diving again, right?

Not long after that, my old pool-deck partner Jim Edge and

I decided to go diving for lobster or fish or whatever we could find in Tampa. We headed into the water near a bridge, must have been under water a long time because by the time we surfaced, it didn't take long for us to realize a strong current had been pushing us out to the Gulf of Mexico at a pretty good pace. We then saw a small island and swam like hell to get to it.

If we had stayed under water or had not noticed it, we would have been swept out into the deep Gulf with no way to return.

Then there was that afternoon in the late 1970s when my buddy Duffy stopped his station-wagon, forcing me to plunge into the hard sand from ninety feet in the air. I had noticed Duffy for days, driving up and down the beach while pulling his "Delta Wing," asking friends and tourists if they wanted to "fly like a bird."

Then he asked me one day, "Want to try it, Ron?"

I usually accepted any challenge back then, but I soon realized this one was a big mistake on my part. I probably weighed 250 and that apparatus just was not built for someone of my weight.

It took me two or three attempts to even get airborne. He would hit the gas and slam! I would crash into the sand. Again. Slam! I hit the beach hard again. Finally, on the third attempt, I suddenly was gliding higher than the nearby telephone poles. I had floated to the west over A1A, the main road that ran parallel to the beach. There was a bar on this thing that went crossways, and I was supposed to push it one way or the other to steer it.

Not feeling comfortable with all the traffic below, me, I then overcompensated my steering and floated over the Atlantic

Ocean. Then suddenly, for whatever reason, Duffy stopped his car, causing me to start falling out of control, just like a bird that had been shot out of the sky. I had to appear to be a blur in the sky to the tourists below me as I crashed hard into the sand.

I really figured I was a goner that day, as I detailed at the beginning. And the moment I crashed into that concrete-like sand did not change my mind much, until I took that one small breath.

So, it was not my time to die via a Delta Wing accident, either.

After I had purchased my airplane, there were a few times when my pilot, Mike, flew us over Cuban airspace, such as on the same day that the U.S. had invaded Grenada in 1983, killing more than twenty Cuban soldiers who were defending against the invasion. We had heard what had happened in Grenada and I instantly thought of the fate of my buddy Bill Schagalis who spent some time in one of Castro's prisons after his airplane ran off the runway.

But there was no way to fly from the Cayman Islands to the U.S. without traveling through Cuban airspace. That is when Mike the pilot, who spoke fluent Spanish, earned his keep. He constantly was on the radio to Cuban air traffic control, speaking Spanish and letting them know we were in a civilian aircraft.

"Do not shoot us down!" he would say in Spanish. "We are civilians. Civilians!"

Every time we flew over Cuba, I had a big knot in my stomach.

Sometimes, simple intuition, or a bad feeling for no reason saved my hide.

One time, I was driving south of Marietta, Georgia, and I came to this area where I had to merge. There was no stop sign or traffic light, but something just did not feel right. Something told me to stop. So, I did.

Just as I looked both ways, a huge tractor-trailer came barreling down through the crossroad directly in front of me. If I would not have stopped, it would have hit me broadside at about eighty miles per hour and surely killed me.

So, it was not my time to die by getting hit by a truck, either.

How and when it all ends for me someday is anybody's guess, but it doesn't worry me. I squeezed every ounce out of life I that could.

After I sold the company in 2007 and had all of my money invested where I thought it should be invested, and I didn't have the daily grind, I realized you really only need four things to live: A roof over your head, a pillow to put your head on at night, food to keep you alive and hopefully, somebody to love you.

Really, if you think about it, that is all you really need in this world.

In recent years, I have started the process of liquidating almost everything I own, with the exception of my main house in Ormond Beach, Florida, and my house in Malibu.

As I write this, my Oregon horse ranch is up for sale. I even sold my sailboat, the Princess Sterling, during the summer of 2019. I have sold several of those oceanfront properties around Daytona Beach that I bought during the recession. I no longer own any fancy sports cars, either.

Some people have told me over the years that if I accidentally stepped into a bucket of shit, I would pull my foot out of it and there would be a one-hundred-dollar bill attached to my shoe.

I guess what they were saying is that I was lucky.

I admit it.

I was.

I still think that way. I was and am the luckiest guy in the world.

I look at it this way: The harder and harder and harder I worked, the luckier and luckier and luckier I became.

And I worked hard from the time I was a kid and knew how to figure things out one way or the other. I was thinking just the other day that when I was young, I could get things done with my looks and my personality. When I grew older, after I created the Hawaiian Tropic models, I learned to have these young beauties around me open doors and get things done.

And I also learned that when I got older, people in business do not care about you as much. It is a form of age discrimination, I suppose, and something that I never thought of when I was younger.

It is true I made a lot of money. I also spent a lot on parties, cars, houses, women and a good time. But I never forgot the big picture and I gave back plenty, both in money and my time, to various charitable causes through the decades, most of which were environmental and animal-rights causes. I was and am a big believer in protecting the environment and I guess that, and our love of snow skiing, was about all John Denver and I had in common.

From the time I grew up on that mountain in Asheville, working all those odd jobs as a kid to help the family, I learned so much. Enough that I forgot some of it. But the most important thing I learned was about true love—you have no idea what it is until you become a parent and raise a child.

The women came and went from my life for decades, but my daughter Sterling is the one true love of my life. She is so beautiful, and I attribute that to Darcy. I did not contribute much to her in that way, other than being the so-called sperm donor.

What a treat it was raising her. I still consider that journey, not the businesses I created, etc., or the money I made, as the greatest achievement of my life.

And I discovered in the past few years I still had the desire to work. To create. To do something worthwhile.

On the morning of December 18, 2014, I read in the newspaper that then President Obama and Cuban president, Raul Castro, announced they were starting the process to normalize relations between the two countries.

I always regarded Cuba as a vast, untapped market and as soon as I read that news, I started to think how I could create another line of suncare products by marketing it with a Cuban theme.

The key factor: The five-year, non-compete clause I had signed when I sold Hawaiian Tropic to Playtex in 2007 had expired a few years earlier. Now I was free to do what I wanted business-wise, and I never did relinquish any rights to the formulas I had created in the first place—only the brand name Hawaiian Tropic.

So, in 2016, I created a new line of products called Havana Sun (which I later changed to "Habana Brisa" since—just like 50 years ago with "Tropic Tan"—the name was already taken).

After three years, our sales are much better than I ever expected. We have four products—oils, lotions, aloes and after-sun—and are adding lip balms, liquid zinc and some products for kids as I write this. And all our products are "reef-friendly."

As far as the actual formula, I never give away too many details, but let me just say it is better than Hawaiian Tropic when I sold it. Much better.

I have had thirteen years, along with the chemists I have hired, to work on it and improve it. I have a core group of great employees. Things are running smoothly, and I see a bright future ahead for the company.

Personally, things have changed dramatically.

I received two phone calls in 2019 that were completely out of the blue, but significant. They were from two prominent people in my past, including one I did not even know existed.

One day in November 2019, my assistant Alexia Meadows—I call her "A.M." for short—picked up the phone and guess who was on the other end of the line?

My former nemesis from the early days of Tropic Tan, none other than Paul Burke.

"Want to meet for lunch?" he asked.

Who was I to refuse?

We met along with Dave Hampton and talked about the old days. I had long forgiven him for his pettiness, his schemes like "roaching the aloe," and all those other tricks, not that he ever apologized for them. I do not want to go to my grave holding grudges, and I can honestly say that we are friends now.

We have nothing to be enemies about. In fact, I am now appreciative of his competitiveness back then, because it pushed me to work harder when I needed to most. The rivalry with him helped me develop Tropic Tan in the first place, which turned into Hawaiian Tropic, which changed my life forever.

But there had been another much more meaningful call

than the one from Burke.

The week before Thanksgiving, A.M. answered the phone and I noticed her jaw drop as she listened to whoever was on the other line. She was not saying much. She listened and listened, and she finally said, "Ron, I think you need to take this call."

She handed me the phone. A woman was on the other line. "Is this Ron Rice?" she asked.

After I confirmed she had the right guy, she said, "I think you are my biological father."

I must have paused for a while, but I do remember saying, "Okay . . ."

She said her name was Valerie and she proceeded to tell me her life story, how she was adopted in Orlando, after she was born in 1968. She now lived in St. Augustine, Florida, and was married and had a college-age daughter. She said that she knew her biological mother was a woman named Sue Ramey.

She recently had taken a DNA test, which confirmed a match to my sister, Barbara, and Sterling, both of whom had entered the country's DNA database a few years earlier. Once she had received the results of her DNA test, she googled my name. And then she found our office phone number on the Internet.

As I listened to her, I knew instantly that she was telling the truth.

One day on the beach in 1967, I had met a beautiful, blonde girl by the name of Sue Ramey.

We started dating a little while I was working to create Tropic Tan and teaching school and all my friends loved her. In fact, several of my lifeguard buddies tried to steal her away from me. I remember we had some great times together. Then she basically disappeared. She just dropped out of my life and I never saw her again.

I had heard that she had moved out of town, but I never pursued her or called her again. There were no cell phones or Internet or any convenient way to track people down back then and I figured that if she wanted to see me or needed me that she would call me.

But she never did, so that was that.

Fifty-two years later, Valerie filled me in on the details of what had happened to her.

Sue had become pregnant and her parents sent her to Orlando to deliver the baby and put it up for adoption.

The more Valerie talked, the more it all made sense of what happened to Sue.

As the years had gone by, I had heard some rumors Sue had gotten pregnant by somebody and that is why she moved away. The Daytona area is a small community in that regard where you hear gossip from time to time. Her family still lived in the area and when Sue's stepfather died in about 2015, I sent a former secretary of mine, Sandy, to the funeral home to see if Sue had shown up or if she could discover any details at all.

But she got nowhere and came back empty.

I basically forgot about it until getting that phone call.

All these years I thought I had only one daughter, and in an instant it took to answer the phone, I had two.

And, I have a grand-daughter I never knew.

Valerie's daughter, Sidney, is a twenty-two-year-old senior at Texas A&M as I write this.

Sadly, Valerie also informed me that Sue, who had married

years ago and moved to Dalton, Georgia, died in 2018. She never got to meet her biological mother and I never got to talk to her or let her know that I knew we had a daughter together.

At the end of Valerie's initial phone call, I invited her and her husband to come visit me, and the next day, they showed up at my front door. She walked into my house and stood there hesitantly for a moment. She had flaming red hair, but I could tell she was my daughter. I approached her and hugged her, and we began to talk.

As she filled me in on her life, she happened to mention that she frequented Rosie O'Grady's in Orlando, where she had grown up, throughout the 1980s and '90s. I thought back to all those times we had made road trips to that very place with many of my staffers. And I figured we had to be there at the same time, perhaps sitting next to each other.

We went to lunch that first day and have been in constant contact ever since.

When I told Darcy and Sterling about it all, they both were skeptical at first, of course. I did go ahead and take a DNA test which confirmed I am her father.

All I can say is that I am extremely happy about it. I have a new family.

It is amazing how fast time flies and how life evolves.

Many of the landmarks of my life and career are long gone, such as the Round House on A1A. Every time I drove past that place for years, I would look over at it and smile. It was a part of me, where it all started. What great memories that place had for me. That lot has nothing but a parking lot on it now.

I do not date that much now, and I really do not miss it, either.

I have a great group of friends, including women who are close friends.

I still attend all the sporting events I fell in love with over the years, such as the NCAA's Final Four and Super Bowls. I love March Madness as well as college football.

When I think back to when I was a boy growing up in Asheville, I knew then that I always wanted to become a productive worthwhile citizen. I wanted to contribute to society somehow. Then when I was a lifeguard, I wanted to get out of the beach-bum lifestyle and make a better living somehow. My dad always wanted to own a business, but he never did. Somehow, someway, I did that. A large part of it was just the fact I had a hard time working for somebody else. That is why I was fired so often before I made it on my own.

He always told me the most productive years financially are your last four years before you retire. It was good advice.

After Dad died in 1975, what made me happy was when Mom told me that he had been so happy for me that I had gone into business for myself. She said that he always wanted to do that, but never did.

I really believe one of the happiest days of my life was when I repaid him that original $500 loan which he had given me in the 1960s to get my business started.

It was not the money. It was the fact that he believed in me.

Like Dad had died, my brother also had died of a heart issue. I really think he lost interest in life and did not care whether he lived or died. The last day I ever spoke to him over the telephone was sometime before Mom died.

Speaking of graves, I recently purchased a mausoleum spot near my home in Ormond Beach.

I think I want to be buried in a Hawaiian shirt. You know I never, ever owned a three-piece suit. I owned a ton of Hawaiian shirts though. Suits and tuxedos were not my thing, although I did have a makeshift tuxedo just for special events.

The idea of death does not scare me at all. At the end of the year, we distribute a Christmas card that celebrates the life of all those people we knew well who had passed away during that particular year and it seems to include more and more faces each year.

One of the guys I enjoyed being around the most was the comedian Robin Williams. He would stand on stage when he performed at those charity auctions and point at our models and make some kind of joke, while saying, "Those are my bee-atches."

One time on stage, he just flatly stated, "Thank God for the Hawaiian Tropic girls!"

I will never forget that line—and I can second that, too.

Then he pointed to me.

"Thank you, Ron, for always bringing them here!" he said.

At that moment, I happened to glance over at Larry David, who was scowling at me. I just smiled back.

Anyway, Robin's suicide really hit me hard. I guess you just never know what is going on with somebody else, I guess.

It all brings me back to reality and I realize my mortality just like anybody else, I guess. When I am driving on a two-lane road, I sometimes wonder if that driver coming at me just flinched or was not a good driver or wanted to end their own life or may be texting . . . it could all end in an instant.

I had survived all those close calls I mentioned, and several others I cannot remember, but you just never know when your time will be up.

When I pictured the ideal life, I pictured living on the beach walking barefoot in the sand while wearing a Hawaiian shirt and a straw hat. And I succeeded at that. I never had to wear a suit to work or punch a time clock, not since leaving the teaching profession anyway. The Campbell High principal could tell you I that I did not like punching time clocks.

I always tried to avoid weddings and funerals like the Plague, but I do realize they are a part of life and sometimes unavoidable. I preferred a good party instead.

I never for once took for granted where I was born, either. What a great country we live in. My life just proves that if you have great ideas, or even one great idea, and you are willing to work hard, it may make you rich beyond your wildest dreams.

Not that money is everything, as we all know.

I want to be known and remembered as a good person who raised a beautiful caring daughter. I worked with charities whenever and wherever I could and gave back something to my community whenever I could.

Nothing more than that.

I started in Asheville, North Carolina, with nothing but my good name which my father passed on to me and plenty of ambition to go with it. I was a childhood entrepreneur of sorts. I worked to help our family. I graduated from college, although it took longer than most. I worked in an engineering firm and sold shoes, however briefly. I lifeguarded, taught school and coached football.

And then I built the second-largest suncare company in the world which helped thousands of employees live productive, happy lives. I like to think those products we created and sold also saved some lives.

And as you know by now, I had a little fun along the way, because most of my memories are great ones.

When I am not working on my new business or talking on the phone to an old friend or former employee, I sit here now looking out at the beach and the ocean . . . and often, many of those memories come flooding back.

And when they do, I am smiling.

AFTERWORD

I hope you enjoyed reading Ron Rice's life story as much as I enjoyed writing it with him.

This project was born in the winter of 2017 when I flipped through channels on a cloudy day, coming across a Showtime special called "Spring Broke."

The two-hour documentary summarized how Spring Break became an annual ritual in Daytona Beach, pumping millions into the local economy and at the center of it all was an entrepreneur named Ron Rice. He not only was the founder of Hawaiian Tropic, but he gladly became the main sponsor of just about any concert or social event held in his adopted hometown. In this documentary, he told several fascinating stories from the good ol' days.

I had heard of Ron before, having covered the Daytona 500 from 1985-99 and was aware of his past racing sponsorships as well as the legendary parties he hosted at his oceanfront Ormond Beach estate as well as noticing his famous Hawaiian Tropic models parade up and down pit lane over the years. It was Ron's "Guerilla Marketing" at work.

So, I quickly found the phone number of his estate and called it. Within a minute or two, Ron was on the line as I pitched the idea of writing his life story.

"Love it," he said in what would become a familiar baritone drawl. "Can you drive up here tomorrow to see me?"

I did, we sat together and talked for the next five hours and instantly became friends. We started to work that very day and the rest is history.

What you just read was what came of our collaboration since that first meeting.

I would spend days at a time sitting with Ron, my tape recorder always running, both of us enjoying the waves rolling onto the beach on the Atlantic where he once lifeguarded, as he ventured from one memory to another. When we went out for lunch—Ron always knew the best spots in town—I placed that tape recorder between us.

He was a self-taught marketing genius and that is how Hawaiian Tropic went from a $4 metal garbage can in his rented garage to a four-billion-dollar business some 40 years later. And along the way, as you just read, he had a blast doing it. Life never cheated Ron Rice because he took a big bite out of it every day. "If it's not fun," he once told me, "Then why do it?"

I finished this manuscript in April of 2020, but Ron continued to add to it. I had instructed him that typically, he could thank around "five to 10" people who were close to him in the acknowledgements section. But as I learned when we first started working together, Ron wasn't good at accepting instructions—he took the time to thank more than a thousand people, as you probably noticed. That had to set some sort of literary record. The thing is, he probably met almost every single one of them at one point in his life and he just didn't want to leave them out. He told me once that every encounter and every conversation had an impact on him in some manner, good or bad, and that was the way he lived his life—"Don't leave anyone out."

As you also have read, Ron faced several close calls with the Grim Reaper throughout his amazing life, as with the example of that Delta wing crashing on the beach in which we opened the book in Chapter 1.

But he couldn't survive the final encounter. He became ill in the winter of 2022.

On May 11, 2022, I visited him for the final time. He was lying in a makeshift hospital bed in front of the large wall of TVs. It was the spot he loved, being able to keep up on sports, politics and news of the day at all once, while still being able to glance over at the beach he loved so much. This time, however, he could barely hold his head up while a hospice worker fed him.

"Good to see you," he whispered. "Sorry, I didn't recognize you at first. We had a good time together . . . didn't we?"

"We sure did," I told him. "Don't worry Ron, the book will still come out and your life story will be told."

"Thank you," he whispered.

After telling me a thousand stories for the previous five years, those were the final words he ever said to me.

Eight days later, he was gone, taking his final breath at about 3 a.m. on the morning of May 19, 2022. He was 81 years old.

As Ron had wanted and you read in the final chapter, he was buried in one of his favorite Hawaiian Tropic shirts. Given the way he lived his life and what he had created, it was only fitting. He never held this finished book in his hands or was able to show it to his friends as he had planned and that saddens me immensely.

However, his incredible story does not stop on the day he died. It lives on in his many friends' memories of him . . . and as I promised him, on these pages. Rest in peace my friend.

▪ JEFF SNOOK

www.ingramcontent.com/pod-product-compliance
Lightning Source LLC
Chambersburg PA
CBHW052050230426
43671CB00011B/1857